John Osborne's plays include: *Look Back in Anger* (1956), *The Entertainer* (1957), *Luther* (1961), *A Patriot For Me* (1966) and *Inadmissible Evidence* (1965). His collected prose, *Damn You, England* was published in 1994 and the two volumes of his autobiography, *A Better Class of Person* (1929–1956) and *Almost a Gentleman* (1955–1966) were published in 1981 and 1991 respectively. John Osborne was born in 1929 and died at Christmas 1994.

JOHN OSBORNE
Plays One

Look Back in Anger,
Epitaph for
George Dillon,
The World of
Paul Slickey
and *Déjàvu*

Introduced by the author

faber and faber
LONDON · BOSTON

This collection first published in 1993 as *Look Back in Anger and other plays*
Reissued as *John Osborne: Plays One* in 1996
by Faber and Faber Limited
3 Queen Square London WC1N 3AU

Photoset by Wilmaset Ltd, Birkenhead, Wirral
Printed by Clays Ltd, St Ives plc

A CIP record for this book is available from the British Library

ISBN 0-571-17766-2

CONTENTS

INTRODUCTION

May 8th, 1956, is one of the few dates usually quoted in accounts of modern theatrical history, and generally regarded as the commencement, for good or ill, of a tangible change in the climate and direction of the English theatre. It was the first performance of *Look Back in Anger* at the Royal Court Theatre, an occasion I only partially remember, but certainly with more accuracy than those who subsequently claimed to have been present and, if they are to be believed, would have filled the theatre several times over.

The compilers of these histories have deduced all sorts of theories about the consequences of that sparsely attended first night and its social, political and even revolutionary implications. Some of these fanciful inventions are fairly wild, based on speculative and disordered hindsight, but they refuse to be swatted or blown away. And all this has served to draw attention to the piece as an historical phenomenon, while the play itself is passed over under the weight of perpetuated misinterpretation.

People cling stubbornly to their fallacies, particularly those who feel constrained to illuminate or 'explain' the intentions of others who are reckless enough to embark upon an act of original creation. The damage such commentators inflict is difficult to restore, even with the refutation of the most authoritative and authentic performance. I will try then, without much hope, to dispose of the most crass misconceptions about *Look Back in Anger*.

First, I would ask anyone reading the play for the first time to disregard anything they may have heard about it. Reading the text of a play is not easy, especially for those who have little experience of playgoing and, most specially, those who have never worked in the theatre itself. It requires the rare gift of technical insight and, above all, imagination. In forty-five years, I have come across barely half a dozen people who could study a script with the instinct to interpret in their heads as a conductor or musician does when reading a score.

I am often asked by students, expecting me to hand over the 'input' of my past to some examination chore, the impatient question: 'Why did you write *Look Back in Anger*?' Why does one wish to breathe, hope for laughter or fall in love? There seems to be an insistent demand for 'motivation' in such things, something concrete and explicable, like an Arts Council grant or the prospect of quick fame. The answer is fairly simple. I was a twenty-five-year-old actor, out of work and separated from my first wife. I had been thinking about the play for a year or more and wrote it over a period of six weeks. The actual writing, as always the most pleasurable and easy part, took a dozen or so days, interrupted half way through when I went up to Morecambe to play a small part in the local repertory company. Most of the second act was written in a deck-chair on the end of the pier, which inspired one speculator to advance the theory that the original title was *On the Pier at Morecambe*.

Look Back was to insinuate itself into theatrical perceptions, poisonously some might say, but it has survived and no one has yet found an antidote to what may be its principal ingredient – vitality. The other claim I would make for it after all these years is honesty. I tried to write it in a language in which it was possible only to tell the truth. When I began to write plays, it seemed to me then (as it does now), that most writers dissemble. They are not to be trusted. They look for intellectual respect, approbation, they flatter, indulge and offer false and easy comfort.

The pursuit of vibrant language and patent honesty, which I always believed the theatre and the now abandoned liturgy of the Anglican church could accommodate, was my intention from the outset, although I never articulated it to myself. The language which actors were called upon to speak when I first began to work was thin and inexpressive. There seemed to be an acceptance that dramatic language shouldn't get above itself, that it was no more than a supernumerary branch of 'Literature'. The *placement* of the most successful playwrights, Priestley, Coward or Rattigan, was well below the salt of the Novelist or Poet. The scholarly efforts of Eliot or the self-conscious high spirits of Fry added to the confusion, while the purple blarney of poesies by O'Casey and, inexplicably, O'Neill, were admired as attempts to elevate English, the world's most defiant and irrepressible language, into a command it had given up with faint heart under the towering shadow of Shakespeare.

Some had tried and acquitted themselves honourably, Congreve for one, but most – Farquhar, Sheridan, Wilde or Shaw – were Irishmen, a race literally allowed to get away with murder. For a long time there was a prevalent feeling that distinguished men of letters who entered the theatre were slumming. Henry James, who tried persistently to invade this lowly brothel, was spectacularly unsuccessful. Somerset Maugham, on the other hand, appeared to have the trick of it and entertained middle-class audiences for a quarter of a century. As a young actor I did a lot of Maugham – *Lady Frederick*, *The Breadwinner*, *The Circle*, *The Sacred Flame* – and one of the things I discovered was that they were extremely difficult to learn. It is one thing to read a play for pleasure, but quite another to study it for commitment to memory. Maugham's language was dead, elusively inert, wobbly like some synthetic rubber substance. The actor's expression 'D.L.P.' ('dead letter perfect') had an impossible application to Maugham because it didn't really matter about the precedence of words or punctuation. You could approximate with little difference in meaning or nuance.

Slovenly writing invites slovenly performance. Later, more skilful dramatists cannot be presented so wilfully, though actors and directors, God rot them, often do their best, protesting that they don't 'feel' a line. And there still prevails a common assumption that a B Flat or C Minor here or there is no matter except to be left to the improvised hindsight of the interpreter. You can't or shouldn't do it to Pinter, Beckett or, I hope, myself. The notations are indicated for meticulously constructed reasons. The 'ands' and the 'buts' are the map-markings of syntax and truth, not the stammering infelicities of another's haphazard personal selection.

A play is an intricate mechanism, and the whole mesh of its engineering logic can be shattered by a misplaced word or emphasis. The most famous example of a playwright preventing an actor from crashing the gears of his fine-tuned machinery is Noël Coward's reproof of Edith Evans when she insisted on inserting the word 'very' into the line: 'On a [very] clear day you can see Marlow.' Having repeatedly corrected her, he exploded: 'No, Edith. On a clear day you can see Marlow. On a *very* clear day you can see Marlow, and Beaumont, *and* Fletcher.'

Many people made the mistake of claiming that the language of *Look Back in Anger* was naturalistic, whatever that means. The language of 'everyday life' is almost incommunicable for the very good reason that it is restricted, inarticulate, dull and boring, and never more so than today when verbal fluency is regarded as suspect if not downright 'elitist'.

They also missed the point, which may not be obvious on the printed page to the uninitiated reader, that it is a comedy. At the Public Dress Rehearsal on May 7th, the mostly young audience had laughed where I hoped they would, to the dismay of George Devine and Tony Richardson, the directors of the theatre and the play. 'But why are they laughing?' Because it's *funny*, I replied. They were not reassured. I remembered that Chekhov had the same trouble. True, the following evening, there were very few laughs indeed. The First Night audience, if they were conscious, seemed transfixed by a tone of voice that was quite alien to them. They were ill at ease; they had no rules of conduct as to how to respond. The obvious one was to walk out, which some did, but with only a vague idea of why. Boredom and anger may have contributed, but mostly they were adrift, like Eskimos watching a Restoration comedy. A performance of *Look Back* without persistent laughter is like an opera without arias. Indeed, Jimmy Porter's inaccurately named 'tirades' should be approached as arias, and require the most adroit handling, delicacy of delivery, invention and timing. This is no play for amateurs, although they frequently attempt it.

In spite of the attention to the play at the time, amounting to something like crazed tumult, it did not transfer to the West End. The misgivings and private distaste of the presiding managements were unpersuaded. Timidity prevailed over agonized avarice. The one producer prepared to compromise his reputation insisted that all references to bears and squirrels be excised. This, I was told, embarrassed the customers; it made them squirm. Even the play's most quoted supporter, Kenneth Tynan, had described them as 'painful whimsy'. A few years on, whole pages of respectable national newspapers would be devoted to Valentine's Day messages from 'Snuggly Bouffel Bears' to 'Squiggly Whiffly Squirrels', far more nauseous than my own prescient invention. In my profession, the surest road to penury is to be ahead of your time.

It took thirty years for the piece to achieve a production which I found satisfying and fulfilled my intentions, dispelling the misunderstandings which had blurred its impact over the decades. None of the interim revivals had done much to challenge the nonsense about the play being a 'monologue'. It still seemed to induce a benighted myopia. Where there were five clearly defined characters on stage, only one was acknow-ledged as visible. The conspiracy had it that Jimmy Porter occupies a vacuum, talking without pause to himself alone. His wife, her father, his temporary mistress, his closest friend, contained no reality, no substance, no impact. Porter was an abortive, loutish Hamlet, who has no Gertrude, Claudius, Polonius, Ophelia or even Horatio to distract the eye and ear of those unwillingly gathered to behold his tedious presence.

If I still sound peevishly impatient after all this time with such commonplace incomprehension of the work whose reput-ation I am doomed to be buried beneath, it is because I am mystified by the myth. Indifference is the most blithely cruel and effective of weaponry. Hamlet is almost devoured by the inefficacy of those who surround him. When Emma Thompson played Alison in Judi Dench's 1989 revival, I tried to explain that it was she, not her husband, who was the most deadly bully. Her silence and her obdurate withdrawal were impregnable. The ironing board was not the plaything of her submission, but the bludgeon and shield which were impenetrable to all Jimmy's appeals to desperate oratory.

Kenneth Branagh succeeded in taking the rant out of the part. He tried to take it trippingly on the tongue. I gave him the same advice I have given actors in other plays of mine (often with dire consequences, as in the abysmal revival of *Inadmissible Evidence* at the National Theatre in 1993): 'Let the text surprise you, as if it took you off-balance, and lift you up even further into the battle of defeat and confusion. Take the words *out of the air*.' I said it again to Peter Egan when he was faced with the same technical problems in *Déjàvu* in 1992. He triumphed, but the attempt was lost on those who had a robot Porter forever fixed in their responses. There seems no remedy against the perception that J.P. is a one-man band, addressing himself in a world of shadows. The facts are there on the printed page, but if you are determined that the play is an unrelieved monologue, not even a perusal of the text will dissuade you.

I once described *Look Back* as a 'formal, old-fashioned play'. I should have been wise enough not to fool about with irony. Certainly it is 'formal' in that it follows a simple narrative impetus. Where it was not 'old-fashioned' was in its deployment of, yes, language and in its indifference to the puny constraints which involved conciliating the audience by confirming their prejudices and not mocking their expectations. This was the school of 'the drama's laws, the drama's patrons give,' one of Dr Johnson's few nonsensical pronouncements. It was also in the Moss Hart American tradition of slavishly obeying the playgoer's direction instead of the playmaker's; the Dramatist as the conniving servant of his master, the Box-Office. 'The audience gets restless, just about here, in the middle of Act Two.' Attention had to be paid.

I have never been a 'popular' writer. Nothing I have ever done has had a London run of more than six months. However, I think that *Look Back* has had some influence, if only in the sense of arousing powerful feelings, hostile or resentful though they may have been. And what *did* happen after 1956 was that attention was no longer necessarily paid. The writer could renounce the obligation to bear the chains of approbation, although there are still plenty left hovering to kiss them.

But that is enough of refutation. Somewhere in the world the play is performed every night. People are bemused, dismayed or, I hope, exhilarated by it and driven to laughter. There have been homosexual and black versions. The lesbian angle must surely be to come. Misogyny is attached to it forever and the American-Freudian view of Jimmy and Cliff as lovers is still irresistible to academics and feminists alike. It's an old war horse that has paid my rent for a lifetime, and seems able to bear the burden of whatever caparison is placed upon its laden back.

Epitaph for George Dillon was written immediately before *Look Back in Anger* in collaboration with an actor-friend, Anthony Creighton. It had an odd passage. I offered it to the English Stage Company after they had accepted *Look Back*. It was clear that they regarded it as an inferior run-up, which was a fair judgement, and little more was said about it, in the way of these things. Then the Oxford Experimental Theatre wrote asking if I had something neglected lying in a drawer. They put it on, every newspaper sent one of its predators to see it and the response seemed to suggest that it might be a superior version of *Look Back*. Certainly, it sorted out the Philistines from the Boys, and the Royal Court perversely decided to stage it.

I was away in America at the time and when I returned it had transferred to the Comedy Theatre. The director, Bill Gaskill, had assembled a supple cast of then little-known actors. His staging was delicate but it seemed that Creighton had coaxed the cast to over-strive for laughs; Heaven knows, the Elliot family is grotesque enough and tip-toe on caricature, as did their models in real life. To guy them robbed them of truthfulness.

However, this was easily put right, and when the play arrived in New York, the production was impeccable. Those who did see it, will never forget the performance of Robert Stephens, the most uncomfortably powerful actor of his generation. When he looked at the photograph of Raymond at the end of Act One, his delivery of the line: 'You stupid looking bastard,' was lacerating. The audience shuddered unfailingly. His crumpled collapse, like an upended beetle, as he unwrapped the Elliots' unconsciously cruel gift of a typewriter, was enough to send the most abstemious, alcohol-fearing American reeling out into 45th Street and the nearest bar. Looking at the text again, it is dispiriting to realize how little in Britain, now the Yookay, has changed. The difference is that the lower-middle classes, instead of being a comic sub-culture, are now firmly on top and in command of the nation's drooping conformism and its resolute addiction to mediocrity in taste, morals and ambition.

In the second volume of my autobiography, *Almost a Gentleman*, I describe how I became the only living playwright to have been pursued down the London streets by an angry mob, the occasion being the first night of *The World of Paul Slickey*. Anyone reading the play now may well wonder what the fuss was all about. I can only refer them to my own account of the strange events and climate of the time which led up to a bizarre, rowdy and ugly event.

There were dispiriting similarities to this in the pre-production and reception of *Déjàvu*. Certainly, the same degree of concerted animosity attended it and the campaigning conspiracy of its suppression was just as malign. However, it is perhaps a little too soon to examine that background and the play is best read for itself. I inserted some brief notes at the beginning which may be helpful in the meantime.

JOHN OSBORNE, *Shropshire, August 1993*

LOOK BACK IN ANGER

For
MY FATHER

CONTENTS

The first performance in Great Britain of *Look Back in Anger* was given at the Royal Court Theatre, Sloane Square, London, on 8 May 1956, by the English Stage Company. It was directed by Tony Richardson, and the décor was by Alan Tagg. The cast was as follows:

JIMMY PORTER	Kenneth Haigh
CLIFF LEWIS	Alan Bates
ALISON PORTER	Mary Ure
HELENA CHARLES	Helena Hughes
COLONEL REDFERN	John Welsh

ACT ONE

*The Porters' one-room flat in a large Midland town. Early evening.
April.*

*The scene is a fairly large attic room, at the top of a large
Victorian house. The ceiling slopes down quite sharply from L. to R.
Down R. are two small low windows. In front of these is a dark oak
dressing table. Most of the furniture is simple, and rather old. Up R.
is a double bed, running the length of most of the back wall, the rest
of which is taken up with a shelf of books. Down R. below the bed is
a heavy chest of drawers, covered with books, neckties and odds and
ends, including a large, tattered toy teddy bear and soft, woolly
squirrel. Up L. is a door. Below this a small wardrobe. Most of the
wall L. is taken up with a high, oblong window. This looks out on to
the landing, but light comes through it from a skylight beyond.
Below the wardrobe is a gas stove, and, beside this, a wooden food
cupboard, on which is a small, portable radio. Down C. is a sturdy
dining table and three chairs, and, below this, L. and R., two deep,
shabby leather armchairs.*

*At rise of curtain, JIMMY and CLIFF are seated in the two
armchairs R. and L., respectively. All that we can see of either of
them is two pairs of legs, sprawled way out beyond the newspapers
which hide the rest of them from sight. They are both reading. Beside
them, and between them, is a jungle of newspapers and weeklies.
When we do eventually see them, we find that JIMMY is a tall, thin
young man about twenty-five, wearing a very worn tweed jacket and
flannels. Clouds of smoke fill the room from the pipe he is smoking.
He is a disconcerting mixture of sincerity and cheerful malice, of
tenderness and freebooting cruelty; restless, importunate, full of
pride, a combination which alienates the sensitive and insensitive
alike. Blistering honesty, or apparent honesty, like his, makes few
friends. To many he may seem sensitive to the point of vulgarity. To
others, he is simply a loudmouth. To be as vehement as he is is to be*

almost non-committal. CLIFF *is the same age, short, dark, big boned, wearing a pullover and grey, new, but very creased trousers. He is easy and relaxed, almost to lethargy, with the rather sad, natural intelligence of the self-taught. If* JIMMY *alienates love,* CLIFF *seems to exact it – demonstrations of it, at least, even from the cautious. He is a soothing, natural counterpoint to* JIMMY.

Standing L., below the food cupboard, is ALISON. *She is leaning over an ironing board. Beside her is a pile of clothes. Hers is the most elusive personality to catch in the uneasy polyphony of these three people. She is tuned in a different key, a key of well-bred malaise that is often drowned in the robust orchestration of the other two. Hanging over the grubby, but expensive, skirt she is wearing is a cherry red shirt of Jimmy's, but she manages somehow to look quite elegant in it. She is roughly the same age as the men. Somehow, their combined physical oddity makes her beauty more striking than it really is. She is tall, slim, dark. The bones of her face are long and delicate. There is a surprising reservation about her eyes, which are so large and deep they should make equivocation impossible. The room is still, smoke filled. The only sound is the occasional thud of Alison's iron on the board. It is one of those chilly Spring evenings, all cloud and shadows. Presently,* JIMMY *throws his paper down.*

JIMMY: Why do I do this every Sunday? Even the book reviews seem to be the same as last week's. Different books – same reviews. Have you finished that one yet?

CLIFF: Not yet.

JIMMY: I've just read three whole columns on the English Novel. Half of it's in French. Do the Sunday papers make *you* feel ignorant?

CLIFF: Not 'arf.

JIMMY: Well, you *are* ignorant. You're just a peasant. (*To* ALISON.) What about you? You're not a peasant are you?

ALISON: (*Absently*) What's that?

JIMMY: I said do the papers make you feel you're not so brilliant after all?

ALISON: Oh – I haven't read them yet.

6

JIMMY: I didn't ask you that. I said –

CLIFF: Leave the poor girlie alone. She's busy.

JIMMY: Well, she can talk, can't she? You can talk, can't you? You can express an opinion. Or does the White Woman's Burden make it impossible to think?

ALISON: I'm sorry. I wasn't listening properly.

JIMMY: You bet you weren't listening. Old Porter talks, and everyone turns over and goes to sleep. And Mrs Porter gets 'em all going with the first yawn.

CLIFF: Leave her alone, I said.

JIMMY: (*Shouting*) All right, dear. Go back to sleep. It was only me talking. You know? Talking? Remember? I'm sorry.

CLIFF: Stop yelling. I'm trying to read.

JIMMY: Why do you bother? You can't understand a word of it.

CLIFF: Uh huh.

JIMMY: You're too ignorant.

CLIFF: Yes, and uneducated. Now shut up, will you?

JIMMY: Why don't you get my wife to explain it to you? She's educated. (*To her.*) That's right, isn't it?

CLIFF: (*Kicking out at him from behind his paper*) Leave her alone, I said.

JIMMY: Do that again, you Welsh ruffian, and I'll pull your ears off.

(*He bangs* CLIFF's *paper out of his hands.*)

CLIFF: (*Leaning forward*) Listen – I'm trying to better myself. Let me get on with it, you big, horrible man. Give it me. (*Puts his hand out for paper.*)

ALISON: Oh, give it to him, Jimmy, for heaven's sake! I can't think!

CLIFF: Yes, come on, give me the paper. She can't think.

JIMMY: Can't think! (*Throws the paper back at him.*) She hasn't had a thought for years! Have you?

ALISON: No.

JIMMY: (*Picks up a weekly*) I'm getting hungry.

7

ALISON: Oh no, not already!

CLIFF: He's a bloody pig.

JIMMY: I'm not a pig. I just like food – that's all.

CLIFF: Like it! You're like a sexual maniac – only with you it's food. You'll end up in the *News of the World*, boyo, you wait. James Porter, aged twenty-five, was bound over last week after pleading guilty to interfering with a small cabbage and two tins of beans on his way home from the Builder's Arms. The accused said he hadn't been feeling well for some time, and had been having black-outs. He asked for his good record as an air-raid warden, second class, to be taken into account.

JIMMY: (*Grins*) Oh, yes, yes, yes. I like to eat. I'd like to live too. Do you mind?

CLIFF: Don't see any use in your eating at all. You never get any fatter.

JIMMY: People like me don't get fat. I've tried to tell you before. We just burn everything up. Now shut up while I read. You can make me some more tea.

CLIFF: Good God, you've just had a great potful! I only had one cup.

JIMMY: Like hell! Make some more.

CLIFF: (*To* ALISON) Isn't that right? Didn't I only have one cup?

ALISON: (*Without looking up*) That's right.

CLIFF: There you are. And she only had one cup too. I saw her. You guzzled the lot.

JIMMY: (*Reading his weekly*) Put the kettle on.

CLIFF: Put it on yourself. You've creased up my paper.

JIMMY: I'm the only one who knows how to treat a paper, or anything else, in this house. (*Picks up another paper.*) Girl here wants to know whether her boyfriend will lose all respect for her if she gives him what he asks for. Stupid bitch.

CLIFF: Just let me get at her, that's all.

JIMMY: Who buys this damned thing? (*Throws it down.*)

Haven't you read the other posh paper yet?

CLIFF: Which?

JIMMY: Well, there are only two posh papers on a Sunday – the one you're reading, and this one. Come on, let me have that one, and you take this.

CLIFF: Oh, all right.

(*They exchange.*)

I was only reading the Bishop of Bromley.

(*Puts out his hand to* ALISON.)

How are you, dullin'?

ALISON: All right thank you, dear.

CLIFF: (*Grasping her hand*) Why don't you leave all that, and sit down for a bit? You look tired.

ALISON: (*Smiling*) I haven't much more to do.

CLIFF: (*Kisses her hand, and puts her fingers in his mouth*) She's a beautiful girl, isn't she?

JIMMY: That's what they all tell me.

(*His eyes meet hers.*)

CLIFF: It's a lovely, delicious paw you've got. Ummmmm. I'm going to bite it off.

ALISON: Don't! I'll burn his shirt.

JIMMY: Give her her finger back, and don't be so sickening. What's the Bishop of Bromley say?

CLIFF: (*Letting go of* ALISON) Oh, it says here that he makes a very moving appeal to all Christians to do all they can to assist in the manufacture of the H-Bomb.

JIMMY: Yes, well, that's quite moving, I suppose. (*To* ALISON.) Are you moved, my darling?

ALISON: Well, naturally.

JIMMY: There you are: even my wife is moved. I ought to send the Bishop a subscription. Let's see. What else does he say. Dumdidumdidumdidum. Ah yes. He's upset because someone has suggested that he supports the rich against the poor. He says he denies the difference of class distinctions. 'This idea has been persistently and wickedly fostered by – the working classes!' Well!

(*He looks up at both of them for reaction, but* CLIFF *is reading, and* ALISON *is intent on her ironing.*)

JIMMY: (*To* CLIFF) Did you read that bit?

CLIFF: Um?

(*He has lost them, and he knows it, but he won't leave it.*)

JIMMY: (*To* ALISON) You don't suppose your father could have written it, do you?

ALISON: Written what?

JIMMY: What I just read out, of course.

ALISON: Why should my father have written it?

JIMMY: Sounds rather like Daddy, don't you think?

ALISON: Does it?

JIMMY: Is the Bishop of Bromley his *nom de plume*, do you think?

CLIFF: Don't take any notice of him. He's being offensive. And it's so easy for him.

JIMMY: (*Quickly*) Did you read about the woman who went to the mass meeting of a certain American evangelist at Earls Court? She went forward, to declare herself for love or whatever it is, and, in the rush of converts to get to the front, she broke four ribs and got kicked in the head. She was yelling her head off in agony, but with 50,000 people putting all they'd got into 'Onward Christian Soldiers', nobody even knew she was there. (*He looks up sharply for a response, but there isn't any.*) Sometimes, I wonder if there isn't something wrong with me. What about that tea?

CLIFF: (*Still behind paper*) What tea?

JIMMY: Put the kettle on.

(ALISON *looks up at him.*)

ALISON: Do you want some more tea?

JIMMY: I don't know. No, I don't think so.

ALISON: Do you want some, Cliff?

JIMMY: No, he doesn't. How much longer will you be doing that?

ALISON: Won't be long.

JIMMY: God, how I hate Sundays! It's always so depressing, always the same. We never seem to get any further, do we? Always the same ritual. Reading the papers, drinking tea, ironing. A few more hours, and another week gone. Our youth is slipping away. Do you know that?

CLIFF: (*Throws down paper*) What's that?

JIMMY: (*Casually*) Oh, nothing, nothing. Damn you, damn both of you, damn them all.

CLIFF: Let's go to the pictures. (*To* ALISON.) What do you say, lovely?

ALISON: I don't think I'll be able to. Perhaps Jimmy would like to go. (*To* JIMMY.) Would you like to?

JIMMY: And have my enjoyment ruined by the Sunday night yobs in the front row? No, thank you. (*Pause.*) Did you read Priestley's piece this week? Why on earth I ask I don't know. I know damned well you haven't. Why do I spend ninepence on that damned paper every week? Nobody reads it except me. Nobody can be bothered. No one can raise themselves out of their delicious sloth. You two will drive me round the bend soon – I know it, as sure as I'm sitting here. I know you're going to drive me mad. Oh heavens, how I long for a little ordinary human enthusiasm. Just enthusiasm – that's all. I want to hear a warm, thrilling voice cry out Hallelujah! (*He bangs his breast theatrically.*) Hallelujah! I'm alive! I've an idea. Why don't we have a little game? Let's pretend that we're human beings, and that we're actually alive. Just for a while. What do you say? Let's pretend we're human. (*He looks from one to the other.*) Oh, brother, it's such a long time since I was with anyone who got enthusiastic about anything.

CLIFF: What did he say?

JIMMY: (*Resentful of being dragged away from his pursuit of* ALISON) What did who say?

CLIFF: Mr Priestley.

JIMMY: What he always says, I suppose. He's like Daddy –
still casting well-fed glances back to the Edwardian
twilight from his comfortable, disenfrachised wilderness.
What the devil have you done to those trousers?

CLIFF: Done?

JIMMY: Are they the ones you bought last weekend? Look at
them. Do you see what he's done to those new trousers?

ALISON: You are naughty, Cliff. They look dreadful.

JIMMY: You spend good money on a new pair of trousers,
and then sprawl about in them like a savage. What do
you think you're going to do when I'm not around to
look after you? Well, what are you going to do? Tell me?

CLIFF: (*Grinning*) I don't know. (*To* ALISON.) What am I
going to do, lovely?

ALISON: You'd better take them off.

JIMMY: Yes, go on. Take 'em off. And I'll kick your behind
for you.

ALISON: I'll give them a press while I've got the iron on.

CLIFF: OK. (*Starts taking them off.*) I'll just empty the
pockets. (*Takes out keys, matches, handkerchief.*)

JIMMY: Give me those matches, will you?

CLIFF: Oh, you're not going to start up that old pipe again,
are you? It stinks the place out. (*To* ALISON.) Doesn't it
smell awful?

(JIMMY *grabs the matches, and lights up.*)

ALISON: I don't mind it. I've got used to it.

JIMMY: She's a great one for getting used to things. If she
were to die, and wake up in paradise – after the first five
minutes, she'd have got used to it.

CLIFF: (*Hands her the trousers*) Thank you, lovely. Give me a
cigarette, will you?

JIMMY: Don't give him one.

CLIFF: I can't stand the stink of that old pipe any longer. I
must have a cigarette.

JIMMY: I thought the doctor said no cigarettes?

CLIFF: Oh, why doesn't he shut up?

JIMMY: All right. They're your ulcers. Go ahead, and have a
   bellyache, if that's what you want. I give up. I give up.
   I'm sick of doing things for people. And all for what?
   (ALISON *gives* CLIFF *a cigarette. They both light up, and
   she goes on with her ironing.*)
   Nobody thinks, nobody cares. No beliefs, no convictions
   and no enthusiasm. Just another Sunday evening.
   (CLIFF *sits down again, in his pullover and shorts.*)
   Perhaps there's a concert on. (*Picks up* Radio Times.)
   Ah.
   (*Nudges* CLIFF *with his foot.*)
   Make some more tea.
   (CLIFF *grunts. He is reading again.*)
   Oh, yes. There's a Vaughan Williams. Well, that's
   something, anyway. Something strong, something
   simple, something English. I suppose people like me
   aren't supposed to be very patriotic. Somebody said –
   what was it – we get our cooking from Paris (that's a
   laugh), our politics from Moscow, and our morals from
   Port Said. Something like that, anyway. Who was it?
   (*Pause.*) Well, you wouldn't know anyway. I hate to
   admit it, but I think I can understand how her Daddy
   must have felt when he came back from India, after all
   those years away. The old Edwardian brigade do make
   their brief little world look pretty tempting. All
   homemade cakes and croquet, bright ideas, bright
   uniforms. Always the same picture: high summer, the
   long days in the sun, slim volumes of verse, crisp linen,
   the smell of starch. What a romantic picture. Phoney
   too, of course. It must have rained sometimes. Still,
   even I regret it somehow, phoney or not. If you've no
   world of your own, it's rather pleasant to regret the
   passing of someone else's. I must be getting sentimental.
   But I must say it's pretty dreary living in the American
   Age – unless you're an American of course. Perhaps all
   our children will be Americans. That's a thought isn't it?

(*He gives* CLIFF *a kick, and shouts at him.*)

I said that's a thought!

CLIFF: You did?

JIMMY: You sit there like a lump of dough. I thought you were going to make me some tea.

(CLIFF *groans.* JIMMY *turns to* ALISON.)

Is your friend Webster coming tonight?

ALISON: He might drop in. You know what he is.

JIMMY: Well, I hope he doesn't. I don't think I could take Webster tonight.

ALISON: I thought you said he was the only person who spoke your language.

JIMMY: So he is. Different dialect but same language. I like him. He's got bite, edge, drive –

ALISON: Enthusiasm.

JIMMY: You've got it. When he comes here, I begin to feel exhilarated. He doesn't like me, but he gives me something, which is more than I get from most people. Not since –

ALISON: Yes, we know. Not since you were living with Madeline. (*She folds some of the clothes she has already ironed, and crosses to the bed with them.*)

CLIFF: (*Behind paper again*) Who's Madeline?

ALISON: Oh, wake up, dear. You've heard about Madeline enough times. She was his mistress. Remember? When he was fourteen. Or was it thirteen?

JIMMY: Eighteen.

ALISON: He owes just about everything to Madeline.

CLIFF: I get mixed up with all your women. Was she the one all those years older than you?

JIMMY: Ten years.

CLIFF: Proper little Marchbanks, you are!

JIMMY: What time's that concert on? (*Checks paper.*)

CLIFF: (*Yawns*) Oh, I feel so sleepy. Don't feel like standing behind that blinking sweet-stall again tomorrow. Why don't you do it on your own, and let me sleep in?

JIMMY: I've got to be at the factory first thing, to get some more stock, so you'll have to put it up on your own. Another five minutes.

(ALISON *has returned to her ironing board. She stands with her arms folded, smoking, staring thoughtfully.*)

She had more animation in her little finger than you two put together.

CLIFF: Who did?

ALISON: Madeline.

JIMMY: Her curiosity about things, and about people was staggering. It wasn't just a naïve nosiness. With her, it was simply the delight of being awake, and watching.

(ALISON *starts to press Cliff's trousers.*)

CLIFF: (*Behind paper*) Perhaps I will make some tea, after all.

JIMMY: (*Quietly*) Just to be with her was an adventure. Even to sit on the top of a bus with her was like setting out with Ulysses.

CLIFF: Wouldn't have said Webster was much like Ulysses. He's an ugly little devil.

JIMMY: I'm not talking about Webster, stupid. He's all right though, in his way. A sort of female Emily Brontë. He's the only one of your friends (*to* ALISON) who's worth tuppence, anyway. I'm surprised you get on with him.

ALISON: So is he, I think.

JIMMY: (*Rising to window R., and looking out*) He's not only got guts, but sensitivity as well. That's about the rarest combination I can think of. None of your other friends have got either.

ALISON: (*Very quietly and earnestly*) Jimmy, please – don't go on. (*He turns and looks at her. The tired appeal in her voice has pulled him up suddenly. But he soon gathers himself for a new assault. He walks C., behind CLIFF, and stands, looking down at his head.*)

JIMMY: Your friends – there's a shower for you.

CLIFF: (*Mumbling*) Dry up. Let her get on with my trousers.

JIMMY: (*Musingly*) Don't think I could provoke her. Nothing

I could do would provoke her. Not even if I were to drop dead.

CLIFF: Then drop dead.

JIMMY: They're either militant like her Mummy and Daddy. Militant, arrogant and full of malice. Or vague. She's somewhere between the two.

CLIFF: Why don't you listen to that concert of yours? And don't stand behind me. That blooming droning on behind me gives me a funny feeling down the spine. (JIMMY *gives his ears a twist and* CLIFF *roars with pain.* JIMMY *grins back at him.*) That hurt, you rotten sadist! (*To* ALISON.) I wish you'd kick his head in for him.

JIMMY: (*Moving in between them*) Have you ever seen her brother? Brother Nigel? The straight-backed, chinless wonder from Sandhurst? I only met him once myself. He asked me to step outside when I told his mother she was evil minded.

CLIFF: And did you?

JIMMY: Certainly not. He's a big chap. Well, you've never heard so many well-bred commonplaces come from beneath the same bowler hat. The Platitude from Outer Space – that's brother Nigel. He'll end up in the Cabinet one day, make no mistake. But somewhere at the back of that mind is the vague knowledge that he and his pals have been plundering and fooling everybody for generations. (*Going upstage, and turning.*) Now Nigel is just about as vague as you can get without being actually invisible. And invisible politicians aren't much use to anyone – not even to *his* supporters! And nothing is more vague about Nigel than his knowledge. His knowledge of life and ordinary human beings is so hazy, he really deserves some sort of decoration for it – a medal inscribed 'For Vaguery in the Field'. But it wouldn't do for him to be troubled by any stabs of conscience, however vague. (*Moving down again.*)

Besides, he's a patriot and an Englishman, and he doesn't like the idea that he may have been selling out his countryman all these years, so what does he do? The only thing he *can* do – seek sanctuary in his own stupidity. The only way to keep things as much like they always have been as possible, is to make any alternative too much for your poor, tiny brain to grasp. It takes some doing nowadays. It really does. But they knew all about character building at Nigel's school, and he'll make it all right. Don't you worry, he'll make it. And, what's more, he'll do it better than anybody else!

(*There is no sound, only the plod of Alison's iron. Her eyes are fixed on what she is doing.* CLIFF *stares at the floor. His cheerfulness has deserted him for the moment.* JIMMY *is rather shakily triumphant. He cannot allow himself to look at either of them to catch their response to his rhetoric, so he moves across to the window, to recover himself, and look out.*)

It's started to rain. That's all it needs. This room and the rain. (*He's been cheated out of his response, but he's got to draw blood somehow. Conversationally.*) Yes, that's the little woman's family. You know Mummy and Daddy, of course. And don't let the Marquess of Queensberry manner fool you. They'll kick you in the groin while you're handing your hat to the maid. As for Nigel and Alison – (*In a reverent, Stuart Hibberd voice.*) Nigel and Alison. They're what they sound like: sycophantic, phlegmatic and pusillanimous.

CLIFF: I'll bet that concert's started by now. Shall I put it on?

JIMMY: I looked up that word the other day. It's one of those words I've never been quite sure of, but always thought I knew.

CLIFF: What was that?

JIMMY: I told you – pusillanimous. Do you know what it means?

(CLIFF *shakes his head*.)

Neither did I really. All this time, I have been married to this woman, this monument to non-attachment, and suddenly I discover that there is actually a word that sums her up. Not just an adjective in the English language to describe her with – it's her name! Pusillanimous! It sounds like some fleshy Roman matron, doesn't it? The Lady Pusillanimous seen here with her husband Sextus, on their way to the Games. (CLIFF *looks troubled, and glances uneasily at* ALISON.) Poor old Sextus! If he were put into a Hollywood film, he's so unimpressive, they'd make some poor British actor play the part. He doesn't know it, but those beefcake Christians will make off with his wife in the wonder of stereophonic sound before the picture's over. (ALISON *leans against the board, and closes her eyes*.) The Lady Pusillanimous has been promised a brighter easier world than old Sextus can ever offer her. Hi, Pusey! What say we get the hell down to the Arena, and maybe feed ourselves to a couple of lions, huh?

ALISON: God help me, if he doesn't stop, I'll go out of my mind in a minute.

JIMMY: Why don't you? That would be something, anyway. (*Crosses to chest of drawers R*.) But I haven't told you what it means yet, have I? (*Picks up dictionary*.) I don't have to tell her – she knows. In fact, if my pronunciation is at fault, she'll probably wait for a suitably public moment to correct it. Here it is. I quote: Pusillanimous. Adjective. Wanting of firmness of mind, of small courage, having a little mind, mean spirited, cowardly, timid of mind. From the Latin pusillus, very little, and animus, the mind. (*Slams the book shut*.) That's my wife! That's *her* isn't it? Behold the Lady Pusillanimous. (*Shouting hoarsely*.) Hi, Pusey! When's your next picture?

(JIMMY *watches her, waiting for her to break. For no more*

than a flash, ALISON's *face seems to contort, and it looks as though she might throw her head back, and scream. But it passes in a moment. She is used to these carefully rehearsed attacks, and it doesn't look as though he will get his triumph tonight. She carries on with her ironing.* JIMMY *crosses, and switches on the radio. The Vaughan Williams concert has started. He goes back to his chair, leans back in it, and closes his eyes.*)

ALISON: (*Handing* CLIFF *his trousers*) There you are, dear. They're not very good, but they'll do for now.
(CLIFF *gets up and puts them on.*)

CLIFF: Oh, that's lovely.

ALISON: Now try and look after them. I'll give them a real press later on.

CLIFF: Thank you, you beautiful, darling girl.
(*He puts his arms round her waist, and kisses her. She smiles, and gives his nose a tug.* JIMMY *watches from his chair.*)

ALISON: (*To* CLIFF) Let's have a cigarette, shall we?

CLIFF: That's a good idea. Where are they?

ALISON: On the stove. Do you want one Jimmy?

JIMMY: No thank you, I'm trying to listen. Do you mind?

CLIFF: Sorry, your lordship.
(*He puts a cigarette in* ALISON's *mouth, and one in his own, and lights up.* CLIFF *sits down, and picks up his paper.* ALISON *goes back to her board.* CLIFF *throws down paper, picks up another, and thumbs through that.*)

JIMMY: Do you have to make all that racket?

CLIFF: Oh, sorry.

JIMMY: It's quite a simple thing, you know – turning over a page. Anyway, that's my paper. (*Snatches it away.*)

CLIFF: Oh, don't be so mean!

JIMMY: Price ninepence, obtainable from any newsagent's. Now let me hear the music, for God's sake. (*Pause. To* ALISON.) Are you going to be much longer doing that?

ALISON: Why?

JIMMY: Perhaps you haven't noticed it, but it's interfering with the radio.

ALISON: I'm sorry. I shan't be much longer.

(*A pause. The iron mingles with the music.* CLIFF *shifts restlessly in his chair.* JIMMY *watches* ALISON, *his foot beginning to twitch dangerously. Presently, he gets up quickly, crossing below* ALISON *to the radio, and turns it off.*)

What did you do that for?

JIMMY: I wanted to listen to the concert, that's all.

ALISON: Well, what's stopping you?

JIMMY: Everyone's making such a din – that's what's stopping me.

ALISON: Well, I'm very sorry, but I can't just stop everything because you want to listen to music.

JIMMY: Why not?

ALISON: Really, Jimmy, you're like a child.

JIMMY: Don't try and patronize me. (*Turning to* CLIFF.) She's so clumsy. I watch for her to do the same things every night. The way she jumps on the bed, as if she were stamping on someone's face, and draws the curtains back with a great clatter, in that casually destructive way of hers. It's like someone launching a battleship. Have you ever noticed how noisy women are? (*Crosses below chairs to L.C.*) Have you? The way they kick the floor about, simply walking over it? Or have you watched them sitting at their dressing tables, dropping their weapons and banging down their bits of boxes and brushes and lipsticks? (*He faces her dressing table.*) I've watched her doing it night after night. When you see a woman in front of her bedroom mirror, you realize what a refined sort of a butcher she is. (*Turns in.*) Did you ever see some dirty old Arab, sticking his fingers into some mess of lamb fat and gristle? Well, she's just like that. Thank God they don't have many women surgeons! Those primitive hands would have your guts out in no time. Flip! Out it comes, like the powder out of its box. Flop! Back it goes, like the powder puff on the table.

CLIFF: (*Grimacing cheerfully*) Ugh! Stop it!

JIMMY: (*Moving upstage*) She'd drop your guts like hair clips and fluff all over the floor. You've got to be fundamentally insensitive to be as noisy and as clumsy as that. (*He moves C., and leans against the table.*) I had a flat underneath a couple of girls once. You heard every damned thing those bastards did, all day and night. The most simple, everyday actions were a sort of assault course on your sensibilities. I used to plead with them. I even got to screaming the most ingenious obscenities I could think of, up the stairs at them. But nothing, nothing, would move them. With those two, even a simple visit to the lavatory sounded like a medieval siege. Oh, they beat me in the end – I had to go. I expect they're still at it. Or they're probably married by now, and driving some other poor devils out of their minds. Slamming their doors, stamping their high heels, banging their irons and saucepans – the eternal flaming racket of the female.

(*Church bells start ringing outside.*)

Oh, hell! Now the bloody bells have started! (*He rushes to the window.*) Wrap it up, will you? Stop ringing those bells! There's somebody going crazy in here! I don't want to hear them!

ALISON: Stop shouting! (*Recovering immediately.*) You'll have Miss Drury up here.

JIMMY: I don't give a damn about Miss Drury – that mild old gentlewoman doesn't fool me, even if she takes in you two. She's an old robber. She gets more than enough out of us for this place every week. Anyway, she's probably in church, (*points to the window*) swinging on those bloody bells!

(CLIFF *goes to the window, and closes it.*)

CLIFF: Come on now, be a good boy. I'll take us all out, and
we'll have a drink.

JIMMY: They're not open yet. It's Sunday. Remember?
Anyway, it's raining.

CLIFF: Well, shall we dance?

(*He pushes* JIMMY *round the floor, who is past the mood for
this kind of fooling.*)

Do you come here often?

JIMMY: Only in the mating season. All right, all right, very
funny.

(*He tries to escape, but* CLIFF *holds him like a vice.*)

Let me go.

CLIFF: Not until you've apologized for being nasty to
everyone. Do you think bosoms will be in or out, this
year?

JIMMY: Your teeth will be out in a minute, if you don't let
go!

(*He makes a great effort to wrench himself free, but* CLIFF
*hangs on. They collapse to the floor C., below the table,
struggling.* ALISON *carries on with her ironing. This is
routine, but she is getting close to breaking point, all the
same.* CLIFF *manages to break away, and finds himself in
front of the ironing board.* JIMMY *springs up. They
grapple.*)

ALISON: Look out, for heaven's sake! Oh, it's more like a zoo
every day!

(JIMMY *makes a frantic, deliberate effort, and manages to
push* CLIFF *on to the ironing board, and into* ALISON. *The
board collapses.* CLIFF *falls against her, and they end up in
a heap on the floor.* ALISON *cries out in pain.* JIMMY *looks
down at them, dazed and breathless.*)

CLIFF: (*Picking himself up*) She's hurt. Are you all right?

ALISON: Well, does it look like it!

CLIFF: She's burnt her arm on the iron.

JIMMY: Darling, I'm sorry.

ALISON: Get out!

JIMMY: I'm sorry, believe me. You think I did it on pur –

ALISON: (*Her head shaking helplessly*) Clear out of my *sight*!

(*He stares at her uncertainly.* CLIFF *nods to him, and he turns and goes out of the door.*)

CLIFF: Come and sit down.

(*He leads her to the armchair. R.*)

You look a bit white. Are you all right?

ALISON: Yes. I'm all right now.

CLIFF: Let's have a look at your arm. (*Examines it.*) Yes, it's quite red. That's going to be painful. What should I do with it?

ALISON: Oh, it's nothing much. A bit of soap on it will do. I never can remember what you do with burns.

CLIFF: I'll just pop down to the bathroom and get some. Are you sure you're all right?

ALISON: Yes.

CLIFF: (*Crossing to door*) Won't be a minute.

(CLIFF *exits.* ALISON *leans back in the chair, and looks up at the ceiling. She breathes in deeply, and brings her hands up to her face. She winces as she feels the pain in her arm, and she lets it fall. She runs her hand through her hair.*)

ALISON: (*In a clenched whisper*) Oh, God!

(CLIFF *re-enters with a bar of soap.*)

CLIFF: It's this scented muck. Do you think it'll be all right?

ALISON: That'll do.

CLIFF: Here we are then. Let's have your arm.

(*He kneels down beside her, and she holds out her arm.*)

I've put it under the tap. It's quite soft. I'll do it ever so gently.

(*Very carefully, he rubs the soap over the burn.*)

All right?

(*She nods.*)

You're a brave girl.

ALISON: I don't feel very brave. (*Tears harshening her voice.*) I really don't, Cliff. I don't think I can take much more. (*Turns her head away.*) I think I feel rather sick.

CLIFF: All over now. (*Puts the soap down.*) Would you like
    me to get you something?
    (*She shakes her head. He sits on the arm of the chair, and
    puts his arm round her. She leans her head back on to him.*)
    Don't upset yourself, lovely.
    (*He massages the back of her neck, and she lets her head fall
    forward.*)
ALISON: Where is he?
CLIFF: In my room.
ALISON: What's he doing?
CLIFF: Lying on the bed. Reading, I think. (*Stroking her
    neck.*) That better?
    (*She leans back, and closes her eyes again.*)
ALISON: Bless you.
    (*He kisses the top of her head.*)
CLIFF: I don't think I'd have the courage to live on
    my own again – in spite of everything. I'm
    pretty rough, and pretty ordinary really, and I'd seem
    worse on my own. And you get fond of people too,
    worse luck.
ALISON: I don't think I want anything more to do with love.
    Any more. I can't take it on.
CLIFF: You're too young to start giving up. Too young, and
    too lovely. Perhaps I'd better put a bandage on that – do
    you think so?
ALISON: There's some on my dressing table.
    (CLIFF *crosses to the dressing table R.*)
    I keep looking back, as far as I remember, and I can't
    think what it was to feel young, really young. Jimmy
    said the same thing to me the other day. I pretended not
    to be listening – because I knew that would hurt him, I
    suppose. And – of course – he got savage, like tonight.
    But I knew just what he meant. I suppose it would have
    been so easy to say 'Yes, darling, I know just what you
    mean. I know what you're feeling.' (*Shrugs.*) It's those
    easy things that seem to be so impossible with us.

(CLIFF *stands down R., holding the bandage, his back to her.*)

CLIFF: I'm wondering how much longer I can go on watching you two tearing the insides out of each other. It looks pretty ugly sometimes.

ALISON: You wouldn't seriously think of leaving us, would you?

CLIFF: I suppose not. (*Crosses to her.*)

ALISON: I think I'm frightened. If only I knew what was going to happen.

CLIFF: (*Kneeling on the arm of her chair*) Give it here.
(*She holds out her arm.*)
Yell out if I hurt you.
(*He bandages it for her.*)

ALISON: (*Staring at her outstretched arm*) Cliff –

CLIFF: Um? (*Slight pause.*) What is it, lovely?

ALISON: Nothing.

CLIFF: I said: what is it?

ALISON: You see – (*Hesitates.*) I'm pregnant.

CLIFF: (*After a few moments*) I'll need some scissors.

ALISON: They're over there.

CLIFF: (*Crossing to the dressing table*) That is something, isn't it? When did you find this out?

ALISON: Few days ago. It was a bit of a shock.

CLIFF: Yes, I dare say.

ALISON: After three years of married life, I have to get caught out now.

CLIFF: None of us infallible, I suppose. (*Crosses to her.*) Must say I'm surprised though.

ALISON: It's always been out of the question. What with – this place, and no money, and oh – everything. He's resented it, I know. What can you do?

CLIFF: You haven't told him yet.

ALISON: Not yet.

CLIFF: What are you going to do?

ALISON: I've no idea.

CLIFF: (*Having cut her bandage, he starts tying it*) That too tight?

ALISON: Fine, thank you.
(*She rises, goes to the ironing board, folds it up, and leans it against the food cupboard R.*)

CLIFF: Is it . . . Is it . . . ?

ALISON: Too late to avert the situation? (*Places the iron on the rack of the stove.*) I'm not certain yet. Maybe not. If not, there won't be any problem, will there?

CLIFF: And if it is too late?
(*Her face is turned away from him. She simply shakes her head.*)
Why don't you tell him now?
(*She kneels down to pick up the clothes on the floor, and folds them up.*)
After all, he does love you. You don't need me to tell you that.

ALISON: Can't you see? He'll suspect my motives at once. He never stops telling himself that I know how vulnerable he is. Tonight it might be all right – we'd make love. But later, we'd both lie awake, watching for the light to come through that little window, and dreading it. In the morning, he'd feel hoaxed, as if I were trying to kill him in the worst way of all. He'd watch me growing bigger every day, and I wouldn't dare to look at him.

CLIFF: You may have to face it, lovely.

ALISON: Jimmy's got his own private morality, as you know. What my mother calls 'loose'. It is pretty free, of course, but it's very harsh too. You know, it's funny, but we never slept together before we were married.

CLIFF: It certainly is – knowing him!

ALISON: We knew each other such a short time, everything moved at such a pace, we didn't have much opportunity. And, afterwards, he actually taunted me with my virginity. He was quite angry about it, as if I had deceived him in some strange way. He seemed to think an untouched woman would defile him.

CLIFF: I've never heard you talking like this about him. He'd be quite pleased.

ALISON: Yes, he would. (*She gets up, the clothes folded over her arm.*) Do you think he's right?

CLIFF: What about?

ALISON: Oh – everything.

CLIFF: Well, I suppose he and I think the same about a lot of things, because we're alike in some ways. We both come from working people, if you like. Oh I know some of his mother's relatives are pretty posh, but he hates them as much as he hates yours. Don't quite know why. Anyway, he gets on with me because I'm common. (*Grins.*) Common as dirt, that's me.

(*She puts her hand on his head, and strokes it thoughtfully.*)

ALISON: You think I should tell him about the baby?

(*He gets up, and puts his arm round her.*)

CLIFF: It'll be all right – you see. Tell him.

(*He kisses her. Enter* JIMMY. *He looks at them curiously, but without surprise. They are both aware of him, but make no sign of it. He crosses to the armchair L., and sits down next to them. He picks up a paper, and starts looking at it.* CLIFF *glances at him,* ALISON's *head against his cheek.*) There you are, you old devil, you! Where have you been?

JIMMY: You know damn well where I've been. (*Without looking at her.*) How's your arm?

ALISON: Oh, it's all right. It wasn't much.

CLIFF: She's beautiful, isn't she?

JIMMY: You seem to think so.

(CLIFF *and* ALISON *still have their arms round one another.*)

CLIFF: Why the hell she married you, I'll never know.

JIMMY: You think she'd have been better off with you?

CLIFF: I'm not her type. Am I, dullin'?

ALISON: I'm not sure what my type is.

JIMMY: Why don't you both get into bed, and have done with it.

ALISON: You know, I think he really means that.

JIMMY: I do. I can't concentrate with you two standing there like that.

CLIFF: He's just an old Puritan at heart.

JIMMY: Perhaps I am, at that. Anyway, you both look pretty silly slobbering over each other.

CLIFF: I think she's beautiful. And so do you, only you're too much of a pig to say so.

JIMMY: You're just a sexy little Welshman, and you know it! Mummy and Daddy turn pale, and face the east every time they remember she's married to me. But if they saw all this going on, they'd collapse. Wonder what they would do, incidentally. Send for the police I expect. (*Genuinely friendly.*) Have you got a cigarette?

ALISON: (*Disengaging*) I'll have a look.

(*She goes to her handbag on the table C.*)

JIMMY: (*Pointing at* CLIFF) He gets more like a little mouse every day, doesn't he? (*He is trying to re-establish himself.*) He really does look like one. Look at those ears, and that face, and the little short legs.

ALISON: (*Looking through her bag*) That's because he *is* a mouse.

CLIFF: Eek! Eek! I'm a mouse.

JIMMY: A randy little mouse.

CLIFF: (*Dancing round the table, and squeaking*) I'm a mouse, I'm a mouse, I'm a randy little mouse. That's a mourris dance.

JIMMY: A what?

CLIFF: A *Mourris Dance*. That's a Morris Dance strictly for mice.

JIMMY: You stink. You really do. Do you know that?

CLIFF: Not as bad as you, you horrible old bear.

(*Goes over to him, and grabs his foot.*)

You're a stinking old bear, you hear me?

JIMMY: Let go of my foot, you whimsy little half-wit. You're making my stomach heave. I'm resting! If you don't let go, I'll cut off your nasty, great, slimy tail!

(CLIFF *gives him a tug, and* JIMMY *falls to the floor.* ALISON *watches them, relieved and suddenly full of affection.*)

ALISON: I've run out of cigarettes.

(CLIFF *is dragging* JIMMY *along the floor by his feet.*)

JIMMY: (*Yelling*) Go out and get me some cigarettes, and stop playing the fool!

CLIFF: OK.

(*He lets go of* JIMMY's *legs suddenly, who yells again as his head bangs on the floor.*)

ALISON: Here's half a crown. (*Giving it him.*) The shop on the corner will be open.

CLIFF: Right you are. (*Kisses her on the forehead quickly.*) Don't forget. (*Crosses upstage to door.*)

JIMMY: Now get to hell out of here!

CLIFF: (*At door*) Hey, shorty!

JIMMY: What do you want?

CLIFF: Make a nice pot of tea.

JIMMY: (*Getting up*) I'll kill you first.

CLIFF: (*Grinning*) That's my boy!

(CLIFF *exits.* JIMMY *is now beside* ALISON, *who is still looking through her handbag. She becomes aware of his nearness, and, after a few moments, closes it. He takes hold of her bandaged arm.*)

JIMMY: How's it feeling?

ALISON: Fine. It wasn't anything.

JIMMY: All this fooling about can get a bit dangerous.

(*He sits on the edge of the table, holding her hand.*)

I'm sorry.

ALISON: I know.

JIMMY: I mean it.

ALISON: There's no need.

JIMMY: I did it on purpose.

ALISON: Yes.

JIMMY: There's hardly a moment when I'm not – watching and wanting you. I've got to hit out somehow. Nearly four years of being in the same room with you, night and day, and I still can't stop my sweat breaking out when I see you doing – something as ordinary as leaning over an ironing board.

(*She strokes his head, not sure of herself yet.*)

(*Sighing.*) Trouble is – Trouble is you get used to people. Even their trivialities become indispensable to you. Indispensable, and a little mysterious.

(*He slides his head forward, against her, trying to catch his thoughts.*)

I think . . . I must have a lot of – old stock . . . Nobody wants it . . .

(*He puts his face against her belly. She goes on stroking his head, still on guard a little. Then he lifts his head, and they kiss passionately.*)

What are we going to do tonight?

ALISON: What would you like to do? Drink?

JIMMY: I know what I want now.

(*She takes his head in her hands and kisses him.*)

ALISON: Well, you'll have to wait till the proper time.

JIMMY: There's no such thing.

ALISON: Cliff will be back in a minute.

JIMMY: What did he mean by 'don't forget'?

ALISON: Something I've been meaning to tell you.

JIMMY: (*Kissing her again*) You're fond of him, aren't you?

ALISON: Yes, I am.

JIMMY: He's the only friend I seem to have left now. People go away. You never see them again. I can remember lots of names – men and women. When I was at school – Watson, Roberts, Davies. Jenny, Madeline, Hugh . . . (*Pause.*) And there's Hugh's mum, of course. I'd almost forgotten her. She's been a good friend to us, if you like.

She's even letting me buy the sweet-stall off her in my
own time. She only bought it for us, anyway. She's so
fond of you. I can never understand why you're so –
distant with her.

ALISON: (*Alarmed at this threat of a different mood*). Jimmy –
please no!

JIMMY: (*Staring at her anxious face*) You're very beautiful. A
beautiful, great-eyed squirrel.
(*She nods brightly, relieved.*)
Hoarding, nut-munching squirrel.
(*She mimes this delightedly.*)
With highly polished, gleaming fur, and an ostrich
feather of a tail.

ALISON: Wheeeeeeeeee!

JIMMY: How I envy you.
(*He stands, her arms around his neck.*)

ALISON: Well, you're a jolly super bear, too. A really
soooooooooooooooooper, marvellous bear.

JIMMY: Bears and squirrels *are* marvellous.

ALISON: Marvellous *and* beautiful. (*She jumps up and down
excitedly, making little 'paw gestures'.*) Ooooooooh!
Ooooooooh!

JIMMY: What the hell's that?

ALISON: That's a dance squirrels do when they're happy.
(*They embrace again.*)

JIMMY: What makes you think you're happy?

ALISON: Everything just seems all right suddenly. That's all.
Jimmy –

JIMMY: Yes?

ALISON: You know I told you I'd something to tell you?

JIMMY: Well?
(CLIFF *appears in the doorway.*)

CLIFF: Didn't get any further than the front door. Miss
Drury hadn't gone to church after all. I couldn't get
away from her. (*To* ALISON.) Someone on the phone for
you.

ALISON: On the phone? Who on earth is it?

CLIFF: Helena something.

(JIMMY *and* ALISON *look at each other quickly*.)

JIMMY: (*To* CLIFF) Helena Charles?

CLIFF: That's it.

ALISON: Thank you, Cliff. (*Moves upstage*.) I won't be a minute.

CLIFF: You will. Old Miss Drury will keep you down there for ever. She doesn't think we keep this place clean enough. (*Comes and sits in the armchair down R*.) Thought you were going to make me some tea, you rotter.

(JIMMY *makes no reply*.)

What's the matter, boyo?

JIMMY: (*Slowly*) That bitch.

CLIFF: Who?

JIMMY: (*To himself*) Helena Charles.

CLIFF: Who is this Helena?

JIMMY: One of her old friends. And one of my natural enemies. You're sitting on my chair.

CLIFF: Where are we going for a drink?

JIMMY: I don't know.

CLIFF: Well, you were all for it earlier on.

JIMMY: What does she want? What would make her ring up? It can't be for anything pleasant. Oh well, we shall soon know. (*He settles on the table*.) Few minutes ago things didn't seem so bad either. I've just about had enough of this 'expense of spirit' lark, as far as women are concerned. Honestly, it's enough to make you become a scoutmaster or something isn't it? Sometimes I almost envy old Gide and the Greek Chorus boys. Oh, I'm not saying that it mustn't be hell for them a lot of the time. But, at least, they do seem to have a cause – not a particularly good one, it's true. But plenty of them do seem to have a revolutionary fire about them, which is more than you can say for the rest of us. Like Webster, for instance. He doesn't like me – they hardly ever do. (*He is talking for the sake of it, only half listening to what he is saying.*) I dare say he suspects me because I refuse to treat him either as a clown or as a tragic hero. He's like a man with a strawberry mark – he keeps thrusting it in your face because he can't believe it doesn't interest or horrify you particularly. (*Picks up Alison's handbag thoughtfully, and starts looking through it.*) As if I give a damn which way he likes his meat served up. I've got my own strawberry mark – only it's in a different place. No, as far as the Michelangelo Brigade's concerned, I must be a sort of right-wing deviationist. If the Revolution ever comes, I'll be the first to be put up against the wall, with all the other poor old liberals.

CLIFF: (*Indicating Alison's handbag*) Wouldn't you say that that was her private property?

JIMMY: You're quite right. But do you know something? Living night and day with another human being has made me predatory and suspicious. I know that the only way of finding out exactly what's going on is to catch them when they don't know you're looking. When she goes out, I go through everything – trunks, cases, drawers, bookcase, everything. Why? To see if there is something of me somewhere, a reference to me. I want to know if I'm being betrayed.

CLIFF: You look for trouble, don't you?

JIMMY: Only because I'm pretty certain of finding it. (*Brings out a letter from the handbook.*) Look at that! Oh, I'm such a fool. This is happening every five minutes of the day. She gets letters. (*He holds it up.*) Letters from her mother, letters in which I'm not mentioned at all because my name is a dirty word. And what does she do? (*Enter ALISON. He turns to look at her.*) She writes long letters back to Mummy, and never mentions me at all, because I'm just a dirty word to her too.

(*He throws the letter down at her feet.*)

Well, what did your friend want?

ALISON: She's at the station. She's – coming over.

JIMMY: I see. She said 'Can I come over?' And you said 'My husband, Jimmy – if you'll forgive me using such a dirty word – will be delighted to see you. He'll kick your face in!'

(*He stands up, unable to sustain his anger, poised on the table.*)

ALISON: (*Quietly*) She's playing with the company at the Hippodrome this week, and she's got no digs. She can't find anywhere to stay –

JIMMY: That I don't believe!

ALISON: So I said she could come here until she fixes something else. Miss Drury's got a spare room downstairs.

JIMMY: Why not have her in here? Did you tell her to bring her armour? Because she's going to need it!

ALISON: (*Vehemently*) Oh why don't you shut up, please!

JIMMY: Oh, my dear wife, you've got so much to learn. I only hope you learn it one day. If only something – something would happen to you, and wake you out of your beauty sleep! (*Coming in close to her.*) If you could have a child, and it would die. Let it grow, let a recognizable human face emerge from that little mass of indiarubber and wrinkles.

(*She retreats away from him.*)

Please – if only I could watch you face that. I wonder if you might even become a recognizable human being yourself. But I doubt it.

(*She moves away, stunned, and leans on the gas stove down L. He stands rather helplessly on his own.*)

Do you know I have never known the great pleasure of lovemaking when I didn't desire it myself. Oh, it's not that she hasn't her own kind of passion. She has the passion of a python. She just devours me whole every time, as if I were some over-large rabbit. That's me. That bulge around her navel – if you're wondering what it is – it's me. Me, buried alive down there, and going mad, smothered in that peaceful looking coil. Not a sound, not a flicker from her – she doesn't even rumble a little. You'd think that this indigestible mess would stir up some kind of tremor in these distended, overfed tripes – but not her! (*Crosses up to the door.*) She'll go on sleeping and devouring until there's nothing left of me.

(JIMMY *exits.* ALISON's *head goes back as if she were about to make some sound. But her mouth remains open and trembling, as* CLIFF *looks on. Curtain.*)

ACT TWO

SCENE ONE

Two weeks later. Evening.

ALISON *is standing over the gas stove, pouring water from the kettle into a large teapot. She is only wearing a slip, and her feet are bare. In the room across the hall,* JIMMY *is playing on his jazz trumpet, in intermittent bursts.* ALISON *takes the pot to the table C., which is laid for four people. The Sunday paper jungle around the two armchairs is as luxuriant as ever. It is late afternoon, the end of a hot day. She wipes her forehead. She crosses to the dressing table R., takes out a pair of stockings from one of the drawers, and sits down on the small chair beside it to put them on. While she is doing this, the door opens and* HELENA *enters. She is the same age as Alison, medium height, carefully and expensively dressed. Now and again, when she allows her rather judicial expression of alertness to soften, she is very attractive. Her sense of matriarchal authority makes most men who meet her anxious, not only to please but impress, as if she were the gracious representative of visiting royalty. In this case, the royalty of that middle-class womanhood, which is so eminently secure in its divine rights, that it can afford to tolerate the parliament, and reasonably free assembly of its menfolk. Even from other young women, like Alison, she receives her due of respect and admiration. In Jimmy, as one would expect, she arouses all the rabble-rousing instincts of his spirit. And she is not accustomed to having to defend herself against catcalls. However, her sense of modestly exalted responsibility enables her to behave with an impressive show of strength and dignity, although the strain of this is beginning to tell on her a little. She is carrying a large salad colander.*

ALISON: Did you manage all right?

HELENA: Of course. I've prepared most of the meals in the last week, you know.

ALISON: Yes, you have. It's been wonderful having someone to help. Another woman, I mean.

HELENA: (*Crossing down L.*) I'm enjoying it. Although I don't think I shall ever get used to having to go down to the bathroom every time I want some water for something.

ALISON: It is primitive, isn't it?

HELENA: Yes. It is rather. (*She starts tearing up green salad on to four plates, which she takes from the food cupboard.*) Looking after one man is really enough, but two is rather an undertaking.

ALISON: Oh, Cliff looks after himself, more or less. In fact, he helps me quite a lot.

HELENA: Can't say I'd noticed it.

ALISON: You've been doing it instead, I suppose.

HELENA: I see.

ALISON: You've settled in so easily somehow.

HELENA: Why shouldn't I?

ALISON: It's not exactly what you're used to, is it?

HELENA: And are you used to it?

ALISON: Everything seems very different here now – with you here.

HELENA: Does it?

ALISON: Yes. I was on my own before –

HELENA: Now you've got me. So you're not sorry you asked me to stay?

ALISON: Of course not. Did you tell him his tea was ready?

HELENA: I banged on the door of Cliff's room, and yelled. He didn't answer, but he must have heard. I don't know where Cliff is.

ALISON: (*Leaning back in her chair*) I thought I'd feel cooler after a bath, but I feel hot again already. God, I wish he'd lose that damned trumpet.

HELENA: I imagine that's for my benefit.

ALISON: Miss Drury will ask us to go soon, I know it. Thank goodness she isn't in. Listen to him.

HELENA: Does he drink?

ALISON: Drink? (*Rather startled.*) He's not an alcoholic, if that's what you mean.

(*They both pause, listening to the trumpet.*)

He'll have the rest of the street banging on the door next.

HELENA: (*Pondering*) It's almost as if he wanted to kill someone with it. And me in particular. I've never seen such hatred in someone's eyes before. It's slightly horrifying. Horrifying (*crossing to food cupboard for tomatoes, beetroot and cucumber*) and oddly exciting.

(ALISON *faces her dressing mirror, and brushes her hair.*)

ALISON: He had his own jazz band once. That was when he was still a student, before I knew him. I rather think he'd like to start another, and give up the stall altogether.

HELENA: Is Cliff in love with you?

ALISON: (*Stops brushing for a moment*) No . . . I don't think so.

HELENA: And what about you? You look as though I've asked you a rather peculiar question. The way things are, you might as well be frank with me. I only want to help. After all, your behaviour together is a little strange – by most people's standards, to say the least.

ALISON: You mean you've seen us embracing each other?

HELENA: Well, it doesn't seem to go on as much as it did, I admit. Perhaps he finds my presence inhibiting – even if Jimmy's isn't.

ALISON: We're simply fond of each other – there's no more to it than that.

HELENA: Darling, really! It can't be as simple as that.

ALISON: You mean there must be something physical too? I suppose there is, but it's not exactly a consuming passion with either of us. It's just a relaxed, cheerful sort of thing, like being warm in bed. You're too comfortable to bother about moving for the sake of some other pleasure.

HELENA: I find it difficult to believe anyone's that lazy!

ALISON: I think *we* are.

HELENA: And what about Jimmy? After all, he is your husband. Do you mean to say he actually approves of it?

ALISON: It isn't easy to explain. It's what he would call a question of allegiances, and he expects you to be pretty literal about them. Not only about himself and all the things he believes in, his present and his future, but his past as well. All the people he admires and loves, and has loved. The friends he used to know, people I've never even known – and probably wouldn't have liked. His father, who died years ago. Even the other women he's loved. Do you understand?

HELENA: Do you?

ALISON: I've tried to. But I still can't bring myself to feel the way he does about things. I can't believe that he's right somehow.

HELENA: Well, that's something, anyway.

ALISON: If things have worked out with Cliff, it's because he's kind and lovable, and I've grown genuinely fond of him. But it's been a fluke. It's worked because Cliff is such a nice person anyway. With Hugh, it was quite different.

HELENA: Hugh?

ALISON: Hugh Tanner. He and Jimmy were friends almost from childhood. Mrs Tanner is his mother –

HELENA: Oh yes – the one who started him off in the sweet business.

ALISON: That's right. Well, after Jimmy and I were married, we'd no money – about eight pounds ten in actual fact – and no home. He didn't even have a job. He'd only left the university about a year. (*Smiles.*) No – left. I don't think one 'comes down' from Jimmy's university. According to him, it's not even red brick, but white tile. Anyway, we went off to live in Hugh's flat. It was over a warehouse in Poplar.

HELENA: Yes. I remember seeing the postmark on your letters.

ALISON: Well, that was where I found myself on my wedding night. Hugh and I disliked each other on sight, and Jimmy knew it. He was so proud of us both, so pathetically anxious that we should take to each other. Like a child showing off his toys. We had a little wedding celebration, and the three of us tried to get tight on some cheap port they'd brought in. Hugh got more and more subtly insulting – he'd a rare talent for that. Jimmy got steadily depressed, and I just sat there, listening to their talk, looking and feeling very stupid. For the first time in my life, I was cut off from the kind of people I'd always known, my family, my friends, everybody. And I'd burnt my boats. After all those weeks of brawling with Mummy and Daddy about Jimmy, I knew I couldn't appeal to them without looking foolish and cheap. It was just before the General Election, I remember, and Nigel was busy getting himself into Parliament. He didn't have time for anyone but his constituents. Oh, he'd have been sweet and kind, I know.

HELENA: (*Moving in C.*) Darling, why didn't you come to me?

ALISON: You were away on tour in some play, I think.

HELENA: So I was.

ALISON: Those next few months at the flat in Poplar were a nightmare. I suppose I must be soft and squeamish, and snobbish, but I felt as though I'd been dropped in a jungle. I couldn't believe that two people, two educated people could be so savage, and so – so uncompromising. Mummy has always said that Jimmy is utterly ruthless, but she hasn't met Hugh. He takes the first prize for ruthlessness – from all comers. Together, they were frightening. They both came to regard me as a sort of hostage from those sections of society they had declared war on.

HELENA: How were you living all this time?

ALISON: I had a tiny bit coming in from a few shares I had left, but it hardly kept us. Mummy had made me sign everything else over to her, in trust, when she knew I was really going to marry Jimmy.

HELENA: Just as well, I imagine.

ALISON: They soon thought of a way out of that. A brilliant campaign. They started inviting themselves – through me – to people's houses, friends of Nigel's and mine, friends of Daddy, oh everyone: The Arksdens, the Tarnatts, the Wains –

HELENA: Not the Wains?

ALISON: Just about everyone I'd ever known. Your people must have been among the few we missed out. It was just enemy territory to them, and, as I say, they used me as a hostage. We'd set out from headquarters in Poplar, and carry out our raids on the enemy in W1, SW1, SW3, and W8. In my name, we'd gatecrash everywhere – cocktails, weekends, even a couple of houseparties. I used to hope that one day, somebody would have the guts to slam the door in our faces, but they didn't. They were too well bred, and probably sorry for me as well. Hugh and Jimmy despised them for it. So we went on plundering them, wolfing their food and drinks, and smoking their cigars like ruffians. Oh, they enjoyed themselves.

HELENA: Apparently.

ALISON: Hugh fairly revelled in the role of the barbarian invader. Sometimes I thought he might even dress the part – you know, furs, spiked helmet, sword. He even got a fiver out of old Man Wain once. Blackmail, of course. People would have signed almost anything to get rid of us. He told him that we were about to be turned out of our flat for not paying the rent. At least it was true.

HELENA: I don't understand you. You must have been crazy.

ALISON: Afraid more than anything.

HELENA: But letting them do it! Letting them get away with it! You managed to stop them stealing the silver, I suppose?

ALISON: Oh, they knew their guerrilla warfare better than that. Hugh tried to seduce some fresh-faced young girl at the Arksdens' once, but that was the only time we were more or less turned out.

HELENA: It's almost unbelievable. I don't understand your part in it all. Why? That's what I don't see. Why did you –

ALISON: Marry him? There must be about six different answers. When the family came back from India, everything seemed, I don't know – unsettled? Anyway, Daddy seemed remote and rather irritable. And Mummy – well, you know Mummy. I didn't have much to worry about. I didn't know I was born as Jimmy says. I met him at a party. I remember it so clearly. I was almost twenty-one. The men there all looked as though they distrusted him, and as for the women, they were all intent on showing their contempt for this rather odd creature, but no one seemed quite sure how to do it. He'd come to the party on a bicycle, he told me, and there was oil all over his dinner jacket. It had been such a lovely day, and he'd been in the sun. Everything about him seemed to burn, his face, the edges of his hair glistened and seemed to spring off his head, and his eyes were so blue and full of the sun. He looked so young and frail, in spite of the tired line of his mouth. I knew I was taking on more than I was ever likely to be capable of bearing, but there never seemed to be any choice.

Well, the howl of outrage and astonishment went up
from the family, and that did it. Whether or no he was
in love with me, that did it. He made up his mind to
marry me. They did just about everything they could
think of to stop us.
HELENA: Yes, it wasn't a very pleasant business. But you can
see their point.
ALISON: Jimmy went into battle with his axe swinging round
his head – frail, and so full of fire. I had never seen
anything like it. The old story of the knight in shining
armour – except that his armour didn't really shine very
much.
HELENA: And what about Hugh?
ALISON: Things got steadily worse between us. He and
Jimmy even went to some of Nigel's political meetings.
They took bunches of their Poplar cronies with them,
and broke them up for him.
HELENA: He's really a savage, isn't he?
ALISON: Well, Hugh was writing some novel or other, and he
made up his mind he must go abroad – to China, or
some God-forsaken place. He said that England was
finished for us, anyway. All the old gang was back –
Dame Alison's Mob, as he used to call it. The only real
hope was to get out, and try somewhere else. He wanted
us to go with him, but Jimmy refused to go. There was a
terrible, bitter row over it. Jimmy accused Hugh of
giving up, and he thought it was wrong of him to go off
for ever, and leave his mother all on her own. He was
upset by the whole idea. They quarrelled for days over
it. I almost wished they'd both go, and leave me behind.
Anyway, they broke up. A few months later we came up
here, and Hugh went off to find the New Millennium on
his own. Sometimes, I think Hugh's mother blames me
for it all. Jimmy too, in a way, although he's never said
so. He never mentions it. But whenever that woman
looks at me, I can feel her thinking 'If it hadn't been for

you, everything would have been all right. We'd have all been happy.' Not that I dislike her – I don't. She's very sweet, in fact. Jimmy seems to adore her principally because she's been poor almost all her life, and she's frankly ignorant. I'm quite aware how snobbish that sounds, but it happens to be the truth.

HELENA: Alison, listens to me. You've got to make up your mind what you're going to do. You're going to have a baby, and you have a new responsibility. Before, it was different – there was only yourself at stake. But you can't go on living in this way any longer. (*To her.*)

ALISON: I'm so tired. I dread him coming into the room.

HELENA: Why haven't you told him you're going to have a child?

ALISON: I don't know. (*Suddenly anticipating* HELENA's *train of thought.*) Oh, it's his all right. There couldn't be any doubt of that. You see – (*She smiles.*) I've never really wanted anyone else.

HELENA: Listen, darling – you've got to tell him. Either he learns to behave like anyone else, and looks after you –

ALISON: Or?

HELENA: Or you must get out of this mad-house. (*Trumpet crescendo.*) This menagerie. He doesn't seem to know what love or anything else means.

ALISON: (*Pointing to chest of drawers up R.*) You see that bear, and that squirrel? Well, that's him, and that's me.

HELENA: Meaning?

ALISON: The game we play: bears and squirrels, squirrels and bears.

(HELENA *looks rather blank.*)

Yes, it's quite mad, I know. Quite mad. (*Picks up the two animals.*) That's him . . . And that's me . . .

HELENA: I didn't realize he was a bit fey, as well as everything else!

ALISON: Oh, there's nothing fey about Jimmy. It's just all we

seem to have left. Or had left. Even bears and squirrels
seem to have gone their own way now.

HELENA: Since I arrived?

ALISON: It started during those first months we had alone
together – after Hugh went abroad. It was the one way of
escaping from everything – a sort of unholy priest-hole of
being animals to one another. We could become little
furry creatures with little brains. Full of dumb,
uncomplicated affection for each other. Playful, careless
creatures in their own cosy zoo for two. A silly symphony
for people who couldn't bear the pain of being human
beings any longer. And now, even they are dead, poor
little silly animals. They were all love, and no brains.
(*Puts them back.*)

HELENA: (*Gripping her arm*) Listen to me. You've got to fight
him. Fight, or get out. Otherwise, he *will* kill you.
(*Enter* CLIFF.)

CLIFF: There you are, dullin'. Hullo, Helena. Tea ready?

ALISON: Yes, dear, it's all ready. Give Jimmy a call, will
you?

CLIFF: Right. (*Yelling back through the door.*) Hey, you
horrible man! Stop that bloody noise, and come and get
your tea! (*Coming in C.*) Going out?

HELENA: (*Crossing to L.*) Yes.

CLIFF: Pictures?

HELENA: No. (*Pause.*) Church.

CLIFF: (*Really surprised*) Oh! I see. Both of you?

HELENA: Yes. Are you coming?

CLIFF: Well . . . I – I haven't read the papers properly yet.
Tea, tea, tea! Let's have some tea, shall we?
(*He sits at the upstage end of the table.* HELENA *puts the four
plates of salad on it, sits down L., and they begin the meal.*
ALISON *is making up her face at her dressing table.*
Presently, JIMMY *enters. He places his trumpet on the
bookcase, and comes above the table.*)
Hullo, boyo. Come and have your tea. That blinkin'

trumpet – why don't you stuff it away somewhere?

JIMMY: You like it all right. Anyone who doesn't like real jazz, hasn't any feeling either for music or people. (*He sits R. end of table.*)

HELENA: Rubbish.

JIMMY: (*To* CLIFF) That seems to prove my point for you. Did you know that Webster played the banjo?

CLIFF: No, does he really?

HELENA: He said he'd bring it along next time he came.

ALISON: (*Muttering*) Oh, no!

JIMMY: Why is it that nobody knows how to treat the papers in this place? Look at them. I haven't even glanced at them yet – not the posh ones, anyway.

CLIFF: By the way, can I look at your *New* –

JIMMY: No, you can't! (*Loudly.*) You want anything, you pay for it. Like I have to. Price –

CLIFF: Price ninepence, obtainable from any bookstall! You're a mean old man, that's what you are.

JIMMY: What do you want to read it for, anyway? You've no intellect, no curiosity. It all just washes over you. Am I right?

CLIFF: Right.

JIMMY: What are you, you Welsh trash?

CLIFF: Nothing, that's what I am.

JIMMY: Nothing are you? Blimey you ought to be Prime Minister. You must have been talking to some of my wife's friends. They're a very intellectual set, aren't they? I've seen 'em.

(CLIFF *and* HELENA *carry on with their meal.*)

They all sit around feeling very spiritual, with their mental hands on each other's knees, discussing sex as if it were the Art of Fugue. If you don't want to be an emotional old spinster, just you listen to your dad! (*He starts eating. The silent hostility of the two women has set him off on the scent, and he looks quite cheerful, although the occasional, thick edge of his voice belies it.*) You know your trouble, son? Too anxious to please.

HELENA: Thank heavens somebody is!

JIMMY: You'll end up like one of those chocolate meringues my wife is so fond of. My wife – that's the one on the tom-toms behind me. Sweet and sticky on the outside, and sink your teeth in it, (*savouring every word*) inside, all white, messy and disgusting. (*Offering teapot sweetly to* HELENA.) Tea?

HELENA: Thank you.

(*He smiles, and pours out a cup for her.*)

JIMMY: That's how you'll end up, my boy – black hearted, evil minded and vicious.

HELENA: (*Taking cup*) Thank you.

JIMMY: And those old favourites, your friends and mine: sycophantic, phlegmatic, and, of course, top of the bill – pusillanimous.

HELENA: (*To* ALISON) Aren't you going to have your tea?

ALISON: Won't be long.

JIMMY: Thought of the title for a new song today. It's called 'You can quit hanging round my counter Mildred 'cos you'll find my position is closed'. (*Turning to* ALISON *suddenly.*) Good?

ALISON: Oh, very good.

JIMMY: Thought you'd like it. If I can slip in a religious angle, it should be a big hit. (*To* HELENA.) Don't you think so? I was thinking you might help me there. (*She doesn't reply.*) It might help you if I recite the lyrics. Let's see now, it's something like this:

> I'm so tired of necking,
> of pecking, home wrecking,
> of empty bed blues –
> just pass me the booze.
> I'm tired of being hetero
> Rather ride on the metero
> Just pass me the booze.
> This perpetual whoring

Gets quite dull and boring
So avoid that old python coil
And pass me the celibate oil.
You can quit etc.

No?

CLIFF: Very good, boyo.

JIMMY: Oh, yes, and I know what I meant to tell you – I wrote a poem while I was at the market yesterday. If you're interested, which you obviously are. (*To* HELENA.) It should appeal to you, in particular. It's soaked in the theology of Dante, with a good slosh of Eliot as well. It starts off 'There are no dry cleaners in Cambodia!'

CLIFF: What do you call it?

JIMMY: 'The Cess Pool'. Myself being a stone dropped in it, you see –

CLIFF: You should be dropped in it, all right.

HELENA: (*To* JIMMY) Why do you try so hard to be unpleasant?

(*He turns very deliberately, delighted that she should rise to the bait so soon – he's scarcely in his stride yet.*)

JIMMY: What's that?

HELENA: Do you have to be so offensive?

JIMMY: You mean now? You think I'm being offensive? You underestimate me. (*Turning to* ALISON.) Doesn't she?

HELENA: I think you're a very tiresome young man.

(*A slight pause as his delight catches up with him. He roars with laughter.*)

JIMMY: Oh dear, oh dear! My wife's friends! Pass Lady Bracknell the cucumber sandwiches, will you?

(*He returns to his meal, but his curiosity about* ALISON's *preparations at the mirror won't be denied any longer. He turns round casually, and speaks to her.*)

Going out?

ALISON: That's right.

JIMMY: On a Sunday evening in this town? Where on earth
　　are you going?

ALISON: (*Rising*) I'm going out with Helena.

JIMMY: That's not a direction – that's an affliction.

　　(*She crosses to the table, and sits down C. He leans forward,
　　and addresses her again.*)

　　I didn't ask you what was the matter with you. I asked
　　you where you were going.

HELENA: (*Steadily*) She's going to church.

　　(*He has been prepared for some plot, but he is as genuinely
　　surprised by this as* CLIFF *was a few minutes earlier.*)

JIMMY: You're doing what? (*Silence.*) Have you gone out of
　　your mind or something? (*To* HELENA.) You're
　　determined to win her, aren't you? So it's come to this
　　now! How feeble can you get? (*His rage mounting within.*)
　　When I think of what I did, what I endured, to get you
　　out –

ALISON: (*Recognizing an onslaught on the way, starts to panic*)
　　Oh yes, we all know what you did for me! You rescued
　　me from the wicked clutches of my family, and all my
　　friends! I'd still be rotting away at home, if you hadn't
　　ridden up on your charger, and carried me off!

　　(*The wild note in her voice has reassured him. His anger
　　cools and hardens. His voice is quite calm when he speaks.*)

JIMMY: The funny thing is, you know, I really did have to
　　ride up on a white charger – off white, really. Mummy
　　locked her up in their eight-bedroomed castle, didn't
　　she? There is no limit to what the middle-aged mummy
　　will do in the holy crusade against ruffians like me.
　　Mummy and I took one quick look at each other, and,
　　from then on, the age of chivalry was dead. I knew that,
　　to protect her innocent young, she wouldn't hesitate to
　　cheat, lie, bully and blackmail. Threatened with me, a
　　young man without money, background or even looks,
　　she'd bellow like a rhinoceros in labour – enough to make
　　every male rhino for miles turn white, and pledge

himself to celibacy. But even I underestimated her strength. Mummy may look over-fed and a bit flabby on the outside, but don't let that well-bred guzzler fool you. Underneath all that, she's armour plated – (*He clutches wildly for something to shock* HELENA *with.*) She's as rough as a night in a Bombay brothel, and as tough as a matelot's arse. She's probably in that bloody cistern, taking down every word we say. (*Kicks cistern.*) Can you 'ear me, mother. (*Sits on it, beats like bongo drums.*) Just about get her in there. Let me give you an example of this lady's tactics. You may have noticed that I happen to wear my hair rather long. Now, if my wife is honest, or concerned enough to explain, she could tell you that this is not due to any dark, unnatural instincts I possess, but because (a) I can usually think of better things than a haircut to spend two bob on, and (b) I prefer long hair. But that obvious, innocent explanation didn't appeal to Mummy at all. So she hires detectives to watch me, to see if she can't somehow get me into the *News of the World*. All so that I shan't carry off her daughter on that poor old charger of mine, all tricked out and caparisoned in discredited passions and ideals! The old grey mare that actually once led the charge against the old order – well, she certainly ain't what she used to be. It was all she could do to carry me, but your weight (*To* ALISON.) was too much for her. She just dropped dead on the way.

CLIFF: (*Quietly*) Don't let's brawl, boyo. It won't do any good.

JIMMY: Why *don't* we brawl? It's the only thing left I'm any good at.

CLIFF: Jimmy, boy –

JIMMY: (*To* ALISON) You've let this genuflecting sin jobber win you over, haven't you? She's got you back, hasn't she?

HELENA: Oh for heaven's sake, don't be such a bully! You've no right to talk about her mother like that!

JIMMY: (*Capable of anything now*) I've got every right. That old bitch should be dead! (*To* ALISON.) Well? Aren't I right?

(CLIFF *and* HELENA *look at* ALISON *tensely, but she just gazes at her plate.*)

I said she's an old bitch, and should be dead! What's the matter with you? Why don't you leap to her defence!

(CLIFF *gets up quickly, and takes his arm.*)

CLIFF: Jimmy, don't!

(JIMMY *pushes him back savagely, and he sits down helplessly, turning his head away on to his hand.*)

JIMMY: If someone said something like that about me, she'd react soon enough – she'd spring into her well-known lethargy, and say nothing! I say she ought to be dead. (*He brakes for a fresh spurt later. He's saving his strength for the knock-out.*) My God, those worms will need a good dose of salts the day they get through her! Oh what a bellyache you've got coming to you, my little wormy ones! Alison's mother is on the way! (*In what he intends to be a comic declamatory voice.*) She will pass away, my friends, leaving a trail of worms gasping for laxatives behind her – from purgatives to purgatory.

(*He smiles down at* ALISON, *but still she hasn't broken.* CLIFF *won't look at them. Only* HELENA *looks at him. Denied the other two, he addresses her.*)

Is anything the matter?

HELENA: I feel rather sick, that's all. Sick with contempt and loathing.

(*He can feel her struggling on the end of his line, and he looks at her rather absently.*)

JIMMY: One day, when I'm no longer spending my days running a sweet-stall, I may write a book about us all. It's all here. (*Slapping his forehead.*) Written in flames a mile high. And it won't be recollected in tranquillity either, picking daffodils with Auntie Wordsworth. It'll be recollected in fire, and blood. My blood.

HELENA: (*Thinking patient reasonableness may be worth a try*)
She simply said that she's going to church with me. I
don't see why that calls for this incredible outburst.

JIMMY: Don't you? Perhaps you're not as clever as I
thought.

HELENA: You think the world's treated you pretty badly,
don't you?

ALISON: (*Turning her face away L.*) Oh, don't try and take his
suffering away from him – he'd be lost without it.
(*He looks at her in surprise, but he turns back to* HELENA.
ALISON *can have her turn again later.*)

JIMMY: I thought this play you're touring in finished up on
Saturday week?

HELENA: That's right.

JIMMY: Eight days ago, in fact.

HELENA: Alison wanted me to stay.

JIMMY: What are you plotting?

HELENA: Don't you think we've had enough of the heavy
villain?

JIMMY: (*To* ALISON) You don't believe in all that stuff. Why
you don't believe in anything. You're just doing it to be
vindictive, aren't you? Why – why are you letting her
influence you like this?

ALISON: (*Starting to break*) Why, why, why, why! (*Putting her
hands over her ears.*) That word's pulling my head off!

JIMMY: And as long as you're around, I'll go on using it.
(*He crosses down to the armchair, and seats himself on the
back of it. He addresses* HELENA's *back.*)
The last time she was in a church was when she was
married to me. I expect that surprises you, doesn't it? It
was expediency, pure and simple. We were in a hurry,
you see. (*The comedy of this strikes him at once, and he
laughs.*) Yes, we were actually in a hurry! Lusting for the
slaughter! Well, the local registrar was a particular pal of
Daddy's, and we knew he'd spill the beans to the Colonel
like a shot. So we had to seek out some local

vicar who didn't know him quite so well. But it was no use. When my best man – a chap I'd met in the pub that morning – and I turned up, Mummy and Daddy were in the church already. They'd found out at the last moment, and had come to watch the execution carried out. How I remember looking down at them, full of beer for breakfast, and feeling a bit buzzed. Mummy was slumped over her pew in a heap – the noble, female rhino, pole-axed at last! And Daddy sat beside her, upright and unafraid, dreaming of his days among the Indian Princes, and unable to believe he'd left his horsewhip at home. Just the two of them in that empty church – them and me. (*Coming out of his remembrance suddenly*.) I'm not sure what happened after that. We must have been married, I suppose. I think I remember being sick in the vestry. (*To* ALISON.) Was I?

HELENA: Haven't you finished?

(*He can smell blood again, and he goes on calmly, cheerfully*.)

JIMMY: (*To* ALISON) Are you going to let yourself be taken in by this saint in Dior's clothing? I will tell you the simple truth about her. (*Articulating with care*.) She is a cow. I wouldn't mind that so much, but she seems to have become a sacred cow as well!

CLIFF: You've gone too far, Jimmy. Now dry up!

HELENA: Oh, let him go on.

JIMMY: (*To* CLIFF) I suppose you're going over to that side as well. Well, why don't you? Helena will help to make it pay off for you. She's an expert in the New Economics – the Economics of the Supernatural. It's all a simple matter of payments and penalties. (*Rises*.) She's one of those apocalyptic share pushers who are spreading all those rumours about a transfer of power. (*His imagination is racing, and the words pour out*.) Reason and Progress, the old firm, is selling out! Everyone get out while the going's good. Those forgotten shares you had in the old traditions, the old beliefs are going up – up and up and up. (*Moves up L.*) There's going to be a change over. A new Board of Directors, who are going to see that the dividends are always attractive, and that they go to the right people. (*Facing them.*) Sell out everything you've got: all those stocks in the old, free inquiry. (*Crosses to above table.*) The big Crash is coming, you can't escape it, so get in on the ground floor with Helena and her friends while there's still time. And there isn't much of it left. Tell me, what could be more gilt-edged than the next world! It's a capital gain, and it's all yours. (*He moves round the table, back to his chair R.*) You see, I know Helena and her kind so very well. In fact, her kind are everywhere, you can't move for them. They're a romantic lot. They spend their time mostly looking forward to the past. The only place they can see the light is the Dark Ages. She's moved long ago into a lovely little cottage of the soul, cut right off from the ugly problems of the twentieth century altogether. She prefers to be cut off from all the conveniences we've fought to get for centuries. She'd rather go down to the ecstatic little shed at the bottom of the garden to relieve her sense of guilt. Our Helena is full of ecstatic wind – (*He leans across the table at her*) aren't you? (*He waits for her to reply.*)

HELENA: (*Quite calmly*) It's a pity you've been so far away all this time. I would probably have slapped your face.
(*They look into each other's eyes across the table. He moves slowly up, above* CLIFF, *until he is beside her.*)
You've behaved like this ever since I first came.

JIMMY: Helena, have you ever watched somebody die?
(*She makes a move to rise.*)
No, don't move away.
(*She remains seated, and looks up at him.*)
It doesn't look dignified enough for you.

HELENA: (*Like ice*) If you come any nearer, I will slap your
face.
(*He looks down at her, a grin smouldering round his mouth.*)
JIMMY: I hope you won't make the mistake of thinking for
one moment that I am a gentleman.
HELENA: I'm not very likely to do that.
JIMMY: (*Bringing his face close to hers*) I've no public-school
scruples about hitting girls. (*Gently.*) If you slap my face
– by God, I'll lay you out!
HELENA: You probably would. You're the type.
JIMMY: You bet I'm the type. I'm the type that detests
physical violence. Which is why, if I find some woman
trying to cash in on what she thinks is my defenceless
chivalry by lashing out with her frail little fists, I lash
back at her.
HELENA: Is that meant to be subtle, or just plain Irish?
(*His grin widens.*)
JIMMY: I think you and I understand one another all right.
But you haven't answered my question. I said: have you
watched somebody die?
HELENA: No, I haven't.
JIMMY: Anyone who's never watched somebody die is
suffering from a pretty bad case of virginity. (*His good
humour of a moment ago deserts him, as he begins to
remember.*) For twelve months, I watched my father dying
– when I was ten years old. He'd come back from the war
in Spain, you see. And certain God-fearing gentlemen
there had made such a mess of him, he didn't have long
left to live. Everyone knew it – even I knew it. (*He moves
R.*) But, you see, I was the only one who cared. (*Turns to
the window.*) His family were embarrassed by the whole
business. Embarrassed and irritated. (*Looking out.*) As for
my mother, all she could think about was the fact that she
had allied herself to a man who seemed to be on the wrong
side in all things. My mother was all for being associated
wth minorities,

provided they were the smart, fashionable ones. (*He moves up C. again.*) We all of us waited for him to die. The family sent him a cheque every month, and hoped he'd get on with it quietly, without too much vulgar fuss. My mother looked after him without complaining, and that was about all. Perhaps she pitied him. I suppose she was capable of that. (*With a kind of appeal in his voice.*) But *I* was the only one who cared! (*He moves L., behind the armchair.*) Every time I sat on the edge of his bed, to listen to him talking or reading to me, I had to fight back my tears. At the end of twelve months, I was a veteran. (*He leans forwards on the back of the armchair.*) All that that feverish failure of a man had to listen to him was a small, frightened boy. I spent hour upon hour in that tiny bedroom. He would talk to me for hours, pouring out all that was left of his life to one, lonely, bewildered little boy, who could barely understand half of what he said. All he could feel was the despair and the bitterness, the sweet, sickly smell of a dying man. (*He moves around the chair.*) You see, I learnt at an early age what it was to be angry – angry and helpless. And I can never forget it. (*Sits.*) I knew more about – love . . . betrayal . . . and death, when I was ten years old than you will probably ever know all your life.

(*They all sit silently. Presently,* HELENA *rises.*)

HELENA: Time we went.

(ALISON *nods.*)

I'll just get my things together. (*Crosses to door.*) I'll see you downstairs.

(*She exits. A slight pause.*)

JIMMY: (*Not looking at her, almost whispering*) Doesn't it matter to you – what people do to me? What are you trying to do to me? I've given you just everything. Doesn't it mean *anything* to you?

(*Her back stiffens. His axe-swinging bravado has vanished, and his voice crumples in disabled rage.*)

You Judas! You phlegm! She's taking you with her, and you're so bloody feeble, you'll let her do it!

(ALISON *suddenly takes hold of her cup, and hurls it on the floor. He's drawn blood at last. She looks down at the pieces on the floor, and then at him. Then she crosses, R., takes out a dress on a hanger, and slips it on. As she is zipping up the side, she feels giddy, and she has to lean against the wardrobe for support. She closes her eyes.*)

ALISON: (*Softly*) All I want is a little peace.

JIMMY: Peace! God! She wants peace! (*Hardly able to get his words out.*) My heart is so full, I feel ill – and she wants peace!

(*She crosses to the bed to put on her shoes.* CLIFF *gets up from the table, and sits in the armchair R. He picks up a paper, and looks at that.* JIMMY *has recovered slightly, and manages to sound almost detached.*)

I rage, and shout my head off, and everyone thinks 'poor chap!' or 'what an objectionable young man!' But that girl there can twist your arm off with her silence. I've sat in this chair in the dark for hours. And, although she knows I'm feeling as I feel now, she's turned over, and gone to sleep.

(*He gets up and faces* CLIFF, *who doesn't look up from his paper.*)

One of us is crazy. One of us is mean and stupid and crazy. Which is it? Is it me? Is it me, standing here like an hysterical girl, hardly able to get my words out? Or is it her? Sitting there, putting on her shoes to go out with that – (*But inspiration has deserted him by now.*) Which is it?

(CLIFF *is still looking down at his paper.*)

I wish to heaven you'd try loving her, that's all. (*He moves up C., watching her look for her gloves.*) Perhaps, one day, you may want to come back. I shall wait for that day. I want to stand up in your tears, and splash about in them, and sing. I want to be there when you grovel. I want to be there, I want to watch it, I want the front seat.

(HELENA *enters, carrying two prayer books*.)

I want to see your face rubbed in the mud – that's all I can hope for. There's nothing else I want any longer.

HELENA: (*After a moment*) There's a phone call for you.

JIMMY: (*Turning*) Well, it can't be anything good, can it?

(JIMMY *goes out*.)

HELENA: All ready?

ALISON: Yes – I think so.

HELENA: You feel all right, don't you?

(ALISON *nods*.)

What's he been raving about now? Oh, what does it matter? He makes me want to claw his hair out by the roots. When I think of what you will be going through in a few months' time – and all for him! It's as if you'd done *him* wrong! These *men*! (*Turning on* CLIFF.) And all the time you just sit there, and do nothing!

CLIFF: (*Looking up slowly*) That's right – I just sit here.

HELENA: What's the matter with you? What sort of a man are you?

CLIFF: I'm not the District Commissioner, you know. Listen, Helena – I don't feel like Jimmy does about you, but I'm not exactly on your side either. And since you've been here, everything's certainly been worse than it's ever been. This has always been a battlefield, but I'm pretty certain that if I hadn't been here, everything would have been over between these two long ago. I've been a – a no-man's land between them. Sometimes, it's been still and peaceful, no incidents, and we've all been reasonably happy. But most of the time, it's simply a very narrow strip of plain hell. But where I come from, we're used to brawling and excitement. Perhaps I even enjoy being in the thick of it. I love these two people very much. (*He looks at her steadily, and adds simply*.) And I pity all of us.

HELENA: Are you including me in that? (*But she goes on quickly to avoid his reply.*) I don't understand him, you or any of it. All I know is that none of you seems to know how to behave in a decent, civilized way. (*In command now.*) Listen, Alison – I've sent your father a wire.

ALISON: (*Numbed and vague by now*) Oh?
(HELENA *looks at her, and realizes quickly that everything now will depend on her own authority. She tries to explain patiently.*)

HELENA: Look, dear – he'll get it first thing in the morning. I thought it would be better than trying to explain the situation over the phone. I asked him to come up, and fetch you home tomorrow.

ALISON: What did you say?

HELENA: Simply that you wanted to come home and would he come up for you.

ALISON: I see.

HELENA: I knew that would be quite enough. I told him there was nothing to worry about, so they won't worry and think there's been an accident or anything. I had to do something, dear. (*Very gently.*) You didn't mind, did you?

ALISON: No, I don't mind. Thank you.

HELENA: And you will go when he comes for you?

ALISON: (*Pause*) Yes. I'll go.

HELENA: (*Relieved*) I expect he'll drive up. He should be here about tea-time. It'll give you plenty of time to get your things together. And, perhaps, after you've gone – Jimmy (*saying the word almost with difficulty*) will come to his senses, and face up to things.

ALISON: Who was on the phone?

HELENA: I didn't catch it properly. It rang after I'd sent the wire off – just as soon as I put the receiver down almost. I had to go back down the stairs again. Sister somebody, I think.

ALISON: Must have been a hospital or something. Unless he knows someone in a convent – *that* doesn't seem very likely, does it? Well, we'll be late, if we don't hurry.
(*She puts down one of the prayer books on the table. Enter* JIMMY. *He comes down C., between the two women.*)

CLIFF: All right, boyo?

JIMMY: (*To* ALISON) It's Hugh's mum. She's – had a stroke.
(*Slight pause.*)

ALISON: I'm sorry.
(JIMMY *sits on the bed.*)

CLIFF: How bad is it?

JIMMY: They didn't say much. But I think she's dying.

CLIFF: Oh dear . . .

JIMMY: (*Rubbing his fist over his face*) It doesn't make any sense at all. Do you think it does?

ALISON: I'm sorry – I really am.

CLIFF: Anything I can do?

JIMMY: The London train goes in half an hour. You'd better order me a taxi.

CLIFF: Right. (*He crosses to the door, and stops.*) Do you want me to come with you, boy?

JIMMY: No thanks. After all, you hardly knew her. It's not for you to go.
(HELENA *looks quickly at* ALISON.)
She may not even remember me, for all I know.

CLIFF: OK.
(*He exits.*)

JIMMY: I remember the first time I showed her your photograph – just after we were married. She looked at it, and the tears just welled up in her eyes, and she said: 'But she's so beautiful! She's so beautiful!' She kept repeating it as if she couldn't believe it. Sounds a bit simple and sentimental when you repeat it. But it was pure gold the way she said it.
(*He looks at her. She is standing by the dressing table, her back to him.*)

She got a kick out of you, like she did out of everything else. Hand me my shoes, will you?

(*She kneels down, and hands them to him.*)

(*Looking down at his feet.*) You're coming with me, aren't you? She (*he shrugs*) hasn't got anyone else now. I . . . need you . . . to come with me.

(*He looks into her eyes, but she turns away, and stands up. Outside, the church bells start ringing.* HELENA *moves up to the door, and waits watching them closely.* ALISON *stands quite still,* JIMMY's *eyes burning into her. Then, she crosses in front of him to the table where she picks up the prayer book, her back to him. She wavers, and seems about to say something, but turns uptage instead, and walks quickly to the door.*)

ALISON: (*Hardly audible*) Let's go.

(*She goes out,* HELENA *following.* JIMMY *gets up, looks about him unbelievingly, and leans against the chest of drawers. The teddy bear is close to his face, and he picks it up gently, looks at it quickly, and throws it downstage. It hits the floor with a thud, and it makes a rattling, groaning sound – as guaranteed in the advertisement.* JIMMY *falls forward on to the bed, his face buried in the covers. Quick curtain.*)

SCENE TWO

The following evening. When the curtain rises, ALISON *is discovered R., going from her dressing table to the bed, and packing her things into a suitcase. Sitting down L. is her father,* COLONEL REDFERN, *a large handsome man, about sixty. Forty years of being a soldier sometimes conceals the essentially gentle, kindly man underneath. Brought up to command respect, he is often slightly withdrawn and uneasy now that he finds himself in a world where his authority has lately become less and less unquestionable. His wife would relish the present situation, but he is only disturbed and bewildered by it. He looks around him, discreetly scrutinizing everything.*

COLONEL: (*Partly to himself*) I'm afraid it's all beyond me. I suppose it always will be. As for Jimmy – he just speaks a different language from any of us. Where did you say he'd gone?

ALISON: He's gone to see Mrs Tanner.

COLONEL: Who?

ALISON: Hugh Tanner's mother.

COLONEL: Oh, I see.

ALISON: She's been taken ill – a stroke. Hugh's abroad, as you know, so Jimmy's gone to London to see her.
(*He nods.*)
He wanted me to go with him.

COLONEL: Didn't she start him off in this sweet-stall business?

ALISON: Yes.

COLONEL: What is she like? Nothing like her son, I trust?

ALISON: Not remotely. Oh – how can you describe her? Rather – ordinary. What Jimmy insists on calling working class. A Charwoman who married an actor, worked hard all her life, and spent most of it struggling to support her husband and her son. Jimmy and she are very fond of each other.

COLONEL: So you didn't go with him?

ALISON: No.

COLONEL: Who's looking after the sweet-stall?

ALISON: Cliff. He should be in soon.

COLONEL: Oh yes, of course – Cliff. Does he live here too?

ALISON: Yes. His room is just across the landing.

COLONEL: Sweet-stall. It does seem an extraordinary thing for an educated young man to be occupying himself with. Why should he want to do that, of all things. I've always thought he must be quite clever in his way.

ALISON: (*No longer interested in this problem*) Oh, he tried so many things – journalism, advertising, even vacuum cleaners for a few weeks. He seems to have been as happy doing this as anything else.

COLONEL: I've often wondered what it was like – where you were living, I mean. You didn't tell us very much in your letters.

ALISON: There wasn't a great deal to tell you. There's not much social life here.

COLONEL: Oh, I know what you mean. You were afraid of being disloyal to your husband.

ALISON: Disloyal! (*She laughs.*) He thought it was high treason of me to write to you at all! I used to have to dodge downstairs for the post, so that he wouldn't see I was getting letters from home. Even then I had to hide them.

COLONEL: He really does hate us doesn't he?

ALISON: Oh yes – don't have any doubts about that. He hates all of us.

COLONEL: (*Sighs*) It seems a great pity. It was all so unfortunate – unfortunate and unnecessary. I'm afraid I can't help feeling that he must have had a certain amount of right on his side.

ALISON: (*Puzzled by this admission*) Right on his side?

COLONEL: It's a little late to admit it, I know, but your mother and I weren't entirely free from blame. I have never said anything – there was no point afterwards – but I have always believed that she went too far over Jimmy. Of course, she was extremely upset at the time – we both were – and that explains a good deal of what happened. I did my best to stop her, but she was in such a state of mind, there was simply nothing I could do. She seemed to have made up her mind that if he was going to marry you, he must be a criminal, at the very least. All those inquiries, the private detectives – the accusations. I hated every moment of it.

ALISON: I suppose she was trying to protect me – in a rather heavy-handed way, admittedly.

COLONEL: I must confess I find that kind of thing rather horrifying. Anyway, I try to think now that it never happened. I didn't approve of Jimmy at all, and I don't suppose I ever should, but, looking back on it, I think it would have been better, for all concerned, if we had never attempted to interfere. At least, it would have been a little more dignified.

ALISON: It wasn't your fault.

COLONEL: I don't know. We were all to blame, in our different ways. No doubt Jimmy acted in good faith. He's honest enough, whatever else he may be. And your mother – in her heavy-handed way, as you put it – acted in good faith as well. Perhaps you and I were the ones most to blame.

ALISON: You and I!

COLONEL: I think you may take after me a little, my dear. You like to sit on the fence because it's comfortable and more peaceful.

ALISON: Sitting on the fence! I married him, didn't I?

COLONEL: Oh yes, you did.

ALISON: In spite of all the humiliating scenes and the threats! What did you say to me at the time? Wasn't I letting you down, turning against you, how could I do this to you etcetera?

COLONEL: Perhaps it might have been better if you hadn't written letters to us – knowing how we felt about your husband, and after everything that had happened. (*He looks at her uncomfortably.*) Forgive me, I'm a little confused, what with everything – the telegram, driving up here suddenly . . .

(*He trails off rather helplessly. He looks tired. He glances at her nervously, a hint of accusation in his eyes, as if he expected her to defend herself further. She senses this, and is more confused than ever.*)

ALISON: Do you know what he said about Mummy? He said she was an over-fed, over-privileged old bitch. 'A good blow-out for the worms' was his expression, I think.

COLONEL: I see. And what does he say about me?

ALISON: Oh, he doesn't seem to mind you so much. In fact, I think he rather likes you. He likes you because he can feel sorry for you. (*Conscious that what she says is going to hurt him.*) 'Poor old Daddy – just one of those sturdy old plants left over from the Edwardian Wilderness that can't understand why the sun isn't shining any more.' (*Rather lamely.*) Something like that, anyway.

COLONEL: He has quite a turn of phrase, hasn't he? (*Simply, and without malice.*) Why did you ever have to meet this young man?

ALISON: Oh, Daddy, please don't put me on trial now. I've been on trial every day and night of my life for nearly four years.

COLONEL: But why should he have married you, feeling as he did about everything?

ALISON: That is the famous American question – you know, the sixty-four dollar one! Perhaps it was revenge.
(*He looks up uncomprehendingly.*)
Oh yes. Some people do actually marry for revenge. People like Jimmy, anyway. Or perhaps he should have been another Shelley, and can't understand now why I'm not another Mary, and you're not William Godwin. He thinks he's got a sort of genius for love and friendship – on his own terms. Well, for twenty years, I'd lived a happy, uncomplicated life, and suddenly, this – this spiritual barbarian – throws down the gauntlet at me. Perhaps only another woman could understand what a challenge like that means – although I think Helena was as mystified as you are.

COLONEL: I am mystified. (*He rises, and crosses to the window R.*) Your husband has obviously taught you a great deal, whether you realize it or not. What any of it means, I

65

don't know. I always believed that people married each other because they were in love. That always seemed a good enough reason to me. But apparently, that's too simple for young people nowadays. They have to talk about challenges and revenge. I just can't believe that love between men and women is really like that.

ALISON: Only some men and women.

COLONEL: But why you? My daughter . . . No. Perhaps Jimmy is right. Perhaps I am a – what was it? an old plant left over from the Edwardian Wilderness. And I can't understand why the sun isn't shining any more. You can see what he means, can't you? It was March 1914 when I left England, and, apart from leaves every ten years or so, I didn't see much of my own country until we all came back in '47. Oh, I knew things had changed, of course. People told you all the time the way it was going – going to the dogs, as the Blimps are supposed to say. But it seemed very unreal to me, out there. The England I remembered was the one I left in 1914, and I was happy to go on remembering it that way. Beside, I had the Maharajah's army to command – that was my world, and I loved it, all of it. At the time, it looked like going on for ever. When I think of it now, it seems like a dream. If only it could have gone on for ever. Those long, cool evenings up in the hills, everything purple and golden. Your mother and I were so happy then. It seemed as though we had everything we could ever want. I think the last day the sun shone was when that dirty little train steamed out of that crowded, suffocating Indian station, and the battalion band playing for all it was worth. I knew in my heart it was all over then. Everything.

ALISON: You're hurt because everything is changed. Jimmy is hurt because everything is the same. And neither of you can face it. Something's gone wrong somewhere, hasn't it?

COLONEL: It looks like it, my dear.

(*She picks up the squirrel from the chest of drawers, is about to put it in her suitcase, hesitates, and then puts it back. The* COLONEL *turns and looks at her. She moves down towards him, her head turned away. For a few moments, she seems to be standing on the edge of choice. The choice made, her body wheels round suddenly, and she is leaning against him, weeping softly.*)

(*Presently.*) This is a big step you're taking. You've made up your mind to come back with me? Is that really what you want?

(*Enter* HELENA.)

HELENA: I'm sorry. I came in to see if I could help you pack, Alison. Oh, you look as though you've finished.

(ALISON *leaves her father, and moves to the bed, pushing down the lid of her suitcase.*)

ALISON: All ready.

HELENA: Have you got everything?

ALISON: Well, no. But Cliff can send the rest on sometime, I expect. He should have been back by now. Oh, of course, he's had to put the stall away on his own today.

COLONEL: (*Crossing and picking up the suitcase*) Well, I'd better put this in the car then. We may as well get along. Your mother will be worried, I know. I promised her I'd ring her when I got here. She's not very well.

HELENA: I hope my telegram didn't upset her too much. Perhaps I shouldn't have –

COLONEL: Not at all. We were very grateful that you did. It was very kind of you, indeed. She tried to insist on coming with me, but I finally managed to talk her out of it. I thought it would be best for everyone. What about your case, Helena? If you care to tell me where it is, I'll take it down with this one.

HELENA: I'm afraid I shan't be coming tonight.

ALISON: (*Very surprised*) Aren't you coming with us?

(*Enter* CLIFF.)

HELENA: I'd like to, but the fact is I've an appointment tomorrow in Birmingham – about a job. They've just sent me a script. It's rather important, and I don't want to miss it. So it looks as though I shall have to stay here tonight.

ALISON: Oh, I see. Hullo, Cliff.

CLIFF: Hullo there.

ALISON: Daddy – this is Cliff.

COLONEL: How do you do, Cliff.

CLIFF: How do you do, sir.

(*Slight pause.*)

COLONEL: Well, I'd better put this in the car, hadn't I? Don't be long, Alison. Good-bye, Helena. I expect we shall be seeing you again soon, if you're not busy.

HELENA: Oh, yes, I shall be back in a day or two.

(CLIFF *takes off his jacket.*)

COLONEL: Well, then – good-bye, Cliff.

CLIFF: Good-bye, sir.

(*The* COLONEL *goes out.* CLIFF *comes down L.* HELENA *moves C.*)

You're really going then?

ALISON: Really going.

CLIFF: I should think Jimmy would be back pretty soon. You won't wait?

ALISON: No, Cliff.

CLIFF: Who's going to tell him?

HELENA: I can tell him. That is, if I'm here when he comes back.

CLIFF: (*Quietly*) You'll be here. (*To* ALISON.) Don't you think you ought to tell him yourself?

(*She hands him an envelope from her handbag. He takes it.*)

Bit conventional, isn't it?

ALISON: I'm a conventional girl.

(*He crosses to her, and puts his arms round her.*)

CLIFF: (*Back over his shoulder, to* HELENA) I hope you're right, that's all.

HELENA: What do you mean? You hope *I'm* right?

CLIFF: (*To* ALISON) The place is going to be really cock-eyed now. You know that, don't you?

ALISON: Please, Cliff –
(*He nods. She kisses him.*)
I'll write to you later.

CLIFF: Good-bye, lovely.

ALISON: Look after him.

CLIFF: We'll keep the old nut-house going somehow.
(*She crosses C., in between the two of them, glances quickly at the two armchairs, the papers still left around them from yesterday.* HELENA *kisses her on the cheek, and squeezes her hand.*)

HELENA: See you soon.
(ALISON *nods, and goes out quickly.* CLIFF *and* HELENA *are left looking at each other.*)
Would you like me to make you some tea?

CLIFF: No, thanks.

HELENA: Think I might have some myself, if you don't mind.

CLIFF: So you're staying?

HELENA: Just for tonight. Do you object?

CLIFF: Nothing to do with me. (*Against the table C.*) Of course, he may not be back until later on.
(*She crosses L., to the window, and lights a cigarette.*)

HELENA: What do you think he'll do? Perhaps he'll look out one of his old girlfriends. What about this Madeline?

CLIFF: What about her?

HELENA: Isn't she supposed to have done a lot for him? Couldn't he go back to her?

CLIFF: I shouldn't think so.

HELENA: What happened?

CLIFF: She was nearly old enough to be his mother. I expect that's something to do with it! Why the hell should I know!

(For the first time in the play, his good humour has completely deserted him. She looks surprised.)

HELENA: You're his friend, aren't you? Anyway, he's not what you'd call reticent about himself, is he? I've never seen so many souls stripped to the waist since I've been here.

(He turns to go.)

HELENA: Aren't you staying?

CLIFF: No, I'm not. There was a train in from London about five minutes ago. And, just in case he may have been on it, I'm going out.

HELENA: Don't you think you ought to be here when he comes?

CLIFF: I've had a hard day, and I don't think I want to see anyone hurt until I've had something to eat first, and perhaps a few drinks as well. I think I might pick up some nice, pleasant little tart in a milk bar, and sneak her in past old mother Drury. Here! *(Tossing the letter at her.)* You give it to him! *(Crossing to door.)* He's all yours. *(At door.)* and I hope he rams it up your nostrils!

(He exits. She crosses to the table, and stubs out her cigarette. The front door downstairs is heard to slam. She moves to the wardrobe, opens it idly. It is empty, except for one dress, swinging on a hanger. She goes over to the dressing table, now cleared but for a framed photograph of Jimmy. Idly, she slams the empty drawers open and shut. She turns upstage to the chest of drawers, picks up the toy bear, and sits on the bed, looking at it. She lays her head back on the pillow, still holding the bear. She looks up quickly as the door crashes open, and JIMMY enters. He stands looking at her, then moves down C., taking off his raincoat and throwing it over the table. He is almost giddy with anger, and has to steady himself on the chair. He looks up.)

JIMMY: That old bastard nearly ran me down in his car! Now, if he'd killed me, that really would have been ironical. And how right and fitting that my wife should have been a passenger. A passenger! What's the matter with everybody? (*Crossing up to her.*) Cliff practically walked into me, coming out of the house. He belted up the other way, and pretended not to see me. Are you the only one who's not afraid to stay?

(*She hands him Alison's note. He takes it.*)

Oh, it's one of these, is it? (*He rips it open. He reads a few lines, and almost snorts with disbelief.*) Did you write this for her! Well, listen to this then! (*Reading.*) 'My dear – I must get away. I don't suppose you will understand, but please try. I need peace so desperately, and, at the moment, I am willing to sacrifice everything just for that. I don't know what's going to happen to us. I know you will be feeling wretched and bitter, but try to be a little patient with me. I shall always have a deep, loving need of you – Alison'. Oh, how could she be so bloody wet! Deep loving need! That makes me puke! (*Crossing to R.*) She couldn't say 'You rotten bastard! I hate your guts, I'm clearing out, and I hope you rot!' No, she has to make a polite, emotional mess out of it! (*Seeing the dress in the wardrobe, he rips it out, and throws it in the corner up L.*) Deep, loving need! I never thought she was capable of being as phoney as that! What is that – a line from one of those plays you've been in? What are you doing here anyway? You'd better keep out of my way, if you don't want your head kicked in.

HELENA: (*Calmly*) If you'll stop thinking about yourself for one moment, I'll tell you something I think you ought to know. Your wife is going to have a baby.

(*He just looks at her.*)

Well? Doesn't that mean anything? Even to you?

(*He is taken aback, but not so much by the news, as by her.*)

JIMMY: All right – yes. I am surprised. I give you that. But, tell me. Did you honestly expect me to go soggy at the knees, and collapse with remorse! (*Leaning nearer.*)

Listen, if you'll stop breathing your female wisdom all over me, I'll tell you something: I don't care. (*Beginning quietly.*) I don't care if she's going to have a baby. I don't care if it has two heads! (*He knows her fingers are itching.*) Do I disgust you? Well, go on – slap my face. But remember what I told you before, will you? For eleven hours, I have been watching someone I love very much going through the sordid process of dying. She was alone, and I was the only one with her. And when I have to walk behind that coffin on Thursday, I'll be on my own again. Because that bitch won't even send her a bunch of flowers – I know! She made the great mistake of all her kind. She thought that because Hugh's mother was a deprived and ignorant old woman, who said all the wrong things in all the wrong places, she couldn't be taken seriously. And you think I should be overcome with awe because that cruel, stupid girl is going to have a baby! (*Anguish in his voice.*) I can't believe it! I can't. (*Grabbing her shoulder.*) Well, the performance is over. Now leave me alone, and *get out*, you evil-minded little virgin.

(*She slaps his face savagely. An expression of horror and disbelief floods his face. But it drains away, and all that is left is pain. His hand goes up to his head, and a muffled cry of despair escapes him.* HELENA *tears his hand away, and kisses him passionately, drawing him down beside her. Curtain.*)

ACT THREE

SCENE ONE

Several months later. A Sunday evening. Alison's personal belongings, such as her make-up things on the dressing table, for example, have been replaced by Helena's.

At rise of curtain, we find JIMMY *and* CLIFF *sprawled in their respective armchairs, immersed in the Sunday newspapers.* HELENA *is standing down L. leaning over the ironing board, a small pile of clothes beside her. She looks more attractive than before, for the setting of her face is more relaxed. She still looks quite smart, but in an unpremeditated, careless way; she wears an old shirt of Jimmy's.*

CLIFF: That stinking old pipe!

    (*Pause.*)

JIMMY: Shut up.

CLIFF: Why don't you do something with it?

JIMMY: Why do I spend half of Sunday reading the papers?

CLIFF: (*Kicks him without lowering his paper*) It stinks!

JIMMY: So do you, but I'm not singing an aria about it.

    (*Turns to the next page.*) The dirty ones get more and more wet round the mouth, and the posh ones are more pompous than ever. (*Lowering paper and waving pipe at* HELENA.) Does this bother you?

HELENA: No. I quite like it.

JIMMY: (*To* CLIFF) There you are – she likes it!

    (*He returns to his paper.* CLIFF *grunts.*)

    Have you read about the grotesque and evil practices going on in the Midlands?

CLIFF: Read about the what?

JIMMY: Grotesque and evil practices going on in the Midlands.

CLIFF: No, what about 'em?

JIMMY: Seems we don't know the old place. It's all in here. Startling Revelations this week! Pictures too. Reconstructions of midnight invocations to the Coptic Goddess of fertility.

HELENA: Sounds madly depraved.

JIMMY: Yes, it's rather us, isn't it? My gosh, look at 'em! Snarling themselves silly. Next week a well-known debutante relates how, during an evil orgy in Market Harborough, she killed and drank the blood of a white cockerel. Well – I'll bet Fortnums must be doing a roaring line in sacrificial cocks! (*Thoughtful.*) Perhaps that's what Miss Drury does on Sunday evenings. She puts in a stint as evil high priestess down at the YW – probably having a workout at this very moment. (*To* HELENA.) You never dabbled in this kind of thing, did you?

HELENA: (*Laughs*) Not lately!

JIMMY: Sounds rather your cup of tea – cup of blood, I should say. (*In an imitation of a Midlands accent.*) Well, I mean, it gives you something to do, doesn't it? After all, it wouldn't do if we was all alike, would it? It'd be a funny world if we was all the same, that's what *I* always say! (*Resuming in his normal voice.*) All I know is that somebody's been sticking pins into *my* wax image for years. (*Suddenly.*) Of course: Alison's mother! Every Friday, the wax arrives from Harrods, and all through the weekend, she's stabbing away at it with a hatpin! Ruined her bridge game, I dare say.

HELENA: Why don't *you* try it?

JIMMY: Yes, it's an idea. (*Pointing to* CLIFF.) Just for a start, we could roast him over the gas stove. Have we got enough shillings for the meter? It seems to be just the thing for these Autumn evenings. After all the whole point of a sacrifice is that you give up something you never really wanted in the first place. You know what I mean? People are doing it around you all the time. They give up their careers, say – or their beliefs – or sex. And everyone thinks to themselves: how wonderful to be able to do that. If only I were capable of doing that! But the truth of it is that they've been kidding themselves, and they've been kidding you. It's not awfully difficult – giving up something you were incapable of ever really wanting. We shouldn't be admiring them. We should feel rather sorry for them. (*Coming back from this sudden, brooding excursion, and turning to* CLIFF.) You'll make and admirable sacrifice.

CLIFF: (*Mumbling*) Dry up! I'm trying to read.

JIMMY: Afterwards, we can make a loving cup from his blood. Can't say I fancy that so much. I've seen it – it looks like cochineal, ever so common. (*To* HELENA.) Yours would be much better – pale Cambridge blue, I imagine. No? And afterwards, we could make invocations to the Coptic Goddess of fertility. Got any idea how you do that? (*To* CLIFF.) Do you know?

CLIFF: Shouldn't have thought *you* needed to make invocations to the Coptic whatever-she-is!

JIMMY: Yes, I see what you mean. (*To* HELENA.) Well, we don't want to *ask* for trouble, do we? Perhaps it might appeal to the lady here – she's written a long letter all about artificial insemination. It's headed: Haven't we tried God's patience enough! (*Throws the paper down.*) Let's see the other posh one.

CLIFF: Haven't finished yet.

JIMMY: Well, hurry up. I'll have to write and ask them to put hyphens in between the syllables for you. There's a particularly savage correspondence going on in there about whether Milton wore braces or not. I just want to see who gets shot down this week.

CLIFF: Just read that. Don't know what it was about, but a Fellow of All Souls seems to have bitten the dust, and the Athenaeum's going up in flames, so the Editor declares that this correspondence is now closed.

JIMMY: I think you're actually acquiring yourself a curiosity, my boy. Oh yes, and then there's an American professor from Yale or somewhere, who believes that when Shakespeare was writing *The Tempest*, he changed his sex. Yes, he was obliged to go back to Stratford because the other actors couldn't take him seriously any longer. This professor chap is coming over here to search for certain documents which will prove that poor old W.S. ended up in someone else's second best bed – a certain Warwickshire farmer's, whom he married after having three children by him.

(HELENA *laughs*. JIMMY *looks up quizzically*.)

Is anything the matter?

HELENA: No, nothing. I'm only beginning to get used to him. I never (*this is to* CLIFF) used to be sure when he was being serious, or when he wasn't.

CLIFF: Don't think he knows himself half the time. When in doubt, just mark it down as an insult.

JIMMY: Hurry up with that paper, and shut up! What are we going to do tonight? There isn't even a decent concert on. (*To* HELENA.) Are you going to Church?

HELENA: (*Rather taken aback*) No. I don't think so. Unless you want to.

JIMMY: Do I detect a growing, satanic glint in her eyes lately? Do you think it's living in sin with me that does it? (*To* HELENA.) Do you feel very sinful my dear? Well? Do you?

(*She can hardly believe that this is an attack, and she can only look at him, uncertain of herself*.)

Do you feel sin crawling out of your ears, like stored up wax or something? Are you wondering whether I'm joking or not? Perhaps I ought to wear a red nose and funny hat. I'm just curious, that's all.

(*She is shaken by the sudden coldness in his eyes, but before she has time to fully realize how hurt she is, he is smiling at her, and shouting cheerfully at* CLIFF.)

Let's have that paper, stupid!

CLIFF: Why don't you drop dead!

JIMMY: (*To* HELENA) Will you be much longer doing that?

HELENA: Nearly finished.

JIMMY: Talking of sin, wasn't that Miss Drury's Reverend friend I saw you chatting with yesterday. Helena darling, I said wasn't that . . .

HELENA: Yes it was.

JIMMY: My dear, you don't have to be on the defensive you know.

HELENA: I'm not on the defensive.

JIMMY: After all, there's no reason why we shouldn't have the parson to tea up here. Why don't we? Did you find that you had much in common?

HELENA: No I don't think so.

JIMMY: Do you think that some of this spiritual beefcake would make a man of me? Should I go in for this moral weight-lifting and get myself some over-developed muscle? I was a liberal skinny weakling. I too was afraid to strip down to my soul, but now everyone looks at my superb physique in envy. I can perform any kind of press there is without betraying the least sign of passion or kindliness.

HELENA: All right, Jimmy.

JIMMY: Two years ago I couldn't even lift up my head – now I have more uplift than a film starlet.

HELENA: Jimmy, can we have one day, just one day, without tumbling over religion or politics?

CLIFF: Yes, change the record, old boy, or pipe down.

JIMMY: (*Rising*) Thought of the title for a new song today. It's called 'My mother's in the madhouse – that's why I'm in love with you.' The lyrics are catchy too. I was thinking we might work it into the act.

HELENA: Good idea.

JIMMY: I was thinking we'd scrub Jock and Day, and call ourselves something else. 'And jocund day stands tiptoed on the misty mountain tops.' It's too intellectual! Anyway, I shouldn't think people will want to be reminded of that peculiar man's plays after Harvard and Yale have finished with him. How about something bright and snappy? I know – What about – T. S. Eliot and Pam!

CLIFF: (*Casually falling in with this familiar routine*) Mirth, mellerdy and madness!

JIMMY: (*Sitting at the table R. and 'strumming' it*) Bringing quips and strips for you!

(*They sing together.*)

> For we may be guilty, darling . . .
> But we're both insane as well!

(JIMMY *stands up, and rattles his lines off at almost unintelligible speed.*)

Ladies and gentlemen, as I was coming to the theatre tonight, I was passing through the stage door, and a man comes up to me, and 'e says:

CLIFF: 'Ere! Have you seen nobody?

JIMMY: Have I seen who?

CLIFF: Have you seen nobody?

JIMMY: Of course, I haven't seen nobody! Kindly don't waste my time! Ladies and gentlemen, a little recitation entitled 'She said she was called little Gidding, but she was more like a gelding iron!' Thank you. 'She said she was called little Gidding – '

CLIFF: Are you quite sure you haven't seen nobody?

JIMMY: Are you still here?

CLIFF: I'm looking for nobody!

JIMMY: *Will* you kindly go away! 'She said she was called little Gidding – '

CLIFF: Well, I can't find nobody anywhere, and I'm supposed to give him this case!

JIMMY: Will you kindly stop interrupting per*lease*! Can't you see I'm trying to entertain these ladies and gentlemen? Who is this nobody you're talking about?

CLIFF: I was told to come here and give this case to nobody.

JIMMY: You were told to come here and give this case to nobody.

CLIFF: That's right. And when I gave it to him, nobody would give me a shilling.

JIMMY: And when you gave it to him, nobody would give you a shilling.

CLIFF: That's right.

JIMMY: Well, what about it?

CLIFF: Nobody's not here!

JIMMY: Now, let me get this straight: when you say nobody's here, you don't mean nobody's here?

CLIFF: No.

JIMMY: No. You mean – nobody's here.

CLIFF: That's right.

JIMMY: Well, why didn't you say so before?

HELENA: (*Not quite sure if this is really her cue*) Hey! You down there!

JIMMY: Oh, it goes on for hours yet, but never mind. What is it, sir?

HELENA: (*Shouting*) I think your sketch stinks! I say – I think your sketch stinks!

JIMMY: He thinks it stinks. And, who, pray, might you be?

HELENA: Me? Oh – (*with mock modesty*) I'm nobody.

JIMMY: Then here's your bloody case!

(*He hurls a cushion at her, which hits the ironing board.*)

HELENA: My ironing board!

(*The two men do a Flanagan and Allen, moving slowly in step, as they sing.*)

Now there's a certain little lady, and you all know who I mean,
She may have been to Roedean, but to me she's still a queen.
Someday I'm goin' to marry her,
When times are not so bad,

Her mother doesn't care for me
So I'll 'ave to ask 'er dad.
We'll build a little home for two,
And have some quiet menage,
We'll send our kids to public school
And live on bread and marge.
Don't be afraid to sleep with your sweetheart,
Just because she's better than you.
Those forgotten middle classes may have fallen on
     their noses,
But a girl who's true blue,
Will still have something left for you,
The angels up above, will know that you're in love
So don't be afraid to sleep with your sweetheart,
Just because she's better than you . . .
          They call me Sydney,
Just because she's better than you.

(*But* JIMMY *has had enough of this gag by now, and he pushes* CLIFF *away.*)

JIMMY: Your damned great feet! That's the second time you've kicked my ankle! It's no good – Helena will have to do it. Go on, go and make some tea, and we'll decide what we're going to do.

CLIFF: Make some yourself!

(*He pushes him back violently,* JIMMY *loses his balance, and falls over.*)

JIMMY: You rough bastard!

(*He leaps up, and they grapple, falling on to the floor with a crash. They roll about, grunting and gasping.* CLIFF *manages to kneel on* JIMMY's *chest.*)

CLIFF: (*Breathing heavily*) I want to read the papers!

JIMMY: You're a savage, a hooligan! You really are! Do you know that! You don't deserve to live in the same house with decent, sensitive people!

CLIFF: Are you going to dry up, or do I read the papers down here?

(JIMMY *makes a supreme effort, and* CLIFF *topples to the floor.*)

JIMMY: You've made me wrench my guts!

(*He pushes the struggling* CLIFF *down.*)

CLIFF: Look what you're doing! You're ripping my shirt. Get *off*!

JIMMY: Well, what do you want to wear a shirt for? (*Rising.*) A tough character like you! Now go and make me some tea.

CLIFF: It's the only clean one I've got. Oh, you big oaf!

(*Getting up from the floor, and appealing to* HELENA.) Look! It's filthy!

HELENA: Yes, it is. He's stronger than he looks. If you like to take it off now, I'll wash it through for you. It'll be dry by the time we want to go out.

(CLIFF *hesitates.*)

What's the matter, Cliff?

CLIFF: Oh, it'll be all right.

JIMMY: Give it to her, and quit moaning!

CLIFF: Oh, all right.

(*He takes it off, and gives it to her.*)

Thanks, Helena.

HELENA: (*Taking it*) Right. I won't be a minute with it.

(*She goes out.* JIMMY *flops into his armchair. R.*)

JIMMY: (*Amused*) You look like Marlon Brando or something. (*Slight pause.*) You don't care for Helena, do you?

CLIFF: You didn't seem very keen yourself once. (*Hesitating, then quickly.*) It's not the same, is it?

JIMMY: (*Irritably*) No, of course it's not the same, you idiot! It never is! Today's meal is always different from yesterday's and the last woman isn't the same as the one before. If you can't accept that, you're going to be pretty unhappy, my boy.

CLIFF: (*Sits on the arm of his chair, and rubs his feet*) Jimmy – I don't think I shall stay here much longer.

JIMMY: (*Rather casually*) Oh, why not?

CLIFF: (*Picking up his tone*) Oh, I don't know. I've just
    thought of trying somewhere different. The sweet-stall's
    all right, but I think I'd like to try something else. You're
    highly educated, and it suits you, but I need something a
    bit better.

JIMMY: Just as you like, my dear boy. It's your business, not
    mine.

CLIFF: And another thing – I think Helena finds it rather a
    lot of work to do with two chaps about the place. It
    won't be so much for her if there's just the two of you.
    Anyway, I think I ought to find some girl who'll just
    look after me.

JIMMY: Sounds like a good idea. Can't think who'd be stupid
    enough to team themselves up with you though. Perhaps
    Helena can think of somebody for you – one of her posh
    girlfriends with lots of money, and no brains. That's
    what you want.

CLIFF: Something like that.

JIMMY: Any idea what you're going to do?

CLIFF: Not much.

JIMMY: That sounds like you all right! Shouldn't think you'll
    last five minutes without me to explain the score to you.

CLIFF: (*Grinning*) Don't suppose so.

JIMMY: You're such a scruffy little beast – I'll bet some
    respectable little madam from Pinner or Guildford
    gobbles you up in six months. She'll marry you, send
    you out to work, and you'll end up as clean as a new
    pin.

CLIFF: (*Chuckling*) Yes, I'm stupid enough for that too!

JIMMY: (*To himself*) I seem to spend my life saying good-bye.
    (*Slight pause.*)

CLIFF: My feet hurt.

JIMMY: Try washing your socks. (*Slowly.*) It's a funny
    thing. You've been loyal, generous and a good friend.
    But I'm quite prepared to see you wander off, find a

new home, and make out on your own. And all because of something I want from that girl downstairs, something I know in my heart she's incapable of giving. You're worth a half a dozen Helenas to me or to anyone. And, if you were in my place, you'd do the same thing. Right?

CLIFF: Right.

JIMMY: Why, why, why, why do we let these women bleed us to death? Have you ever had a letter, and on it is franked 'Please Give Your Blood Generously'? Well, the Postmaster-General does that, on behalf of all the women of the world. I suppose people of our generation aren't able to die for good causes any longer. We had all that done for us, in the thirties and the forties, when we were still kids. (*In his familiar, semi-serious mood.*) There aren't any good, brave causes left. If the big bang does come, and we all get killed off, it won't be in aid of the old-fashioned, grand design. It'll just be for the Brave New-nothing-very-much-thank-you. About as pointless and inglorious as stepping in front of a bus. No, there's nothing left for it, me boy, but to let yourself be butchered by the women.
(*Enter* HELENA.)

HELENA: Here you are, Cliff. (*Handing him the shirt.*)

CLIFF: Oh, thanks, Helena, very much. That's decent of you.

HELENA: Not at all. I should dry it over the gas – the fire in your room would be better. There won't be much room for it over the stove.

CLIFF: Right, I will. (*Crosses to door.*)

JIMMY: And hurry up about it, stupid. We'll all go out, and have a drink soon. (*To* HELENA.) OK?

HELENA: OK.

JIMMY: (*Shouting to* CLIFF *on his way out*) But make me some tea first, you madcap little Charlie.
(*She crosses down L.*)

JIMMY: Darling, I'm sick of seeing you behind that damned ironing board!

HELENA: (*Wryly*) Sorry.

JIMMY: Get yourself glammed up, and we'll hit the town. See you've put a shroud over mummy, I think you should have laid a Union Jack over it.

HELENA: Is anything wrong?

JIMMY: Oh, don't frown like that – you look like the presiding magistrate!

HELENA: How should I look?

JIMMY: As if your heart stirred a little when you looked at me.

HELENA: Oh, it does that all right.

JIMMY: Cliff tells me he's leaving us.

HELENA: I know. He told me last night.

JIMMY: Did he? I always seem to be at the end of the queue when they're passing information out.

HELENA: I'm sorry he's going.

JIMMY: Yes, so am I. He's a sloppy, irritating bastard, but he's got a big heart. You can forgive somebody almost anything for that. He's had to learn how to take it, and he knows how to hand it out. Come here.

(*He is sitting on the arm of his chair. She crosses to him, and they look at each other. Then she puts out her hand, and runs it over his head, fondling his ear and neck.*)

Right from that first night, you have always put out your hand to me first. As if you expected nothing, or worse than nothing, and didn't care. You made a good enemy, didn't you? What they call a worthy opponent. But then, when people put down their weapons, it doesn't mean they've necessarily stopped fighting.

HELENA: (*Steadily*) I love you.

JIMMY: I think perhaps you do. Yes, I think perhaps you do. Perhaps it means something to lie with your victorious general in your arms. Especially, when he's heartily sick of the whole campaign, tired out, hungry and dry.

(His lips find her fingers, and he kisses them. She presses his head against her.)

You stood up, and came out to meet me. Oh, Helena –
(His face comes up to hers, and they embrace fiercely.)
Don't let anything go wrong!

HELENA: *(Softly)* Oh, my darling –

JIMMY: Either you're with me or against me.

HELENA: I've always wanted you – always!
(They kiss again.)

JIMMY: T. S. Eliot and Pam, we'll make a good double. If you'll help me. I'll close that damned sweet-stall, and we'll start everything from scratch. What do you say? We'll get away from this place.

HELENA: *(Nodding happily)* I say that's wonderful.

JIMMY: *(Kissing her quickly)* Put all that junk away, and we'll get out. We'll get pleasantly, joyfully tiddly, we'll gaze at each other tenderly and lecherously in 'The Builder's Arms', and then we'll come back here, and I'll make such love to you, you'll not care about anything else at all.
(She moves away L., after kissing his hand.)

HELENA: I'll just change out of your old shirt. *(Folding ironing board.)*

JIMMY: *(Moving upstage to door)* Right. I'll hurry up the little man.
(But before he reaches the door, it opens and ALISON enters. She wears a raincoat, her hair is untidy, and she looks rather ill. There is a stunned pause.)

ALISON: *(Quietly)* Hullo.

JIMMY: *(To HELENA after a moment)* Friend of yours to see you.
(He goes out quickly, and the two women are left looking at each other. Quick curtain.)

It is a few minutes later. From Cliff's room, across the landing, comes the sound of Jimmy's jazz trumpet. At rise of the curtain, HELENA *is standing L. of the table, pouring out a cup of tea.* ALISON *is sitting on the armchair R. She bends down and picks up Jimmy's pipe. Then she scoops up a little pile of ash from the floor, and drops it in the ashtray on the arm of the chair.*

ALISON: He still smokes this foul old stuff. I used to hate it
　　　at first, but you get used to it.
HELENA: Yes.
ALISON: I went to the pictures last week, and some old man
　　　was smoking it in front, a few rows away. I actually got
　　　up, and sat right behind him.
HELENA: (*Coming down with cup of tea*) Here, have this. It
　　　usually seems to help.
ALISON: (*Taking it*) Thanks.
HELENA: Are you sure you feel all right now?
ALISON: (*Nods*) It was just – oh, everything. It's my own
　　　fault – entirely. I must be mad, coming here like this.
　　　I'm sorry, Helena.
HELENA: Why should you be sorry – you of all people?
ALISON: Because it was unfair and cruel of me to come back.
　　　I'm afraid a sense of timing is one of the things I seem to
　　　have learnt from Jimmy. But it's something that can be
　　　in very bad taste. (*Sips her tea.*) So many times, I've just
　　　managed to stop myself coming here – right at the last
　　　moment. Even today, when I went to the booking office
　　　at St Pancras, it was like a charade, and I never believed
　　　that I'd let myself walk on to that train. And when I was
　　　on it, I got into a panic. I felt like a criminal. I told
　　　myself I'd turn round at the other end, and come
　　　straight back. I couldn't even believe that this place
　　　existed any more. But once I got here, there was nothing
　　　I could do. I had to convince myself that everything I

remembered about this place had really happened to me once. (*She lowers her cup, and her foot plays with the newspapers on the floor.*) How many times in these past few months I've thought of the evenings we used to spend here in this room. Suspended and rather remote. You make a good cup of tea.

HELENA: (*Sitting L. of table*) Something Jimmy taught *me*.

ALISON: (*Covering her face*) Oh, why am I here! You must all wish me a thousand miles away!

HELENA: I don't wish anything of the kind. You've more right to be here than I.

ALISON: Oh, Helena, don't bring out the book of rules –

HELENA: You are his wife, aren't you? Whatever I have done, I've never been able to forget that fact. You have all the rights –

ALISON: Helena – even I gave up believing in the divine rights of marriage long ago. Even before I met Jimmy. They've got something different now – constitutional monarchy. You are where you are by consent. And if you start trying any strong-arm stuff, you're out. And I'm out.

HELENA: Is that something you learnt from him?

ALISON: Don't make me feel like a blackmailer or something, please! I've done something foolish, and rather vulgar in coming here tonight. I regret it, and I detest myself for doing it. But I did not come here in order to gain anything. Whatever it was – hysteria or just macabre curiosity, I'd certainly no intention of making any kind of breach between you and Jimmy. You must believe that.

HELENA: Oh, I believe it all right. That's why everything seems more wrong and terrible than ever. You didn't even reproach me. You should have been outraged but you weren't. (*She leans back, as if she wanted to draw back from herself.*) I feel so – *ashamed*.

ALISON: You talk as though he were something you'd swindled me out of –

HELENA: (*Fiercely*) And you talk as if he were a book or
something you pass around to anyone who happens to
want it for five minutes. What's the matter with you?
You sound as though you were quoting *him* all the time. I
thought you told me once you couldn't bring yourself to
believe in him.

ALISON: I don't think I ever believed in your way either.

HELENA: At least I still believe in right and wrong! Not even
the months in this madhouse have stopped me doing
that. Even though everything I have done is wrong, at
least I have known it was wrong.

ALISON: You loved him, didn't you? That's what you wrote,
and told me.

HELENA: And it was true.

ALISON: It was pretty difficult to believe at the time. I
couldn't understand it.

HELENA: I could hardly believe it myself.

ALISON: Afterwards, it wasn't quite so difficult. You used to
say some pretty harsh things about him. Not that I was
sorry to hear them – they were rather comforting then.
But you even shocked me sometimes.

HELENA: I suppose I was a little over-emphatic. There doesn't
seem much point in trying to explain everything, does
there?

ALISON: Not really.

HELENA: Do you know – I have discovered what is wrong
with Jimmy? It's very simple really. He was born out of
his time.

ALISON: Yes. I know.

HELENA: There's no place for people like that any longer – in
sex, or politics, or anything. That's why he's so futile.
Sometimes, when I listen to him, I feel he thinks he's still
in the middle of the French Revolution. And that's where
he ought to be, of course. He doesn't know where he is,
or where he's going. He'll never do anything, and he'll
never amount to anything.

ALISON: I suppose he's what you'd call an Eminent Victorian. Slightly comic – in a way . . . We seem to have had this conversation before.

HELENA: Yes, I remember everything you said about him. It horrified me. I couldn't believe that you could have married someone like that. Alison – it's all over between Jimmy and me. I can see it now. I've got to get out. No – listen to me. When I saw you standing there tonight, I knew that it was all utterly wrong. That I didn't believe in any of this, and not Jimmy or anyone could make me believe otherwise. (*Rising.*) How could I have ever thought I could get away with it! He wants one world and I want another, and lying in that bed won't ever change it! I believe in good and evil, and I don't have to apologize for that. It's quite a modern, scientific belief now, so they tell me. And, by everything I have ever believed in, or wanted, what I have been doing is wrong and evil.

ALISON: Helena – you're not going to leave him?

HELENA: Yes, I am. (*Before* ALISON *can interrupt, she goes on.*) Oh, I'm not stepping aside to let you come back. You can do what you like. Frankly, I think you'd be a fool – but that's your own business. I think I've given you enough advice.

ALISON: But he – he'll have no one.

HELENA: Oh, my dear, he'll find somebody. He'll probably hold court here like one of the Renaissance popes. Oh, I know I'm throwing the book of rules at you, as you call it, but, believe me, you're never going to be happy without it. I tried throwing it away all these months, but I know now it just doesn't work. When you came in at that door, ill and tired and hurt, it was all over for me. You see – I didn't know about the baby. It was such a shock. It's like a judgement on us.

ALISON: You saw me, and I had to tell you what had happened. I lost the child. It's a simple fact. There is no judgement there's no blame –

HELENA: Maybe not. But I feel it just the same.

ALISON: But don't you see? It isn't logical!

HELENA: No, it isn't. (*Calmly.*) But I know it's right.
(*The trumpet gets louder.*)

ALISON: Helena, (*going to her*) you mustn't leave him. He
needs you, I know he needs you –

HELENA: Do you think so?

ALISON: Maybe you're not the right one for him – we're
neither of us right –

HELENA: (*Moving upstage*) Oh, why doesn't he stop that
damned noise!

ALISON: He wants something quite different from us. What
it is exactly I don't know – a kind of cross between a
mother and a Greek courtesan, a henchwoman, a
mixture of Cleopatra and Boswell. But give him a little
longer –

HELENA: (*Wrenching the door open*) Please! Will you stop that!
I can't think!
(*There is a slight pause, and the trumpet goes on. She puts her
hands to her head.*)
Jimmy, for God's sake!
(*It stops.*)
Jimmy, I want to speak to you.

JIMMY: (*Off*) Is your friend still with you?

HELENA: Oh, don't be an idiot, and come in here!
(*She moves down L.*)

ALISON: (*Rising*) He doesn't want to see me.

HELENA: Stay where you are, and don't be silly. I'm sorry. It
won't be very pleasant, but I've made up my mind to go,
and I've got to tell him now.
(*Enter* JIMMY.)

JIMMY: Is this another of your dark plots? (*He looks at*
ALISON.) Hadn't she better sit down? She looks a bit
ghastly.

HELENA: I'm so sorry, dear. Would you like some more tea,
or an aspirin or something?

(ALISON *shakes her head, and sits. She can't look at either of them.*)

(*To* JIMMY, *the old authority returning*) It's not very surprising, is it? She's been very ill, she's –

JIMMY: (*Quietly*) You don't have to draw a diagram for me – I can see what's happened to her.

HELENA: And doesn't it mean anything to you?

JIMMY: I don't exactly relish the idea of anyone being ill, or in pain. It was my child too, you know. But (*he shrugs*) it isn't my first loss.

ALISON: (*On her breath*) It was mine.

(*He glances at her, but turns back to* HELENA *quickly.*)

JIMMY: What are you looking so solemn about? What's she doing here?

ALISON: I'm sorry, I'm – (*Presses her hand over her mouth.*)

(HELENA *crosses to* JIMMY *C., and grasps his hand.*)

HELENA: Don't please. Can't you see the condition she's in? She's done nothing, she's said nothing, none of it's her fault.

(*He takes his hand away, and moves away a little downstage.*)

JIMMY: What isn't her fault?

HELENA: Jimmy – I don't what a brawl, so please –

JIMMY: Let's hear it, shall we?

HELENA: Very well. I'm going downstairs to pack my things. If I hurry, I shall just catch the 7.15 to London.

(*They both look at him, but he simply leans forward against the table, not looking at either of them.*)

This is not Alison's doing – you must understand that. It's my own decision entirely. In fact, she's just been trying to talk me out of it. It's just that suddenly, tonight, I see what I have really known all along. That you can't be happy when what you're doing is wrong, or is hurting someone else. I suppose it could never have worked, anyway, but I do love you, Jimmy. I shall never love anyone as I have loved you. (*Turns away L.*) But I

can't go on. (*Passionately and sincerely.*) I can't take part –
in all this suffering. I can't!

(*She appeals to him for some reaction, but he only looks down
at the table, and nods.* HELENA *recovers, and makes an
effort to regain authority.*)

(*To* ALISON.) You probably won't feel up to making
that journey again tonight, but we can fix you up at an
hotel before I go. There's about half an hour. I'll just
make it.

(*She turns up to the door, but* JIMMY's *voice stops her.*)

JIMMY: (*In a low, resigned voice*) They all want to escape from
the pain of being alive. And, most of all, from love.
(*Crosses to the dressing table.*) I always knew something
like this would turn up – some problem, like an ill wife –
and it would be too much for those delicate, hot-house
feelings of yours. (*He sweeps up Helen's things from the
dressing table, and crosses over to the wardrobe. Outside, the
church bells start ringing.*) It's no good trying to fool
yourself about love. You can't fall into it like a soft job,
without dirtying up your hands. (*Hands her the make-up
things, which she takes. He opens the wardrobe.*) It takes
muscle and guts. And if you can't bear the thought (*takes
out a dress on a hanger*) of messing up your nice, clean
soul, (*crossing back to her*) you'd better give up the whole
idea of life, and become a saint. (*Puts the dress in her
arms.*) Because you'll never make it as a human being.
It's either this world or the next.

(*She looks at him for a moment, and then goes out quickly.
He is shaken, and he avoids* ALISON's *eyes, crossing to the
window. He rests against it, then bangs his fist against the
frame.*)

Oh, those bells!

(*The shadows are growing around them.* JIMMY *stands, his
head against the window pane.* ALISON *is huddled forward
in the armchair R. Presently, she breaks the stillness, and
rises to above the table.*)

ALISON: I'm . . . sorry. I'll go now.

(*She starts to move upstage. But his voice pulls her up.*)

JIMMY: You never even sent any flowers to the funeral. Not – a little bunch of flowers. You had to deny me that too, didn't you?

(*She starts to move, but again he speaks.*)

The injustice of it is almost perfect! The wrong people going hungry, the wrong people being loved, the wrong people dying!

(*She moves to the gas stove. He turns to face her.*)

Was I really wrong to believe that there's a – a kind of – burning virility of mind and spirit that looks for something as powerful as itself? The heaviest, strongest creatures in this world seem to be the loneliest. Like the old bear, following his own breath in the dark forest. There's no warm pack, no herd to comfort him. That voice that cries out doesn't *have* to be a weakling's, does it? (*He moves in a little.*) Do you remember that first night I saw you at that grisly party? You didn't really notice me, but I was watching you all the evening. You seemed to have a wonderful relaxation of spirit. I knew that was what I wanted. You've got to be really brawny to have that kind of strength – the strength to relax. It was only after we were married that I discovered that it wasn't relaxation at all. In order to relax, you've first got to sweat your guts out. And, as far as you were concerned, you'd never had a hair out of place, or a bead of sweat anywhere.

(*A cry escapes from her, and her fist flies to her mouth. She moves down to below the table, leaning on it.*)

I may be a lost cause, but I thought if you loved me, it needn't matter.

(*She is crying silently. He moved down to face her.*)

ALISON: It doesn't matter! I was wrong, I was wrong! I don't want to be neutral, I don't want to be a saint. I want to be a lost cause. I want to be corrupt and futile!

(*All he can do is watch her helplessly. Her voice takes on a little strength, and rises.*)

Don't you understand? It's gone! It's gone! That – that helpless human being inside my body. I thought it was so safe, and secure in there. Nothing could take it from me. It was mine, my responsibility. But it's lost. (*She slides down against the leg of the table to the floor.*) All I wanted was to die. I never knew what it was like. I didn't know it could be like that! I was in pain, and all I could think of was you, and what I'd lost. (*Scarcely able to speak.*) I thought: if only – if only he could see me now, so stupid, and ugly and ridiculous. This is what he's been longing for me to feel. This is what he wants to splash about in! I'm in the fire, and I'm burning, and all I want is to die! It's cost him his child, and any others I might have had! But what does it matter – this is what he wanted from me! (*She raises her face to him.*) Don't you see! I'm in the mud at last! I'm grovelling! I'm crawling! Oh, God –

(*She collapses at his feet. He stands, frozen for a moment, then he bends down and takes her shaking body in his arms. He shakes his head, and whispers:*)

JIMMY: Don't. Please don't . . . I can't –

(*She gasps for her breath against him.*)

You're all right. You're all right now. Please, I – I . . . Not any more . . .

(*She relaxes suddenly. He looks down at her, full of fatigue, and says with a kind of mocking, tender irony:*)

We'll be together in our bear's cave, and our squirrel's drey, and we'll live on honey, and nuts – lots and lots of nuts. And we'll sing songs about ourselves – about warm trees and snug caves, and lying in the sun. And you'll keep those big eyes on my fur, and help me keep my claws in order, because I'm a bit of a soppy, scruffy sort of a bear. And I'll see that you keep that sleek, bushy tail glistening as it should, because you're a very beautiful squirrel, but you're none too bright either, so we've got to be careful. There are cruel steel traps lying about everywhere, just waiting for rather mad, slightly satanic, and very timid little animals. Right?

(ALISON *nods.*)

(*Pathetically.*) Poor squirrels!

ALISON: (*With the same comic emphasis*) Poor bears! (*She laughs a little. Then looks at him very tenderly, and adds very, very softly.*) Oh, poor, poor bears!

(*Slides her arms around him. Curtain.*)

EPITAPH FOR
GEORGE DILLON

A Play in Three Acts

JOHN OSBORNE · ANTHONY CREIGHTON

TO E.M.C.
with our love

The first professional performance in Great Britain of *Epitaph for George Dillon* was given at the Royal Court Theatre, Sloane Square, London, on 11 February 1958 by the English Stage Company. It was directed by William Gaskill and the décor was by Stephen Doncaster. The cast was as follows:

JOSIE ELLIOT	Wendy Craig
RUTH GRAY	Yvonne Mitchell
MRS ELLIOT	Alison Leggatt
NORAH ELLIOT	Avril Elgar
PERCY ELLIOT	Toke Townley
GEORGE DILLON	Robert Stephens
GEOFFREY COLWYN-STUART	Philip Locke
MR WEBB	Paul Bailey
BARNEY EVANS	Nigel Davenport

The action of the play takes place in the home of the Elliot family just outside London.

Act I   Spring
Act II   Summer
Act III *scene I*   Autumn
Act III *scene II* Winter

ACT ONE

The home of the Elliot family, just outside London. Spring, late afternoon.

The action takes place in the sitting-room and hall. The front door being stage right. In the hall, immediately facing, are the stairs which turn off left. Flat against the staircase is a hat and coat stand, shelving hats, coats, magazines, umbrellas, etc., in the midst of which is a vase of everlasting flowers. Upstage of the hall, under the arch formed by the stairs is the door leading into the room called the lounge. Next to this upstage is the invisible wall which divides the hall from the sitting-room. The only object suggesting the wall is a door set upstage. Downstage of this, set against the 'wall' facing into the sitting-room is a radiogram, upon which stands a biscuit barrel and a silver-plated dish containing wax or real fruit. Nearby an armchair of the 'contemporary' kind faces downstage. Against the upstage wall, right, is a dining-chair. Centre, an ornate cocktail cabinet and another dining-chair. On the wall, flanking this, are two wall lights, in the centre of which is painted a group of wild ducks, in flight.

Left centre is the door leading to the kitchen, next to which is the kitchen hatch, which when raised, reveals the kitchen beyond. Below the hatch is a tea-trolley. Above the hatch, on the wall, is a tinted photograph of a wedding group. In the stage left wall, french windows which look out on to a small back garden. Below the french windows, a half-round occasional table, above hangs a mirror. In front of the french windows a settee, again of the utility-contemporary period. At the head a white-painted wrought-iron floor lamp. Upstage, left centre, a draw-leaf table with dining-chair and arm-dining-chair in position. On the cocktail cabinet stands a large china model of an Alsatian dog, and a photograph of a soldier in a silver frame, decorated with 'Haig' poppies.

At rise of curtain, JOSIE *is on stage alone. She is about twenty,*

*pretty in a hard, frilly way and nobody's fool. At the moment she is
not looking her best. The turban she is wearing reveals a couple of
curlers above her forehead, her jumper is grubby and her slacks
baggy, stained and not very fetching. She is sprawled in the
armchair. In a vicious idleness she stares at a highly coloured
weekly. Mozart is on the radio, delicate, liquid. She flips through the
magazine, is about to put it down when something catches her
attention.*

She reads.

JOSIE: Fancy writing up and asking *that*! (*She laughs and goes
on with her reading, fondling one of her curlers as she does
so. Presently she throws the magazine down.*) Soppy cow!
(*She sighs and leans back, thrusts her hands into the top of
her slacks, rubbing her stomach and frowning. She gets up
and stares at her reflection in the mirror. Pursing her lips
experimentally, she watches the effect. She leans forward
and tries fluffing up her eyebrows. It doesn't seem very
successful and she sighs again.*) Oh, that damn row! (*She
goes to the radio, stabs at the knobs, then gives up and
switches it off. Her eye catches the magazine again and she
goes through it again until she finds what she is looking for.
She stares at it sullenly and flings the paper on the floor. At
the mirror again she tries several grimaces, puts out her
tongue. A little more speculation, and she goes over to the
settee, and sinks down on her knees. She stretches, and,
catching sight of the resulting white space between her
jumper and slacks, strokes herself dreamily. She slides
forward on to her stomach, her hands moving over the arm
of the settee, curiosity in her fingers and boredom in her
body. She starts to sing, in a studied, offhand way, one of
those downward-inflection popular hits.*)
　　Why don't you Give Me . . . Give Me . . .
　(*Pause.*)
　　All that you have to share.
　　Why don't you Give Me . . . Give Me . . .

(*She picks her nose daintily, and turns over on her back.*)
   And tell me you really c-are . . .
(*Her hand trails the space beside her, like a hand in rippling water, then stops, as she says deliberately:*) I wonder – what it *would* be like? (*She is about to swing her legs above her head, when the front door bell rings.*) Good-O! (*She rushes off to the front door, almost reaches it, when she remembers something, and comes back into the dining-room. Her eyes light on her handbag, and she snatches it up, taking it with her, through the hall, straight to the front door. The bell is still ringing, and she calls out:*) Oh, all right! Wait a minute! Wait a minute!
(*Opens front door. We hear a voice saying:* 'Parcel for Mrs Elliot. Three pounds fifteen and ninepence to pay.') *Miss* Elliot, if you please. I thought you were never coming. Here you are. You have been a long time. I thought you'd have been here this morning. I haven't even been able to go up the road, waiting for you to come. What? I haven't got it. Well, you'll have to change it.
(*A few minutes of change fumbling before she slams the front door, and goes into the sitting-room with a square cardboard box in her arms, which she starts to open excitedly, kneeling on the floor. Off comes the string and paper, then the lid and a layer of tissue paper. She rises quickly, places the box on the settee, takes a cigarette from her handbag, which she puts in her mouth, kicks off her slippers, and goes to the radiogram, unzipping her slacks at the same time. She raises the lid, switches it on, and takes off her slacks, leaving them on the floor, one leg inside out. She selects a record from the pile beside her, and puts it on. Cigarette in mouth, she waits expectantly until the corncrake growl of a New Orleans trumpet strides off into a piece of fairly traditional jazz. She runs back to her parcel and takes out the contents, in a scurry of paper and impatience, which turn out to be a pair of black, tapering trousers. She puts them on, zipping up the*

*sides with a little difficulty. Hands on hips, she looks down
at the result anxiously, then delightedly. She goes nearer to
the mirror, to get a better view of herself. She bounces up
and down, looking at this angle and that, patting her
stomach, feeling the seat until she is finally satisfied. She
lights her cigarette, then, putting her hands in her unfamiliar
pockets, strikes a more or less elegant attitude and a bored
expression, one black undeniably slim leg straight out in
front of the other. She inclines her head back, and blows out
a cloud of smoke. JOSIE may be funny at times, but she is
never consciously so. She begins to dance, slowly at first, and
surprisingly well, across R., ending up by lying with her
back on the floor, and her knees up. The front door opens
and RUTH enters hall. JOSIE sits up quickly.)*
That you, Mum?

(RUTH *closes the door, but makes no reply.* JOSIE *takes off
her new trousers, and starts slipping them back in their box.
As she is doing this,* RUTH *enters from the hall. She is about
forty, slim, smartly dressed, attractive. She carries a small
weekend case, which she puts down when she gets into the
sitting-room.)*
You're in early.

(RUTH *goes to the radiogram and switches it off.)*

RUTH: Do you mind if we do without New Orleans just for
the moment? (*She crosses and picks up Josie's old slacks
from the floor.*) Are you looking for these?

(*She throws them over, and* JOSIE *manages to catch them.*)

JOSIE: Thought you were Mum.

RUTH: I don't suppose you'd made any tea?

JOSIE: (*Putting on her slacks*) I had some at dinner time.

(RUTH *goes into the kitchen, and puts the kettle on to boil.*)
You're in early.

RUTH: (*Off*) Why aren't you at work today?

JOSIE: Wasn't feeling very good this morning.

RUTH: (*Off*) Oh?

JOSIE: So Mum said I'd better stay indoors. (*She is staring at the case* RUTH *has left on the floor.*) Going on your holidays?

RUTH: (*Off*) No – coming back. Satisfied?

JOSIE: How can you be coming back, when you haven't been away? Anyway, I haven't had a day off work for ages – it won't hurt them. (*Picking up the case to see if it is empty.*) New case?

RUTH: (*Off*) I picked it up from where I left it last night – at Leicester Square Left Luggage Office. And it's full of obscene photographs.

JOSIE: Oh?

RUTH: (*Appearing in the doorway*) Josie: give me a cigarette, will you? I came all the way back in the train without one. (*Back into kitchen.*) There wasn't any post for me was there?

JOSIE: (*Crossing to her handbag R.*) Package came for you – registered.

RUTH: (*Off*) No letters?

JOSIE: Just the pools. It's only a small one. Doesn't weigh anything hardly.

RUTH: (*Off*) And what's inside it?

JOSIE: (*Searching in her handbag*) How should I know?

RUTH: (*Off*) Didn't you open it?

JOSIE: What do you mean? Course I didn't open it.

RUTH: (*Coming back in*) If you must fry yourself food when you're feeling ill, you might have the decency to clear up afterwards. The gas stove is covered in grease and muck – it's filthy. (*She takes off her hat, and moves to the occasional table down L., where she sees a small package.*) Is this it? (*Examines it, and goes on, rather absently.*) You've even left the breakfast things in the sink. (JOSIE *is holding her packet of cigarettes, watching her curiously.* RUTH *stares at the packet.*)

JOSIE: Typewritten.

RUTH: You've had damn-all to do all day. It's like a slum when your mother comes in.

JOSIE: Aren't you going to open it?

RUTH: (*A quick glance at her*) I said you're a slut.

JOSIE: Oh, did you? I didn't hear.

(*After a momentary hesitation, RUTH unwraps the package. JOSIE slips her cigarettes back into her handbag, and moves over to the kitchen door. From a small cardbox box, RUTH takes out a man's wrist watch. JOSIE takes it in, and goes into the kitchen.*)

JOSIE: I'll get a cup of tea.

(*The watch is lying in RUTH's hand, as with the other, she takes out a piece of notepaper, and reads it. Then she places the box on the table. She stares at the paper, stroking her temples with her fingers, as if she felt a weight in her head. Presently, she calls out to JOSIE in the kitchen. The edge has gone out of her voice, and she sounds tired.*)

RUTH: Josie: be a good girl and get me that cigarette, will you?

(*JOSIE enters with a cup of tea, which she hands to her.*)

JOSIE: That man was here again this afternoon, asking for you.

RUTH: I've asked you twice to let me have one of your cigarettes. Please! I'll pay you back tonight.

JOSIE: Haven't got one. Sorry.

RUTH: (*Turning back to the table*) Oh well, I suppose I'll have to go upstairs, anyway. There may be some in the bedroom somewhere. (*She replaces the watch and note in the little box.*) Who was here, did you say?

JOSIE: That man. I don't know who he is. The one who came on Saturday, and again the other day. That's the third time he's been.

RUTH: I thought you told him I didn't get in till 5.30?

JOSIE: I did. He said he'd come back one evening.

RUTH: (*To armchair and sitting*) Well, what time did he come today?

JOSIE: About four, I suppose.

RUTH: He doesn't sound very bright, whoever he is. What's he look like?

JOSIE: Not bad. Bit like Frankie Vaughan.

RUTH: Who the hell's Frankie Vaughan. (*Sipping tea.*) You make a putrid cup of tea, don't you. Doesn't he say what he wants?

JOSIE: Just that he wants to see you – that's all.

RUTH: Strange way to go about it. Calling at the time when you've specifically told him I shall be out. You didn't tell him anything did you?

JOSIE: Tell him what? That he looked like Frankie Vaughan?

RUTH: Oh, Josie, for heaven's sake, can't you see I'm tired? All I want is a cigarette and a bath.

(*The front door opens and* MRS ELLIOT *comes in. She is a sincere, emotionally restrained little woman in her early fifties, who firmly believes that every cloud has a silver lining. She carries various carrier-bags filled with shopping. At the hall-stand she removes her coat.*)

RUTH: That's your mother. For heaven's sake make a start on that kitchen so that she can get started on the supper without having to clear up your mess first.

JOSIE: (*Moving to kitchen*) OK.

MRS E.: Are you there, Josie? (*Taking off hat.*)

JOSIE: Hullo, Mum. You're not in any trouble are you, Auntie?

RUTH: In trouble? Do you mean in the general or the popular sense?

JOSIE: What?

MRS E.: (*Coming into sitting-room with bags*) Hullo, dear, hullo, Josie. Managed to get a seat on the train today, thank goodness. (*Into kitchen.*)

RUTH: Hullo, Kate.

JOSIE: Hullo, Mum.

MRS E.: Oh Josie, you are a naughty girl, you really are. (*Into sitting-room.*) I was hoping you'd have everything nice and clean and tidy when I came in.

JOSIE: I was just going to do it.

MRS E.: Just look at it out there. It would be tonight too,
when there's so much to do.

RUTH: Here, let me take that from you. (*Taking one of the
bags.*)

MRS E.: Thank you, Ruth.

JOSIE: I'm sorry, Mum. Auntie Ruth was talking to me just as
I was going to do it. Everyone seems a bit early tonight.
(*Into kitchen.*)

MRS E.: (*Unpacking carrier*) I asked Mr Beamish to let me off
five minutes early. Didn't like it either. I thought I'd
just miss the rush. Funny what a difference a few
minutes makes. Anyway, I managed to get some
shopping up the road before they closed. Oh dear, what
a rush. There we are. You're back early, Ruth dear.
Weren't you feeling well? Wonder if George likes parsley
sauce.

RUTH: It wasn't anything. Central heating in the office, I
expect.

MRS E.: Well – Josie complained she wasn't too great this
morning at breakfast time, so I made her stay at home. I
hope you haven't gone and caught something off of her –
food poisoning or something.

RUTH: Yes.

MRS E.: You do look tired, I must say.

RUTH: Oh, I'm better now. Josie gave her *Auntie* a cup of tea.

MRS E.: You always hate her calling you Auntie don't you.
What can you expect dear when that's what you are?
Now, I wanted you to do something for me. What was it?
Josie, don't bother with those things now. Lay the table
for me in here instead, there's a good girl.

RUTH: You seem a bit overloaded.

MRS E.: Well, I had to get a few extras.

JOSIE: (*In from kitchen*) Where's the fire, Mum?

MRS E.: Now try and help me a little, Josie. I'm rather cross
with you over that kitchen, my girl.

JOSIE: Well, I'm doing it, aren't I?

RUTH: All right you two, I'll help, only don't go on about it, please. (*Into kitchen.*)

JOSIE: Well, she was 'going on' a bit herself just now.

MRS E.: That's enough, Josie. (*Clearing table.*) I had hoped that at least you could have had the table laid.

JOSIE: Yes, Mum, all right.

MRS E.: I'm in such a muddle, I don't know where I am. I haven't a chance to do a thing. Hope your father comes in on time.

JOSIE: What's all the panic? Don't tell me you've got somebody coming?

MRS E.: Yes, I have.

JOSIE: Who on earth is it?

(RUTH *comes in with loaded tray, puts it down and she and* MRS E. *start laying the table.*)

MRS E.: Young George is coming, that's all.

RUTH: George?

MRS E.: George Dillon. The young fellow that works at my place. You know. I told you about him.

RUTH: Oh, did you. I don't remember.

JOSIE: Oh, him. (*She yawns loudly and flops into the armchair.*)

MRS E.: Of course I told you. I've often spoken about him. I've asked him down to tea lots of times. But each time some appointment seems to turn up, and he can't come. Well, he's coming now, for certain. He's a very busy chap. Always on the go.

RUTH: Oh, that one. The rather superior young man who's so much younger than the rest of you. Is he still there? I thought you said the job wasn't quite good enough for him.

MRS E.: I've always felt a bit sorry for him, that's all. He seemed so much on his own all the time. And, one day, I started telling him about our Raymond, and he was most interested. He was in the services as well, you see.

RUTH: Quite a coincidence.

MRS E.: Yes. He went right through the war.
RUTH: I had the idea we all did.
  (*Pause.*)
MRS E.: No, Ruth, some boys didn't get to see the end of it.
RUTH: I'm sorry, Kate. I've had a bit of a day, I'm afraid. I'm
  not in the right frame of mind to talk to young men,
  refined or not. If I can't do anything for you down here,
  I'll go and run myself a bath, if you don't mind.
MRS E.: Oh! Were you going to have a bath now?
RUTH: Yes. Why?
MRS E.: Well, I can't go into a long rigamarole now – I've too
  much to do before George comes. But you see – well,
  you've got to know sometime, I suppose – I've asked him
  to stay.
JOSIE: Stay? What, here?
MRS E.: It won't be for long – just till he finds somewhere else
  to go.
JOSIE: What's wrong with where he is?
MRS E.: He's not very happy there. I'll tell you later. Don't
  worry me with a lot of questions now, Josie. There's too
  much to do.
RUTH: Well, it's your business. It's your house – not mine.
  What about Percy?
MRS E.: Nothing about Percy. It's got nothing to do with
  him.
RUTH: You're right, of course. (*Rather dryly.*) It isn't his
  house, either.
MRS E.: There's just one thing –
JOSIE: There won't half be an atmosphere when he finds out.
  You know what Dad's like – he hasn't got over those
  budgerigars you bought yet.
MRS E.: He knows what he can do, and it won't take me long
  to tell him. Oh, do clear up that paper and stuff, Josie.
  The place looks awful. What was I saying?
RUTH: 'There's just one thing.'
MRS E.: Oh yes, Ruth. I was going to ask if you would mind

very much moving out of your room for a few days, and going in with Norah.

RUTH: Why yes, I do mind. Is it really necessary? Does George Whats-his-name have to have my room?

MRS E.: No, he doesn't have to, but I thought it would be nicer – being Ray's old room, he'd like it. More like a man's room. Still –

RUTH: (*Quietly*) You know, I do like to have at least some time to myself. And anyway, Norah sleeps with her mouth open.

MRS E.: Oh, very well, Ruth. Josie can go in with her. You won't mind, will you, Josie?

JOSIE: (*Folding up paper*) Oh, all right. All this blessed fuss! (*Into kitchen.*)

RUTH: I'm sorry, Kate, but you do understand.

MRS E.: Never mind. I just thought it would be nicer, that's all. It doesn't matter, dear. And there's no fuss, Madame Josie, thank you. God pays debts without money, I always say.

RUTH: You haven't any aspirin, have you? I don't seem to know where any of my things are –

MRS E.: There are some in the medicine chest, I think. And if you're going up, would you mind getting some of Josie's stuff into Norah's room – as that's going to be the arrangement?

RUTH: Right.

(*She is lost in her own thoughts and does not move.* MRS E. *is too preoccupied to notice. Pause.*)

MRS E.: Only would you mind doing it now, while Josie and I get straight down here? George'll be here very soon – he's only got to pick up his bag from his digs. Is that your case?

RUTH: (*Picking it up, and into hall*) I'll take it up with me. (*Taking off scarf and hanging it up.*) Is there anything else?

MRS E.: No, thank you very much, Ruth. I must get started now.

(RUTH *goes upstairs.*)

Oh, yes – (*into hall*) – Ruth, dear, would you put a clean towel in the bathroom for George? I expect he'd like a wash when he comes in.

RUTH: (*Halfway upstairs*) Yes.

MRS E.: I'm sorry you're not feeling well, dear.

(RUTH *goes on upstairs.* MRS E. *returns to sitting-room*) Now, where are we? (*The table by now is almost laid, and* MRS E. *completes it.*)

JOSIE: (*In from kitchen*) Will it be the boiled pork, Mum? There isn't much left – least, not after Dad get his hands on it.

MRS E.: He can have it all, as far as I'm concerned. Anyway, it won't worry George, he's a vegetarian. (*To cocktail cabinet.*)

JOSIE: A what?

MRS E.: (*Triumphantly*) A vegetarian. Now, where's the sherry got to, I wonder? Oh, yes. (*She finds the bottle, and puts it on the table.*)

JOSIE: Oh, one of them. He sounds a bit wishy-washy to me.

MRS E.: Well, he's not – he's a real gentleman.

JOSIE: That's what I mean. My, we are going posh, aren't we? Sherry! Anybody'd think it was Christmas.

MRS E.: (*To kitchen*) That's enough of that, young lady. Now go and get dressed and make yourself a bit more presentable, or else George will think I brought you up in the slums.

JOSIE: (*Idly round the room*) George, George, George. Georgie Porgie puddeny-pie, kissed the girls and made them cry –

MRS E.: (*From kitchen*) Now do as I say, dear, please.

JOSIE: All right, Mum. (*She starts to sing.*)

Why don't you Give Me . . .
Give Me. Give Me . . .
All that you –

All that you
Have to share . . .

(*Her eyes light on the small package on the table down L. She moves over to it. She extracts the note from the package, and unfolds it.*)

MRS E.: (*Off*) Draw the curtains before you go, will you, dear? Thank goodness the days are drawing out again, though. I'm so sick of the winter.

JOSIE: OK, Mum. (*She moves to the french windows L., draws one of the curtains, and begins reading the letter. Reading.*) 'My dear – You have just left, and I have found that you have left two pounds for me on the desk. How thoughtful of you, and, after that catechism of smug deficiencies you had just recited to me, how very practical and how like you. I suppose you must have slipped it there while I was swallowed up in the damned misery of our situation. Make no mistake – for the money, I'm grateful. But your setting up as a kind of emotional soup kitchen makes me spit.

(RUTH *is seen to fold her arms to her and shiver.*)

If you had any understanding at all, you would know what a bitter taste this kind of watery gruel must have. This is the Brown Windsor of love all right, and the only fit place for it is the sink. If this is the kind of thing you and your pals would dole out for the proletariat and its poor, grubby artists, you had better think again. I'm just going out for some beer. PS. Was just going to post this, when I thought I would return this watch to you. It seems to be the one thing I have left that you ever gave me. I'd like to think that my returning it would hurt you, but I know it won't.'

(*Bell rings. The lights in the sitting-room blaze on.* MRS E. *has switched them on. The door bell goes on ringing furiously.*)

MRS E.: My goodness, Josie, can't you please answer the front door for me? I've got milk on the stove. (*Into*

kitchen.) And I asked you to draw those curtains, didn't
I?

JOSIE: OK. (*Draws curtains*.) All right, all right, I'm coming.
(*Goes through hall to front door*.) Oh, it's you. It's only
Norah, Mum.

(NORAH *comes in, wearing outdoor clothes. She is in her
middle thirties. She has some of her mother's restraint but this
is due more to having 'been let down twice'. There is no
bitterness, only a naïve simplicity in all things and at all
times*.)

MRS E.: That you, Norah?

JOSIE: (*Going into sitting-room*) Well, I've just said so, haven't
I?

NORAH: (*Following her*) Can't think where I left my key.
It's probably in my other bag. I'll have a look in a
minute. (*Takes off hat and coat*.) Blessed train, packed
as usual. (*Fetches her slippers from under the settee and
changes her shoes*.) I saw Father coming up the road,
but I wasn't going to wait for *him* to let me in. Not
after this morning.

(JOSIE *takes out her 'jazz' trousers and holds them against
her waist, dancing and humming quietly*.)

MRS E.: (*In kitchen*) Had a nice day, dear?

NORAH: Not bad, thanks, Mum. (*To* JOSIE.) You going to the
club tonight?

JOSIE: I might. Why?

NORAH: Nothing.

JOSIE: Len's got a new motor-bike. It's a smasher.

NORAH: Fancy.

JOSIE: Mum says he can come to dinner on Sunday.

MRS E.: (*In from kitchen*) Well, Mum has changed her mind.
He can't.

JOSIE: Oh, Mum! Why?

MRS E.: I'll tell you why later. For goodness' sake take that
blessed box upstairs. Supper's nearly ready and there's
only George and him to come.

(JOSIE *picks up box and trousers and goes upstairs, singing her favourite song.*)

NORAH: George who?

MRS E.: Young George from the office, you know the one who gave me the necklace.

NORAH: Oh, him.

MRS E.: Would you like to start your supper, dear? It's all ready, and I expect you're hungry. (*She goes into the kitchen.*)

NORAH: You know I'm never hungry, Mum.

MRS E.: Too many sweets, my girl, that's your trouble. (NORAH *sits at her usual place at the table.*) You know what a state your teeth are in already. (*In with a plate of food which she places in front of* NORAH.) I'm sure those sweets are half the trouble. There, see how you like that.

NORAH: Thanks, Mum.

(MRS E. *goes to the foot of stairs and calls.*)

MRS E.: Ruth – Ruth, dear! Don't be long will you? And don't forget that towel. (*She returns to sitting-room.*) Is it all right dear?

NORAH: Yes, thanks.

MRS E.: That's good.

(MRS E. *goes into kitchen as the front door opens.* PERCY, *her husband, comes in with a briefcase, mac and umbrella, all of which he deposits at the hat-stand. He is a small, mean little man. Small in every sense of the word, with a small man's aggression. He goes upstairs.*)

NORAH: Mum!

MRS E.: (*Coming in*) Yes, dear? Something wrong?

NORAH: *He's* just come in, I think.

MRS E.: Oh! (*Going to foot of stairs.*) Percy! – Was that you, Percy? (*She returns to sitting-room.*) I suppose it was him, Norah?

NORAH: Of course it was. I'd know that cat-like tread

anywhere. Trust him not to give a civil answer to a civil question.

MRS E.: The only time your father ever gave a civil answer to a civil question was when he said 'I will' at the wedding. Hope George isn't long, then we can all clear off into the lounge and watch the telly – leave your father to it. Anything on tonight? Not one of them morbid plays, I hope.

NORAH: There's some skating, I think.

MRS E.: That'll be nice. (*Into kitchen.*) They usually have some nice music with that.

(PERCY *comes downstairs and, after taking an evening paper from his briefcase, goes into the sitting-room and sits at the table in the arm-dining-chair.*)

MRS E.: (*Lifting kitchen hatch*) Will you have boiled pork or boiled eggs?

PERCY: (*Reading paper*) Nothing.

MRS E.: You heard what I said – boiled pork or boiled eggs?

PERCY: And you heard what I said – nothing. Just a cup of tea.

(MRS E. *slams down the hatch.* NORAH *pours out tea for her father and herself.*)

NORAH: Must put some more water in the pot.

PERCY: You'll drown it.

NORAH: And I know something else that needs drowning.

(*Into kitchen with teapot.* MRS E. *comes in with plate of food, and sets it in front of* PERCY.)

PERCY: I said I didn't want anything.

MRS E.: You'll no doubt eat it just the same. Josie! Ruth! Come along, now! And another thing: I hope you'll mind your manners, Percy, in future, particularly as I have a young gentleman from the office coming to stay here for a little while. (*To herself.*) It'll be like having Raymond in the house again.

PERCY: Accch! So you've taken to cradle-snatching, have you. Not content with taking another woman's husband,

you have to pick up a 'young gentleman' as well. Where
did all this happen – Dean Street?

MRS E.: (*With an effort*) Look, Percy, I'm warning you, once
and for all, this is *my* house, and I have worked for every
penny I bought it with, and everything in it. As far as I'm
concerned, you're just the lodger here. Why you've got
your knife into Jack Livings, goodness only knows.
They're nice, respectable people, and well you know it.
I'm sure I don't know what Mrs Livings would say if she
knew about your horrible accusations. Just because Mr
Livings comes in now and again to do a few useful things
about the house, that's all it is – things you're too *damn*
lazy to do for me.

NORAH: (*Mildly*) Mum!

MRS E.: I'm sorry, Norah, but there it is. There are times
when your father goes too far with his insults. And I'll
have you know this too: George is a fine, clean, upright
young man. And he's clever too. He's in the theatrical
line, he is, and one day he's going to be as famous as that
Laurence Olivier, you see, and then perhaps you'll laugh
on the other side of your face.

PERCY: Accch! Theatrical line! Don't give me that nonsense.
I bet you he hasn't got two ha'pennies for a penny – they
never have, these people.

MRS E.: No – it's true that, at the moment, he hasn't a lot of
money to throw around, but he will have, he's that type.
He's used to money, you can tell that. He's very
cultured.

NORAH: Not like some people we know.

PERCY: How is it he's only a tuppenny-ha'penny penpusher
then?

MRS E.: He's not a clerk any longer. There was a little upset
at the office today and he walked out. And a good job
too, I say. Wasting his time and talent in a place like that.
It's not right, and I wouldn't like to see any boy of mine
going to waste like that – especially when George

has so many plans and ideas to make himself famous. There isn't much he can't turn his hand to in the theatrical line, believe me. Why he doesn't only act in plays, he writes them as well. As a matter of fact, he's bang in the middle of one at the moment. I expect he'll finish it while he's here.

PERCY: That's all very interesting, I'm sure. You've got it all nicely worked out between you, haven't you? But what about me? I'm going to look a proper bloody fool, aren't I? What are the neighbours going to think, I'd like to know?

MRS E.: No more than they do now, believe me. They know very well what you're like. I haven't forgotten yesterday either – shouting and swearing at the top of your voice. At the front door too. The humiliation of it! I don't mind you swearing at the back door, but the front door – well –

PERCY: Accch! You women – nag, nag, nag.

(JOSIE *comes downstairs, and goes into the 'lounge'. She is now 'respectable'.*)

MRS E.: Is that you, Ruth? Josie? Oh, for heaven's sake don't start looking at that thing till we've had supper.

(JOSIE *comes out of lounge into sitting-room.*)

JOSIE: Oh, all right. It's only the newsreel.

(*She gets a chair and sits at the table.* MRS E. *goes into the kitchen and returns immediately with two plates of food.*) It's panel-game night, isn't it?

MRS E.: There you are. (*She places plate in front of* JOSIE.) And I may as well have mine while I'm about it. And what do you say, Miss Josie? (*Sits at table.*)

JOSIE: Sorry. Thanks, Mum.

MRS E.: That's better.

(*They are all eating now. Pause.*)

JOSIE: Silence in the pig-market, let the old sow speak first.

MRS E.: Pudding, Percy?

PERCY: No.

JOSIE: Trouble with you, Dad, is you talk too much.

PERCY: Accch!

JOSIE: Can I put a record on, liven things up a bit. Ever so
sordid in here, like a mortuary.

PERCY: That blessed racket. If I had my way –

MRS E.: It's Norah's wireless.

(JOSIE *puts on a record and returns to her seat.*)

JOSIE: The girls are taking a coach up to Salisbury on
Sunday. You coming, Mum?

(RUTH *comes slowly down the stairs. Halfway down, there
is a knock at the door.*)

MRS E.: No, I don't think so, dear. I expect Norah will
though. She's coach mad.

(RUTH *answers the front door and a man's voice is heard
outside. It is* GEORGE DILLON.)

NORAH: That would be lovely.

GEORGE: I'm awfully sorry, but does Mrs Elliot live here?

RUTH: Yes, she does. Did you want to speak to her?

GEORGE: Well, as a matter of fact she asked me to –

RUTH: Oh, I am sorry. Of course, you must be George. Do
come in.

(GEORGE DILLON *enters. He is a little over thirty, boyish,
yet still every year his age. He is short, not good-looking, but
with an anti-romantic kind of charm. He displays at
different times a mercurial, ironic passion, lethargy,
offensiveness, blatant sincerity and a mentally picaresque
dishonesty – sometimes almost all of these at the same time.
A walking confliction in fact. Just at the moment he is rather
shy, feeling his way. He is carrying a suitcase and a 'carry-
all' bag.*)

GEORGE: Yes, that's right. Thank you.

RUTH: I'm Ruth Gray. Mrs Elliot's sister.

GEORGE: How do you do?

(*They shake hands.*)

I seem to think we've met somewhere before, haven't
we?

RUTH: Yes, I had that feeling too.

MRS E.: There's someone in the hall. Is that you, Ruth? (*She rises and goes into the hall.*)

RUTH: Mr Dillon has arrived, Kate.

MRS E.: Oh, good. You found your way all right, then? Glad you remembered it was Targon Wood station you had to get out at – most people think Pelham Junction is nearer, but it isn't really. I didn't hear you ring the bell. I expect you're hungry, aren't you? Would you like a wash before supper? Bring your things up. (*Going upstairs.*) I'll show you where your room is and where you can find the toilet.

(GEORGE *follows her up.*)

GEORGE: That's very nice of you. I couldn't find the bell, so I knocked instead.

MRS E.: Yes, I thought I didn't hear you ring.

(*They both disappear.* RUTH *stands looking up the stairs for a moment.*)

JOSIE: Must be nearly time for 'Classics on Ice'. I'm going to get a good seat before that fellow pinches it. (*Rising, she puts chair under table.*) Sounds ever so posh, doesn't he?

NORAH: I thought you were going to the club.

JOSIE: It's a woman's privilege to change her mind. (*Crosses into hall.*) Well, what's he like, Auntie?

(RUTH *does not move.*)

Auntie, what's he like?

RUTH: I don't know. Of course I don't. Why should I?

JOSIE: Oh, all right. I was only asking. Keep your hair on.

(*Goes into lounge.* RUTH *walks slowly into sitting-room and sits in armchair.* NORAH *collects dirty plates.* PERCY *is still reading.* MRS E. *comes downstairs into sitting-room.*)

MRS E.: Well, that's that. Have you finished, Percy?

(PERCY *folds newspaper.*)

PERCY: Where's Henry Irving?

MRS E.: Never you mind. I'd be grateful if you made yourself useful for once and made up the lounge fire.

(PERCY *rises and switches off radiogram and goes into lounge.* NORAH *takes things into the kitchen.*)

That's right, dear. Can't keep his hands off that wireless, can he? Now, Ruth, what about your supper, dear?

RUTH: (*Rising*) Oh, nothing for me, thanks. (*Crosses to small table.*) I think I'll just have some hot milk and go to bed. (*She picks up the small package containing the watch. The note is missing.*) Kate.

MRS E.: Yes, dear? Why, Ruth, what is it? You look quite pale. If I were you –

RUTH: Has anyone been at this table at all? Have they, Kate?

MRS E.: My dear, I'm sure I don't know. What a funny thing to ask. Why shouldn't they if they want to?

RUTH: There was a letter of mine here. Quite personal. A private letter. Someone has moved it.

MRS E.: Now, Ruth, dear, don't go upsetting yourself over a little thing like that. I expect you'll come across it later on. You go upstairs and I'll bring you up some hot milk later on.

(MRS E. *goes into the kitchen. Then* RUTH *goes into hall, halfway upstairs she stops for a moment, then comes down again, goes to lounge door, opens it and calls. There is the sound of the 'Skater's Waltz' from within.*)

RUTH: Josie, come here a minute, will you?

JOSIE: Oh, what do you want, can't you see I'm watching the telly?

RUTH: Come here, please, when I ask you. (*She moves to the foot of the stairs as she waits.*)

JOSIE: (*At lounge door*) What do you want?

RUTH: Shut the door and come here.

(JOSIE *goes to her.*)

JOSIE: Well?

RUTH: Where is it?

JOSIE: Where's what? I don't know what you're talking about.

RUTH: You know damn well what. Give me that letter.

JOSIE: Oh, that. Oh, yes. (*Slowly, reluctantly, she withdraws letter from her jumper.*)

RUTH: Thank you very much. Kindly learn to keep your nose clean in future, will you?

JOSIE: So that's where you've been all these weekends, with Jock. Does he wear a kilt?

RUTH: Mind your own damned business.
(*Gives her a resounding smack across the face.* JOSIE *yells. Enter* MRS E.)

MRS E.: Why, whatever's going on?

JOSIE: Going on! It's Auntie Ruth what's been going on. *Carrying* on more like – with a man – and paying him for it what's more.

RUTH: Just you dare read my letters again, and I'll do more than slap your face.

JOSIE: Don't you talk to me like that – you're not my mum.

MRS E.: If what Ruth says is true, Josie, then I'm very ashamed. I thought I'd brought you up to behave like a lady. Never, never do that again, do you hear? Now kindly leave the room – but first say you're sorry to Auntie Ruth.

JOSIE: (*After some hesitation*) I'm sorry, Auntie Ruth. (*Goes off to lounge singing 'If Jock could love me, love me . . .'*)

RUTH: Slut! slut! slut!

MRS E.: Ruth – that's no way to talk, and you know it.
(RUTH *turns away.*)

MRS E.: So things didn't work out then?

RUTH: No – I've just walked out on him, for better or for worse.

MRS E.: But I don't understand. Josie said something about paying him –

RUTH: I don't have to buy my love – or do I? Yes, I gave him the odd pound or two, to keep him alive.

MRS E.: But surely he could do a job of work?

RUTH: Job of work? He's a writer – the original starving artist in the attic – and I believed he had promise.

MRS E.: Then why did you leave him?

RUTH: He's been a promising young man for too long. Youthful promise doesn't look too well with receding hair. I've misjudged him – he's the complete flop, and I've spent nearly six years giving all I could to him, giving my love to him – such as it is.

MRS E.: It's beyond me, dear. It's funny – you're the only one in the family who doesn't have patience or understanding. While you were enjoying yourself at college, we all had to go out to work. I can only say that college gave you a lot of funny ideas.

RUTH: That's right. Funny enough to make me do an inexcusable thing. When he told me he hadn't a penny, not even the price of a packet of cigarettes, I went to his jacket pocket, and inside I found a cheque for eight guineas for some book review or other he'd written. He hadn't even told me about it. Not only did he lie about the money, but he even kept his piffling little success from me. A brainless, cheap little lie. And that did it – the whole works collapsed, the whole flimsy works. (*She walks to the door.*) I suppose that's really why I left him. (*Exits upstairs.*)

MRS E.: (*Crossing to hallway*) George! Supper's ready dear. (*Returns to kitchen.* GEORGE *comes down, looking over his shoulder. As* GEORGE *crosses hall,* NORAH *comes out of kitchen into hall. 'Skater's Waltz' comes up good and loud.*)

NORAH: Hullo.

GEORGE: Hullo.

NORAH: Your supper's in there. I'm going to watch the skating.

(*She goes into lounge.* GEORGE *goes into sitting-room. He coughs slightly.*)

MRS E.: That's right, dear, make yourself at home. Oh, that blessed telly, it's much too loud, isn't it? (*She crosses to lounge and opens door*.) Do put that telly down a bit, there's good children. We can't hear ourselves think in here. (*She goes back into sitting-room*.) There, that's better isn't it? You sit there, dear. (*He sits in Percy's place*.) They're all watching the telly, so you can have your supper in peace. And while we're alone, dear – I want you to treat this just as if it were your home, just do whatever you like, won't you?

GEORGE: That's very kind of you, Mrs Elliot. I just don't know what to say. (*He puts out his hand*.) I can only say that I won't impose myself on you for one minute longer than I can help. You're so very kind.

MRS E.: I've never mentioned this before, but I'm helping you all I can because I feel that in some small way I'm helping my son, Raymond. He was killed in the war, you know. That's his picture over there.

GEORGE: Yes, I'm sorry.

MRS E.: (*Very simply*) He was a lovely boy. Clever, like you, artistic, too, but somehow he didn't seem to have that drive, that sort of initiative. Well, he didn't really have much chance to get on. But *you* will, George, I'm sure. With all your talent, you just can't go wrong. You're always planning things – and all the things you've already done too. You've got your acting and your plays and I don't know what, haven't you?

GEORGE: Oh, yes, Mrs Elliot, don't you worry – the play I'm writing now is just about in the bag. I can finish it in no time here. And I've already got someone interested in it – for the West End, I mean.

MRS E.: Well, there you are – what did I say? You certainly are one for irons in the fire, aren't you? And to think we shall all come and see your piece, and sit in the posh seats. That will be nice. Well, there we are, dear. And if Ray was here now, I'd be talking to him just as I'm talking to you. What I'm trying to say is that I want you to feel that you are taking his place in the home, and if

there's anything you want – anything – please don't
hesitate to ask. And don't, please, ever go short of
money. Ray used to send me home so much a week
when he was in the army, for me to save for him when
he came home. I'd like to think it's being put to good
use at last by helping you.

GEORGE: Bless you, Mrs Elliot. (*He coughs slightly.*) You're
so very kind and thoughtful. I just don't know how to
thank you. I only hope I'll prove worthy of your
kindness. I promise I won't let you down in any way. I
promise you that.

MRS E.: (*Patting his cheek*) Good. Now we must see about
getting you something to eat. Being a vegetarian you
must eat lots of strange things. You'll have to tell me
about them as we go along. (*Into kitchen.*)

GEORGE: I don't want you to put yourself out. (*He sits
looking around him.*)

MRS E.: (*Lifting hatch*) I've got some nice boiled cod and
parsley sauce. You do eat fish, don't you? (*She sees him
staring at the birds on the wall C.*) Yes, Ray painted those.
I told you he was artistic, didn't I?
(*Hatch down.* GEORGE *rises and walks round the room
restlessly, looking at the photographs on the wall, the
cocktail cabinet, the general dressings. He then picks up the
photograph of Raymond and looks at it steadily.*)

GEORGE: You stupid-looking bastard.
(*Quick curtain.*)

ACT TWO

Summer. There is now a telephone standing on small table in hall. The french windows are open. The settee brought round to face slightly downstage. NORAH, JOSIE, MRS E. *and* PERCY *are sitting in their customary places at the meal table, eating. After curtain rises, a slight pause.*

MRS E.: Pudding, Percy?

PERCY: No.

> (MRS E. *rises, taking plates into kitchen. As she does so, the telephone rings and she stops dead.*)

NORAH: (*With awe*) It's ringing!

JOSIE: The phone's ringing!

MRS E.: Our first call.

PERCY: What a racket – wireless, TV, and now the blinking telephone.

MRS E.: Who's it for, I wonder?

NORAH: Answer it and see.

JOSIE: Yes, that's the best way to find out. (*Jumps up and goes into hall.*) I'll go, Mum. (*Lifts receiver.*) Yes, yes it is. Who? Yes. All right, I'll fetch her. (*Into sitting-room.*) It's for you, Mum. Ever such a funny man – he's got a sort of Chinese accent.

MRS E.: (*Giving plates to* JOSIE) Chinese?

JOSIE: Yes.

MRS E.: But I don't know any Chinamen.

JOSIE: Well, you'd better hurry up and answer it, Mum – he's waiting.

NORAH: Perhaps he's from *Chu Chin Chow on Ice*.

> (MRS E. *goes into hall, and picks up receiver.*)

MRS E.: Hullo. Yes, it is.

> (JOSIE *stands in doorway, listening.*)

Have we what? Well, I don't know. I'll see. (*To* JOSIE.)
He wants to know if we've got any laundry that wants
doing. (*In phone.*) No, I don't think so, thank you.
What are you laughing at? (*She laughs.*) Oh, you are a
naughty boy, you really are – you took us all in. (*To*
JOSIE.) It's George.

JOSIE: Oh, silly. (*She goes into kitchen.*)

MRS E.: What's that, dear? Have you? Oh, I am pleased.
Yes, oh we will! All right, dear. Good-bye. (*Replaces
receiver, goes into sitting-room.*) Says he's got some good
news – he's got a job, and something about his play. I
didn't quite catch what it was. Fancy young George
being the first to ring up – and I had it put in specially
for him too. Isn't that nice? Oh, I must sit down a
minute – the excitement's too much for me!

(NORAH *pours tea.*)

NORAH: Needs more water. (*Into kitchen.*)

PERCY: *What's* he gone and got?

MRS E.: You heard, didn't you? A job. What did you think it
was?

JOSIE: (*In from kitchen*) Must be something good for him to
ring up like that.

MRS E.: Yes – silly boy. He was only at the station. He'll be
home in a minute. I'm so glad. That awful day he left
that office, he swore he'd stick it out until he got
something really worthwhile.

(NORAH *comes in with teapot.*)

MRS E.: And it's turned up at last. He always said he
wouldn't take anything tatty.

NORAH: What's 'tatty'?

MRS E.: I don't really know, dear – George is always saying it.

JOSIE: Well, now I can really tell the whole of Targon
Broadway that we've got a real actor staying with us.
That's if he doesn't get too stuck up, and want to go and
live in Berkeley Square or something.

MRS E.: Of course he won't. George has settled down here

very well. This is his home now. There's no reason at all
why he should have to go.

JOSIE: Well, he'll have to get married sometime, won't he?

MRS E.: Well, yes, there is that, of course.

NORAH: How do you know he hasn't got a girfriend already?
(*Phone rings.*)

MRS E.: Well! There it is again – twice in a couple of minutes.
(JOSIE *goes to it quickly, lifts receiver.*)

JOSIE: (*On phone*) Hullo. Who? No, I think you must have
the wrong number. You're welcome. (*Puts phone down
and returns to sitting-room.*) Wrong number.

MRS E.: Oh.

JOSIE: What were we talking about?

MRS E.: George. I was just going to say that I think you're a
bit gone on him aren't you. What about poor old Len
Cook now, eh!

JOSIE: Well, George will do to fill in while Len does his
National Service. I wouldn't mind going to Germany
with Len though.

NORAH: You'd have to marry him first, wouldn't you? I mean
it wouldn't be very proper just to go and – well – 'live'
with him –

JOSIE: Oh, I don't know. I don't mind what I do or where I
go, so long as my man's got money.

PERCY: The trouble with young girls today is that they spend
too much time thinking about love and S-E-X.

JOSIE: S-E-X? Oh, sex. Sex doesn't mean a thing to me. To
my way of thinking, love is the most important and
beautiful thing in this world and that's got nothing to do
with sex.

PERCY: (*Producing irrelevances like a bombshell*) Well, I may be
a crank and all that, but if I can persuade the council to
close the park gates after dark, I shall die a happy man.

NORAH: What on earth's that got to do with sex?

MRS E.: Well, I don't think we need go on with this
conversation – but Josie is quite right. You keep those

beautiful thoughts dear and you can be sure you won't come to any harm. Put the kettle on for George, there's a dear.

(JOSIE *goes into kitchen.* GEORGE *appears at the french window, waving a bottle of wine.*)

GEORGE: Friends, Romans and countrymen, lend me your ears!

MRS E.: Oh, George! You did make me jump!

(GEORGE *goes up and hugs her.*)

And I'm so pleased about your job dear – we're all dying to hear about it.

JOSIE: Where is it, George, Drury Lane?

GEORGE: Could be, Josie, could be! Come on Norah, cheer up and find the corkscrew for the big Bacchanalia.

MRS E.: I'll find it. (*Goes to cocktail cabinet.*)

GEORGE: Cast of thousands, ten years in the making. Starring the one and only Mrs Elliot as Juno!

(*They all laugh with the exception of* PERCY. RUTH *comes in at the front door and stands listening at the foot of the stairs.*)

GEORGE: (*Assuming a thick Dublin accent*) And you, Norah, me darlin', you shall play Ariadne.

NORAH: I'm not being a man for you or nobody.

GEORGE: And Josie, let me see, yes, you'll play Semele.

JOSIE: Oh! There's a name to go to bed with!

GEORGE: And that's exactly what you do my sweet – with me, Jupiter.

(*More general laughter.* RUTH *goes upstairs.*)

PERCY: Aaacch!

MRS E.: There you are, Josie, what was I saying only a minute ago? (*Handing* GEORGE *corkscrew.*)

GEORGE: Now let the wine flow on this day of days. And what a day it's been. Do you know, one agent I went to see this morning looked me up and down in this duffel-coat and said: 'No, we ain't got to *Biblical* parts today.' Must have thought I looked like John the Baptist. Perhaps if I go in a kilt, he'll offer me a gangster part. Glasses, Mrs E.

Bring out the golden goblets. That's right. For in spite of George continually being told he's too young, too old, too short – in spite of his wig, glass eye, false teeth and wooden leg, George has got himself a job. (*He hands wine to* MRS ELLIOT.) There we are.

MRS E.: I mustn't have more than one. I can't go to the meeting tiddly, can I? I don't know what Mr Colwyn-Stuart would say.

GEORGE: Josie?

JOSIE: I certainly won't say no. (*Takes glass.*)

GEORGE: And what about you, Percy. Will you have a tipple?

PERCY: Well, seeing as how you are in the money.

GEORGE: And Norah! A glass for Norah Mavourneen – me darlin' gal.

NORAH: Not for me, thank you.

GEORGE: No?

NORAH: No, thank you.

MRS E.: Oh, go on, Norah. It's no use you pretending you're teetotal. You had some on Boxing Day, I remember. Go on, be sociable.

NORAH: I really don't think I could after seeing those great fat men on the telly last night trampling on the grapes half naked. It was horrible.

GEORGE: So Norah isn't going to touch any more wine until they bath in a respectable manner? Never mind, dear, just one sip won't hurt you. (*Gives her a glass.*)

NORAH: Oh, all right then, just a sip.

MRS E.: Well, good health, George, and congratulations.

ALL: Good luck, Down the hatch, *etc*.

JOSIE: Well, now tell us what it is.

GEORGE: First of all, there's every chance of my play going on at the Trident Theatre.

MRS E.: Oh, good.

JOSIE: Where's that, George? In the West End?

GEORGE: Well, no, not exactly. Bayswater. And it means I should get plenty of managers and agents to see it.

MRS E.: Oh, good.

GEORGE: I saw Ronnie Harris this morning – you know the film man and he said he's got a part for me coming up shortly.

NORAH: What sort of film, George?

GEORGE: Don't really know yet – to do with some Army job or something, so he says.

MRS E.: That'll be nice.

GEORGE: And finally, I've got a TV job coming up in three weeks' time.

JOSIE: George! You going to be on the telly?

GEORGE: Well, yes. But it's not exactly the lead, mind you, but it's something, anyway.

JOSIE: Oh, I'll say it is. Our George on the telly! What are you going to be in, George?

GEORGE: Ever heard of a play called *Hamlet*?

JOSIE: Of course I have.

NORAH: Yes, I saw that a long time ago. That's a very *old* one, isn't it. Very good though. He dies in the end, doesn't he?

GEORGE: He does indeed, Norah, he does.

NORAH: I always like a good laugh really. What I always say is –

NORAH *and* GEORGE: There's enough misery in the world without paying to see it.

GEORGE: I don't think you really like the theatre very much, do you, Norah?

NORAH: Oh, yes I do.

GEORGE: Not really.

NORAH: Yes, but I don't ever go.

GEORGE: Oh, but you should. The theatre is like a shrine, Norah. A cathedral. Do you ever go to church, Norah?

MRS E.: The only time she goes to church is when she's got a blessed banner stuck in her hand.

NORAH: Oh, Mum. (*Rises and goes into lounge*.)

MRS E.: And talking of church – I must pop your Saviar in the oven. You'll be able to look after it, won't you? I'm off to the meeting as soon as Mr Colwyn-Stuart gets here. (*Exit kitchen.*)

GEORGE: Lord, is he coming? I'm in no mood for Mr Colwyn-pussy-Stuart. Josie, how long will you be?

JOSIE: How long will I be? Oooooh! It's jazz night! I must get changed. (*She runs upstairs.*)

GEORGE: (*Sinking exhausted in armchair*). Tired as I am, anything would be better than having to put up with that moron.

PERCY: For once, young man, I agree with you. Thanks for the drink.

GEORGE: (*Absently*) Not at all. A pleasure.

PERCY: Now that you're a celebrity, I'm surprised that you want to go jazzing at the Jubilee Hall with Josie.

GEORGE: (*Singing*) 'Jazzing at the Jubilee with Josie!'

PERCY: And I certainly hope that now you are earning money, you will be able to pay for yourself instead of sponging off other people.

GEORGE: (*Looks at him sharply*) What do you mean?
(*The front doorbell rings.*)

MRS E.: (*In from kitchen*) That's him now. Right on the dot as usual. Do I look all right?
(RUTH *comes downstairs.*)

GEORGE: Ravishing.

PERCY: Accch!

MRS E.: (*Into hall*) Answer that, Ruth dear, will you? (*Into sitting-room.*) And if you can't make an effort to make yourself a little more pleasant, you'd better go and watch the telly.

PERCY: (*Sitting down*) I'm busy.
(RUTH *opens front door.*)

MRS E.: All right then. But I don't want any upsets tonight.
(GEOFFREY COLWYN-STUART *comes in and follows* RUTH *into sitting-room. He wears an elegant suit, with a beautifully laundered shirt, a carefully chosen green spotted tie, and*

breast-pocket handkerchief to match. He is a pale, balding man in his late thirties, all sweetness and light.)

MRS E.: Oh come in Mr Stuart, I'm nearly ready. You know everyone don't you?

GEOFFREY: Yes. Good evening everyone. Why, Mrs Elliott, you look blooming tonight.

MRS E.: Oh not really. I haven't had a minute since I came in.

GEOFFREY: But that's the secret, isn't it? Good evening Mr Elliot. How are you?

PERCY: (*Half rises, turning to greet* GEOFFREY *but finally doesn't*) How are you?

MRS E.: You've met George, haven't you?

GEOFFREY: Oh, yes, we've met several times, haven't we?

MRS E.: Yes. He's been here a long time now.

GEOFFREY: Like one of the family, in fact.

MRS E.: Well, I won't keep you long. I'll just pop upstairs and put on a spot of powder, then I'm ready. George'll keep you entertained. He keeps *us* entertained, doesn't he?

(PERCY *makes a noise like an aborted whistle, which he keeps up for the next few minutes.* RUTH *sits at the table, drinking tea.*)

MRS E.: Didn't you want to watch the television, Percy? George has had some good news today, haven't you George? We've been ever so excited. He's going to be on the telly himself soon. You'll have to come round and see him when he is. I expect he'll tell you all about it. Make Mr Colwyn-Stuart comfortable. Don't go without me, now! (*Into hall and upstairs.*)

GEOFFREY: It's all right, you needn't hurry. We're early yet. (*Crossing left.*) What a dear she is.

GEORGE: Rather.

GEOFFREY: Mind if I sit here? (*At table.*)

RUTH: Do. There's some tea left, if you'd care for some.

GEOFFREY: No, thank you so much. I've just had dinner.

RUTH: Have you? We've just had supper.

(*Removes wine to cocktail cabinet.* PERCY *taps the sides of his armchair pensively.*)

GEOFFREY: And how's the world treating you, Mr Elliot? I suppose I should say 'how are *you* treating the world?' After all, that's what really counts, isn't it?

PERCY: Not too badly, thank you.

GEOFFREY: Your wife's been telling me that you've not been sleeping very well lately. I'm sorry to hear that.

PERCY: (*Rubbing his nose*) Oh? She told you that, did she?

GEOFFREY: She mentioned it at our last meeting actually.

PERCY: The last meeting, was it? Actually?

GEOFFREY: How are you feeling now? Any better?

PERCY: Nothing the matter with me. Don't sleep so good sometimes, that's all.

GEOFFREY: Mrs Elliot says she can't persuade you to go to a doctor about it.

PERCY: Don't believe in them.

GEOFFREY: Well, I think you'll find plenty of people to support you there – including you, eh, George?

GEORGE: Right.

PERCY: I don't believe in a lot of vegetarian rot either. I'm not making *my*self ill. Meatless steaks! (*Grins.*)

RUTH: Yes, I must say, that was rather too much for me. Nut cutlet I can take, but meatless steak's a bit too much of a paradox. Do you think Oscar Wilde could possibly have been a vegetarian?

PERCY: It's just that I have a lot of things on my mind.

GEOFFREY: In your own words, Mr Elliot. Exactly. The old ravelled sleeve of care, am I right, George?

GEORGE: (*Absently*) Eh?

RUTH: Shakespeare, George, Aren't you supposed to stand to attention, or something?

GEOFFREY: The number of people one sees every day, with tired, haggard eyes, dark circles of care underneath them.

GEORGE: I always thought that had another significance.

GEOFFREY: (*Smiling*) You're a pretty free sort of chap, aren't you? I hope you don't shock everyone in this respectable household with your Bohemian ways.

GEORGE: By 'Bohemian' I suppose you mean crummy. It's rather like calling bad breath 'halitosis', don't you think?

RUTH: He's straight out of *Trilby* – didn't you know?

GEORGE: Frankly, I always touch mine up with a brown liner.

GEOFFREY: What?

GEORGE: The rings under my eyes – helps me when I play clergymen's parts. I'm rather good at them.

GEOFFREY: (*Refusing to be stung*) You know, you surprise me a little, George. You seem such an intelligent, vital young man, so much in the swim. After all, it's not even considered fashionable to be sceptical nowadays. The really *smart* thing is the spiritual thing.

RUTH: That's true enough.

GEOFFREY: And you too, Ruth. Of course, your interests are political, I know. But shall I tell you something? If I were to invite the Foreign Secretary, say, down here to speak, he wouldn't be able to half fill the Jubilee Hall.

RUTH: Are we supposed to be surprised?

GEOFFREY: On the other hand, if were to invite someone like Billy Graham – well, take my word for it, you wouldn't be able to get within a mile of the place.

RUTH: With his message of love and all that? Love isn't everything, you know, Mr Stuart.

GEOFFREY: That's where we disagree, Ruth. I believe that it is.

RUTH: Take justice away from love, and it doesn't mean a thing.

GEOFFREY: Love can change the face of the world.

RUTH: Tell that to the poor black devils in South Africa. Why don't you do something for them?

GEOFFREY: Dear, oh dear – we're going to get involved already if we're not careful. I can see that. Oh, there's nothing I enjoy more than a good old intellectual rough and tumble, and I only wish I could stay and slog it out with the two of you, but there isn't time, unfortunately. The fact is, we've probably got a great deal in common. You know: I have discovered a new way of judging people.

RUTH: You have?

GEOFFREY: I simply ask myself whether their lights are shining.

GEORGE: What about their livers?

GEOFFREY: (*Laughing*) Yes. I did phrase it badly didn't I? Perhaps I should have said 'lamps'. I ask myself whether their lamps are shining. You see, my theory is that inside every one of us is a lamp. When it's alight, the loves and hates, the ambitions, desires and ideas inside it are burning, and that person is really alive. But there are people who go around every day, at work, at home with their families – they seem normal, but their lamps have gone out. They've simply given up. They've give up being alive.

RUTH: And are our lamps alight, do you think, Mr Stuart?

GEOFFREY: Oh, very definitely. It struck me the moment I came into the room.

GEORGE: Tell me. (*Nodding at* PERCY.) What about Mr Elliot's lamp?

GEOFFREY: Oh, yes, I think so. I think so. It's burning all right.

GEORGE: You *think* so! You hear that, Percy? You need a new wick.

GEOFFREY: Oh, I hope I didn't sound rude. I think Mr Elliot is on edge about things a little perhaps, principally because he's tired and can't sleep.

PERCY: All I said was –

GEOFFREY: People are wearing themselves out, worrying about a whole lot of things, unimportant things that don't matter one jot. You, Ruth, you worry about who's going to win the next election.

RUTH: Believe me – I no longer give a *damn*.

GEOFFREY: It's not important. And you, George, you worry about whether you're going to rise to the top of your profession. That's not important.

GEORGE: Thank you. We'll let you know.

GEOFFREY: One day – a few years ago this was – I happened to speak to a very famous clergyman – oh, he's dead now –

PERCY: He's all right then.

GEOFFREY: For years that man was in the habit of addressing as many as six different meetings in one day, often in the same number of towns. So I asked him how it was that he never seemed to get even a little bit tired. And he explained it to me. He said: 'Because I believe in every single word that I utter.'

GEORGE: Lucky him.

GEOFFREY: You could see his lamp burning at the very back of the hall. He was on fire for what he believed in. And that's the secret. It's no use sitting around moaning. (*Enter* MRS E. *from hall.*)

MRS E.: Who's been moaning? I'm all ready. The television's started, Percy. Have you been having a little chat with George?

GEOFFREY: Well, not exactly. I'm afraid I've been rather bad mannered.

MRS E.: I'm quite sure you haven't. *You're* never bad mannered with anyone.

GEOFFREY: I have been rather monopolizing the conversation. In fact, I've a teeny-weeny feeling that George and Ruth think I'm rather an old bore.

MRS E.: Of course he doesn't. He's a very deep one, George – I know that.

GEOFFREY: What really started us off was – we were talking about tiredness. It's a long time since I heard *you* complaining of tiredness, Mrs Elliot. Not since those very early days just after – just after the end of the war. I think she's a good advertisement for the system, don't you? No doubt, it sounds a little odd to you, but it's all a question of what *we* call synchronizing yourself with Providence. Of getting into step with the Almighty.

MRS E.: Yes. Well, I think we ought to be getting in step ourselves, Mr Stuart, don't you?

GEOFFREY: Yes, I suppose we had.

(*She turns to go, and* GEOFFREY *rises.* GEORGE *has hardly been listening, but suddenly he responds, almost as an afterthought to himself.*)

GEORGE: Yes. If only it were as simple as that, Mr Stuart. But life isn't simple, and, if you've any brains in your head at all, it's frankly a pain in the arse.

MRS E.: George! Really!

GEORGE: I'm sorry. I apologize. But I've said it now. You see, to me there is something contemptible about a man who can't face it all without drugging himself up to the rings round his eyes with a lot of comforting myths – like all these bird-brains who batten off the National Health. I don't care who it is – you or anyone – you must have a secret doubt somewhere. You know that the only reason you do believe in these things is because they *are* comforting.

GEOFFREY: So you think that religion is just a series of useful untruths?

GEORGE: Yes, I do.

PERCY: Hear! Hear!

MRS E.: You be quiet!

GEOFFREY: It's all right, Mrs Elliot. George is like so many young men – he believes that the great thing about the truth is that it must always be unpleasant.

GEORGE: It's just that I believe it's easy to answer the ultimate questions – it saves you bothering with the immediate ones.

MRS E.: There's such a thing as faith, George.

GEORGE: I believe in evidence. And faith is believing in

something for which there *is* no evidence. You don't say: I have faith that two and two are four, do you? Or that the earth is round? And why? Because they're both easily verified.

GEOFFREY: So it all has to be verified for you, does it, George? I think I understand you better than you know.

GEORGE: Oh?

GEOFFREY: You see, I come into contact with a great many artistic people. What *do* you believe in? Yourself?

GEORGE: Right. (*Adding in vocal parenthesis.*) He said, striking attitude of genius.

GEOFFREY: You have faith. You have faith in yourself – in your talent. Am I right?

GEORGE: Well?

GEOFFREY: Your talent, George. You believe in that with all your heart. And your evidence? Where is that, George? Can you show it to me?
(*Pause. They all look at him.*)

RUTH: *Touché.*
(GEORGE *is still for a moment. Then he laughs.*)

GEORGE: What a performance! All this Jesuit subtlety! You're too much for me. Just say that I'm like Christopher Columbus – I haven't discovered America yet. But it's there all right, waiting to be yes, verified.

GEOFFREY: Yes, I'm quite sure it is. You see, I have faith too. I can see the lamp burning. Well, we really must be off. Come along, Mrs Elliot. Good night, everybody.

MRS E.: Yes. Well, I shan't be back late.
(*They both go into hall, and out through the front door.*)

PERCY: (*Rising and crossing to doorway*). Lamps! (*Chuckling. Turns.*) 'E ought to be on the bleeding stage – not you! (*Exit to lounge.*)

RUTH: Are you all right? You look a bit shaken.

GEORGE: I'm all right. I rather stupidly let the conducting of divine lip-service irritate me.

RUTH: So I noticed.

GEORGE: It's just been a pretty awful day, that's all.

RUTH: You surprise me.

GEORGE: Do I?

RUTH: Not really. You aren't very impressed with Geoffrey, I take it?

GEORGE: Right. What the Americans call 'strictly for the birds'. If there should be any heavenly purpose at all behind Mr Colwyn-phoney-Stuart, it's that he's God's own gift to the birds. Hope I didn't upset Mrs Elliot though. She's obviously pretty taken up with the whole racket.

RUTH: It might help if you weren't quite so vicious about it. You sound like a man with a secret doubt yourself.

GEORGE: Why is it you distrust me so much? I had a feeling we were the same kind.

RUTH: Did you? I suppose it's given poor Kate something to think about since Raymond was killed.

GEORGE: Tell me –

RUTH: Yes?

GEORGE: What was he really like?

RUTH: Raymond? Nice enough boy. Hard working, conscientious. Like most decent, ordinary lads of his age. (*Their eyes meet.*) You aren't remotely alike.

GEORGE: I thought you were in the habit of pitching into her yourself, hammer and sickle, over the Colwyn-Stuart.

RUTH: I should have thought that was different.

GEORGE: You mean that you're one of the family, and I'm not?

RUTH: If you like.

GEORGE: Suppose I'd better apologize.

RUTH: I shouldn't worry. I can't image what you could do wrong in her eyes. Well – I can imagine it all right, but I can't see you being stupid enough to lose the only good friend you've got.

GEORGE: What makes you think I haven't any good friends?

RUTH: Have you?

GEORGE: I thought you steel-hardened cadres of the far-away left had a better defence against the little jokies of right-wing deviationists like me. Or is it Wall Street jackal? No – I don't really look much like a jackal. Villiers Street wolf perhaps.

RUTH: Very droll – but not very well timed for someone who is supposed to be an actor.

GEORGE: Join my fan club, won't you?

RUTH: I'm not in the right frame of mind for shoddy little gags. (*Pause.*) I looked up the Party secretary tonight.

GEORGE: So you've packed it in at last.

RUTH: No doubt you think it's pretty funny.

GEORGE: No. I don't think it's funny.

RUTH: Seventeen years. It's rather like walking out on a lover. All over, finished, kaput. He hardly listened to my explanation – just sat there with a sneer all over his face. He didn't even have the manners to get up and show me out. I think that's what I've hated most of all, all these years – the sheer, damned bad manners of the lot of them.

GEORGE: Farther left you go, the worse the manners seem to get.

RUTH: Well! The house is still fairly ringing with the bloody shovel of *your* opinions.

GEORGE: *I* have a sense of humour. 'Bloody shovel of your opinions!' Is that a quotation?

RUTH: Just someone I used to know. Someone rather like you, in fact.

GEORGE: I thought you'd tied me up with someone the moment I met you.

RUTH: Where are you going tonight?

GEORGE: Dancing, I believe. Somewhere Josie knows.

RUTH: Don't sound so apologetic about it. It doesn't suit you. Pass my handbag, will you?
(*He does so.*)
Looks as though you've a long wait ahead of you, my lad.
(*She offers him a cigarette.*)

GEORGE: Have one of mine. (*Fumbles in his pockets.*)

RUTH: You needn't go through the pantomime for me, George. Take one.

GEORGE: No, thank you.

RUTH: Oh, don't look like that, for God's sake! You make me feel as though I'm – setting up as a soup kitchen or something. Please.
(*She throws a cigarette. He catches it, fumbles for a light. She snaps a lighter at him, and he goes over to her. He bends over her for a light.*)

GEORGE: How young you look sometimes.

RUTH: So do you when you're silent, and no longer trying to justify yourself.

GEORGE: What's the time?

RUTH: Seven-fifteen. Where's your watch?

GEORGE: Being repaired.

RUTH: Pawned, I suppose.

GEORGE: Just as you like. I think I'll give Josie a yell.

RUTH: It won't do any good – not for ages yet. I didn't mean to hurt you just now.

GEORGE: Didn't you?

RUTH: Yes. You're quite right. I did mean to hurt you. I wish I hadn't.

GEORGE: What are you doing tonight?

RUTH: I don't know yet. I'm getting rather used to being at home every night. I *did* apologize.

GEORGE: We're neither of us as steel-hardened as we should be, are we? I used to smoke my mother's cigarettes too. Right up until the time she died.

RUTH: When was that?

GEORGE: Couple of years ago. We often used to go out together – she enjoyed that more than anything. She'd pay for the lot: drinks, meals, cinemas – even the bus fares. When the conductor came up the stairs, I would always grope in my pockets. And my mother would bring out her purse, and push my empty, fumbling hands away. 'It's all right, dear. I've got change.' I used to wonder whether perhaps there might come just *one* day when it might not have to happen. When I might actually have that two shillings or half-crown in my pocket. But it always did. It had become a liturgy. We went through it the last time we went out together – on my thirtieth birthday. During the war it was different. I was well paid then.

RUTH: What did he give you for it?

GEORGE: What?

RUTH: The pawnbroker – for the watch?

GEORGE: Fifteen shillings. I was lucky to get that – it wasn't a very good one.

RUTH: Here. (*Takes out Jock's watch from handbag, and holds it out to him.*) Well, take it.

GEORGE: What's this?

RUTH: What does it look like? Try it on.

GEORGE: (*Taking it*) Are you giving me this?

RUTH: Yes, but you don't have to make a meal out of it.

GEORGE: It must have cost a fortune.

RUTH: It did. Try not to pawn it. Or, if you do, tell me, and I can renew the ticket or something.

GEORGE: I shan't pawn it, I promise you. I think it must be the nicest present I've had. How do you fix it?

RUTH: Here –
(*She adjusts it for him, he watches her.*)

GEORGE: Your – friend?

RUTH: Oh, he doesn't want it any more. He told me.

GEORGE: Can you get the Third Programme on it?

RUTH: There!

GEORGE: Perhaps it'll change my luck.

RUTH: Superstitious too?

GEORGE: Thank you. Very much.
(*She still has his hand in hers.*)

RUTH: How beautiful your hands are – they're like marble, so white and clear.

GEORGE: Nonsense.

RUTH: But they are. I've never seen such beautiful hands.

GEORGE: You make it sound as if I were half dead already.
  (*She looks up quickly, disturbed. Quite suddenly, he kisses her. Almost as quickly, he releases her. She soon recovers and moves away.*)

RUTH: Did you notice what I did with my lighter? My cigarette's gone out.

GEORGE: Didn't you put it back in your bag?
  (*She opens it.*)

RUTH: So I did. What sort of parts do you play? On the stage, I mean.

GEORGE: Good ones.

RUTH: Stupid question deserves a stupid answer. I mean: any particular type.

GEORGE: I suppose so. Reminds me of the actor who was asked at an audition what sort of parts he played, and he replied 'Scornful parts'. I think I play 'scornful' parts – anyone a bit loud-mouthed, around my height, preferably rough and dirty, with a furnace roaring in his belly. The rougher and dirtier the better.

RUTH: A character actor in fact.

GEORGE: I'm sorry I kissed you. So you needn't try to pay me back for it.

RUTH: Don't apologize. I was flattered for a moment. I'm sure there's an explanation somewhere, but I'd rather you didn't try to tell me what it is.

GEORGE: Just as you like.

RUTH: First time I've tasted Brown Windsor.

GEORGE: Tasted what?

RUTH: (*Laughing*) The Brown Windsor of love, George. Haven't you come across it.

GEORGE: That – friend of yours sounds rather pretentious to me.

RUTH: It's funny how rhetorical gentle spirits can become.

GEORGE: He's a poet or something?

RUTH: I used to hope so.

(GEORGE *stretches himself.*)

GEORGE: God, I feel tired! (*He looks all round the room. His eyes rest on Raymond's painted birds on the back wall C.*) Blimey! Those birds! (*Goes upstage and walks around and is finally stopped by the sight of the cocktail cabinet.*) I've sat here for weeks now and looked at that. Oh, I've often marvelled at them from afar in a shop window. But I never thought I'd ever see one in someone's house. I thought they just stood there, in a pool of neon, like some sort of monstrous symbol, surrounded by bilious dining-room suites and mattresses and things. It never occurred to me that anyone bought them!

RUTH: Norah's cocktail cabinet? Well, she didn't actually buy it – she won it.

GEORGE: What was her reaction?

RUTH: I think we were all a little over-awed by it.

(GEORGE *goes nearer to it.*)

GEORGE: It looks as though it has come out of a jelly-mould like an American car. What do you suppose you *do* with it? You don't keep drinks in it – that's just a front, concealing its true mystery. What do you keep in it – old razor blades? I know, I've got it!

(*He sits down and 'plays' it vigorously, like a cinema organ, humming a 'lullaby-lane' style signature tune. He turns a beaming face to* RUTH.)

And now I'm going to finish up with a short selection of popular symphonies, entitled 'Evergreens from the Greats', ending up with Beethoven's Ninth! And don't forget – if you're enjoying yourself, then all join in. If you can't remember the words, let alone understand 'em, well, just whistle the tune. Here we go then!

(*Encouraged by* RUTH's *laughter, he turns back and crashes away on the cocktail cabinet, pulling out the stops and singing:*)

I fell in love with ye- ieuw!

145

While we were dancing

The Beethoven Waltz! . . .

(*A final flourish on the invisible keyboard; he turns and bows obsequiously.* RUTH's *response has exhilarated him, and he stands in front of her, rather flushed.*)

It ought to disappear somehow, but I couldn't find the combination. (*He watches her with pleasure.*) That's the first time you've ever laughed.

RUTH: Oh, yes, you can be funny, George. These flashes of frenzy, the torrents of ideas they can be quite funny, even exciting at times. If I don't laugh, it's because I know I shall see fatigue and fear in your eyes sooner or later.

GEORGE: Oh?

RUTH: You're burning yourself out. And for what?

GEORGE: Go on – but don't think you can kill my confidence. I've had experts doing it for years.

RUTH: I just can't make up my mind about you.

GEORGE: Meaning?

RUTH: Do you really have any integrity?

GEORGE: What's *your* verdict?

RUTH: I'm still not sure. It just seems to me that for someone who makes a religion out of being brilliant, you must be very unlucky.

GEORGE: You don't even begin to understand – you're no different from the rest. Burning myself out! You bet I'm burning myself out! I've been doing it for so many years now – and who in hell cares? At this moment I feel about as empty and as threadbare as my pockets. You wonder that I should be tired. I feel played out.

(*She applauds.*)

RUTH: Bravo! Not bad at all, George. Bit ragged maybe, but it'll do. Perhaps you may not be so bad after all. Tell me about this television job.

GEORGE: That? It's a walk-on – one line which will be drowned by the rest anyway. And if I know Lime Grove, it'll be so dark, I shan't be seen at all. All for twelve guineas. It's a fortune. But what am I going to do? How can I let them all sit in there – and probably half the street as well – staring stupidly at the telly for two and a half hours to watch me make one thirty-second appearance at the very end? What a triumph for dear old Percy! And Mr Colwyn-Stuart and his Hallelujah Chorus!

RUTH: Quite a problem.

GEORGE: As it is, I owe Mrs Elliot God-knows how much. But I suppose you knew that.

RUTH: It's not exactly a surprise.

GEORGE: She was buying me cigarettes every day up until last week. I did manage to put a stop to that. I told her I was giving it up for my health. To my surprise, she actually believed me.

RUTH: *Are* you any good, George?

GEORGE: (*Almost like a child*) That's a moron's question.

RUTH: As you like.

GEORGE: Well, ask yourself. Isn't it? Listen: all I ever got – inside and outside the theatre – is the raves of a microscopic minority, and the open hostility of the rest. I attract hostility. I seem to be on heat for it. Whenever I step out on to those boards – immediately, from the very first moment I show my face – I know I've got to fight almost every one of those people in the auditorium. Right from the stalls to the gallery, to the Vestal Virgins in the boxes! My God, it's a gladiatorial combat! Me against Them! Me and mighty Them! Oh, I may win some of them over. Sometimes it's a half maybe, sometimes a third, sometimes it's not even a quarter. But I *do* beat them down. I beat them down! And even in the hatred of the majority, there's a kind of triumph because I know that, although they'd never admit it, they secretly respect me.

RUTH: What about this film you're going to be in?

GEORGE: It doesn't mean a thing. The old line. You know? Keep in touch – we'll let you know. You *don't* understand, do you?

RUTH: I just don't see much virtue in trying to ignore failure.

GEORGE: There's no such thing as failure – just waiting for success.

RUTH: George – really!

GEORGE: All right, forget it.

RUTH: I know what it is to go on waiting.

GEORGE: And do you think I don't! I spend my life next to a telephone. Every time it rings is like death to me.

RUTH: (*Relentless*) What about these plays you write. You do do that as well, don't you?

GEORGE: Oh yes – you think I'm a dabbler. A dilettante who can't afford it.

RUTH: This Trident Theatre – the 'three uplifted fingers of Drama, Ballet and Poetry –'

GEORGE: A so-called club theatre, meaning a preciously over-decorated flea-pit, principally famous for its rather tarty bar, and frequented almost exclusively by intense students, incompetent longhairs, and rather flashy deadbeats generally.

RUTH: I see. I'd like to read some of your work.

GEORGE: Thank you, I'll think about it.

RUTH: Do you charge a fee?

GEORGE: You're not being very funny yourself now.

RUTH: Perhaps your sense of humour has deserted you after all. My politics and your art – they seem to be like Kate's religion, better not discussed. Rationally, at any rate.

GEORGE: I knew you were suspicious of me, that you distrusted me. I didn't realize you detested me this much.

RUTH: George: Why don't you go?

GEORGE: Go?

RUTH: Leave this house. Get out of here. If you're what you believe yourself to be, you've no place in a house like this. It's unfair to you. It's stifling. You should be with your own kind. And if you're not what you say you are, you've no right to be here anyway, and you're being unfair to everyone.

GEORGE: Are you serious? I haven't got a penny in the world.

RUTH: You'll manage. You've got to. It's your only chance of survival. Am I being harsh, George? Perhaps, as you say, we're the same kind.

GEORGE: (*Savagely*) That's good! Oh yes! And what about you?

RUTH: (*Off her balance*) What about me?

GEORGE: What are *you* doing here? All right, you've had your go at me. But what about yourself?

RUTH: Well?

GEORGE: Oh, don't be so innocent, Ruth. This house! This room! This hideous, God-awful room!

RUTH: Aren't you being just a little insulting?

GEORGE: I'm simply telling you what you very well know. They may be your relations, but have you honestly got one tiny thing in common with any of them? These people –

RUTH: Oh, no! Not 'these people'! Please – not that! After all, they don't still keep coals in the bath.

GEORGE: I didn't notice. Have you looked at them? Have you listened to them? They don't merely act and talk like caricatures, they *are* caricatures! That's what's so terrifying. Put any one of them on a stage, and no one would take them seriously for one minute! They think in clichés, they talk in them, they even feel in them – and, brother, that's an achievement! Their existence is one great cliché that they carry about with them like a snail in his little house – and they live in it and die in it!

RUTH: Even if it's true – and I don't say it is – you still sound pretty cheap saying it.

GEORGE: Look at that wedding group. (*Points to it.*) Look at it! It's like a million other grisly groups – all tinted in unbelievable pastels; round-shouldered girls with crinkled-up hair, open mouths, and bad teeth. The bridegroom looks as gormless as he's feeling lecherous, and the bride – the bride's looking as though she's just been thrown out of an orgy at a Druids' reunion! Mr and Mrs Elliot at their wedding. It stands there like a comic monument to the macabre farce that has gone on between them in this house ever since that greatest day in a girl's life thirty-five years ago.

RUTH: Oh, a good delivery, George. You're being brilliant, after all. They're very easy people to score off, but, never mind, go on!

GEORGE: There's Josie – at this moment putting all she's got into misapplying half Woolworths on to her empty, characterless little face. Oh, sneer at me for my snobbery, for my bad taste, but, say what you like: I have a mind and feelings that are all fingertips. Josie's mind. She can hardly spell it. And her feelings – what about them? All thumbs, thumbs that are fat and squashy – like bananas, in fact, and rather sickly.

RUTH: You should look an intriguing couple on the dance floor tonight. I'm tempted to come myself.

GEORGE: Why don't you?

RUTH: I should hate to break up this marriage of true minds.

GEORGE: You know damned well why I'm going. People like me depend upon the Josies of this world. The great, gaping mass that you're so fond of. You know? And for tonight, Josie is that mass, all rolled into one. And do you know what? Behind that brooding cloud of mascara, she's got her eye on George, Josie has. Because not only does she suffer from constipation, but night starvation as well. And then, there's Norah. Now what can you say about her? Norah doesn't even exist – she's just a hole in the air!

RUTH: You've a lot to learn yet, George. If there weren't people like the Elliots, people like you couldn't exist.

Don't forget that. Don't think it's the other way around, because it's not. They can do without you, take my word for it. But without them, you're lost – nothing.

GEORGE: Don't give me that, Ruth. They drive you mad, and you know it. It's like living in one of those really bad suitable-for-all-the-family comedies they do all the year round in weekly rep. in Wigan. How have you stuck it here? What's the secret? Tell me. Since that mysterious divorce of yours that they all heavy-handedly avoid mentioning – and the weekend trips you don't make any more. How long is it you've been here? How long? Nine years is it? Ten years? Twelve? Oh no, Ruth – *you* can't afford to sneer at me!

RUTH: You've made your point. Don't get carried away with it. Why do I stay? Because I don't earn enough to get me out of it, and somewhere else. I spend too much on clothes, cigarettes –

GEORGE: And – 'incidentals'? (*Holding up wrist-watch.*)

RUTH: The job I do is so hysterically dull that every time I go into that office, and see myself surrounded by those imitation human beings, I feel so trapped and helpless, that I could yell my lungs out with the loneliness and the boredom of it.

GEORGE: So you do!

RUTH: But, at my age, and with my lack of the right kind of qualifications, there's not much else I can do. Perhaps I haven't the courage to try. At least, I'm safe. And so I go on, from spring, through the summer, to the autumn and another winter, meaningless; just another caricature.

GEORGE: I knew it! I knew it!

RUTH: Thank you for reminding me of it.

GEORGE: The truth is a caricature.

RUTH: Is that meant to be profound?

GEORGE: You hate them, don't you? Shall I tell you why they horrify me?

RUTH: I suppose I give you what is known as the 'feed' line now. No – tell me, why do they horrify you.

GEORGE: They've no curiosity. There are no questions for them, and, consequently, no answers. They've no apprehension, no humility –

RUTH: Humility! (*Laughing.*) Good old George!

GEORGE: And, above all, no real laughter. Tell me, have you ever heard any of them, even once, laugh? I mean really laugh – not make that choked, edgy sound that people make all the time. Or, to put it more unintelligibly: I don't mean that breaking wind people make somewhere between their eyebrows and their navels, when they hear about the old lady's most embarrassing moment. I mean the real thing – the sound of the very wit of being alive. Laughter's the nearest we ever get, or should get, to sainthood. It's the state of grace that saves most of us from contempt.

RUTH: Hooray!

GEORGE: No, it wasn't really spontaneous. Singing and dancing 'Jazzing at the Jubilee with Josie'.

RUTH: Why haven't we talked like this before. A few moments ago you made me feel old. Now, I suddenly feel younger.

GEORGE: 'If you can't give a dollar, give me a lousy dime . . .'

RUTH: Can't say I've exactly heard *you* falling about with mirth since you came here.

GEORGE: No, you haven't. I suppose it does sound as though I'm complaining because everyone doesn't go around as if they were on parole from *Crime and Punishment*, muttering about God, and laughing their blooming heads off.

RUTH: Oh yes, you are a character! I think your little performance has done me good.

GEORGE: You're a good audience. Even if I do have to beat you down. That's all I need – an audience.

RUTH: And do you – think you'll find it?

GEORGE: I don't know.

(*He takes a deep breath, and sits down quickly, suddenly drained. She watches him, fascinated.*)

RUTH: How quickly you change! That's what's so frightening about you. These agonizing bubbles of personality, then phut! Nothing. Simply tiredness and pain.

GEORGE: I've been trailing around all day. I've had a few drinks, and nothing to eat. It suddenly hit me, that's all.

RUTH: Perhaps you have got talent, George. I don't know. Who can tell? Even the experts can't always recognize it when they see it. You may even be great. But don't make a disease out of it. You're sick with it.

GEORGE: It's a disease some of us long to have.

RUTH: I know that. I met it once before.

GEORGE: Then you must know it's incurable.

RUTH: Galloping – like a consumption.

GEORGE: (*Sharply*) What did that mean?

RUTH: Nothing.

GEORGE: But do you know what is worse? Far, far worse?

RUTH: No, Brother Bones, tell me what is worse.

GEORGE: What is worse is having the same symptoms as talent, the pain, the ugly swellings, the lot – but never knowing whether or not the diagnosis is correct. Do you think there may be some kind of euthanasia for that? Could you kill it by burying yourself here – for good?

RUTH: Why do you ask me?

GEORGE: Would the warm, generous, honest-to-goodness animal lying at your side every night, with its honest-to-goodness love – would it make you forget?

RUTH: All you're saying is that it's a hard world to live in if you're a poet – particularly if it should happen that you're not a very good poet.

GEORGE: Unquote.

RUTH: Unquote. Life is hard, George. Anyone who thinks it isn't is either very young or a fool. And you're not either.

Perhaps even bad artists have their place in the scheme of things.

GEORGE: Scheme of flaming things! Get us with our intellectual sets on! And we're not even tight. I wish we were spending the evening together, all the same.

RUTH: Why are you so morbidly self-conscious? I thought all actors revelled in exhibitionism.

GEORGE: Don't you believe it. Only insincere old bastards who carried spears with Martin Harvey, and have been choking themselves silly with emotion ever since. 'Emotion, laddie – that's the secret!' Shall I tell you a story. Yes, do tell me a story. Well, it happened to me when I was in the RAF during the war.

RUTH: I didn't know you were. You've never mentioned it.

GEORGE: The one thing I never shoot lines about is the RAF. Just a gap in my life. That's all. Well, it happened like this: It was one night in particular, when it wasn't my turn to go on ops. Instead, we got a basinful of what we gave the Jerries, smack bang in the middle of the camp. I remember flinging myself down, not so much on to the earth as into it. A wing commander type pitched himself next to me, and, together, we shared his tin-helmet. Fear ran through the whole of my body, the strange fear that my right leg would be blown off, and how terrible it would be. Suddenly, the winco shouted at me above the din: 'What's your profession?' 'Actor,' I said. The moment I uttered that word, machine-gun fire and bombs all around us, the name of my calling, my whole reason for existence – it sounded so hideously trivial and unimportant, so divorced from living, and the real world, that my fear vanished. All I could feel was shame. (*He is lost for a moment or two. Then he looks at her quickly, and adds brightly.*) Gifted people are always dramatizing themselves. It provides its own experience, I suppose.

RUTH: How pompous can you get? You had me under your

spell for a moment. Now you've broken it. I'm beginning not to know when you're being real, and when you're not.

GEORGE: Always put the gun in the other man's hand. It's my rule of life.

RUTH: Yes. You're play-acting all right. You've done it all your life, and you'll go on doing it. You can't tell what's real and what isn't any more, can you, George? I can't sit here drivelling all night.

(*She turns to go.*)

GEORGE: (*Taking her by the arm*) And what if I do? What does it matter? My motives aren't as simple as you like to think –

RUTH: – You're being phoney, George, aren't you? We're a pair of –

GEORGE: – What if I am? Or you, for that matter? It's just as –

RUTH: (*Sings*) It's a Barnum and Bailey world,
Just as phoney as it can be!
You've got us both acting it now –

GEORGE: – just as serious and as complex as any other attitude. Ruth! Believe me, it isn't any less –

RUTH: – haven't you, George? Cutting in on each other's lives –

GEORGE: – real or sincere. You just never stop standing outside –

RUTH: – fluffing your emotions –

GEORGE: – it's a penance –

RUTH: – that's the word, isn't it? You're fluffing it –

GEORGE: – the actor's second sense –

RUTH: – all studied, premeditated –

GEORGE: – watching, observing, watching me now, commenting, analysing, giggling –

RUTH: – timed for effect, deliberate, suspect –

GEORGE: – just at this moment, don't you want me more than anything else –

RUTH:	I've had my lot, George.
GEORGE:	More than anything?
RUTH:	We've both had our lots!
GEORGE:	You're as arrogant as I am!
RUTH:	You know what, George?
GEORGE:	That's one of the reasons you're drawn to me! If only you knew – how much – at this moment –

RUTH: No, not me. Somebody else – not me!

GEORGE: I mean it, damn you!

RUTH: Strictly for the birds, George! Strictly for the birds!

GEORGE: Ruth!

RUTH: Let me go!

> (*He does so.*)

GEORGE: (*Simply*) I've botched it. (*Pause.*) Haven't I?

> (*The descent has been so sudden, and they are both dazed.*)

RUTH: I'm not sure what has happened. Nothing I suppose. We're just two rather lost people – nothing extraordinary. Anyway, I'm past the stage for casual affairs. (*Turns away.*) You can't go on being Bohemian at forty.

> (JOSIE *comes running down the stairs into the sitting-room. She is wearing her 'jazz trousers'.*)

JOSIE: Ready?

GEORGE: Yes. Yes. I suppose so.

> (RUTH *goes quickly out through the french windows.*)

JOSIE: Well, come on then. Had your supper?

GEORGE: No. I don't want anything. Let's have a drink, shall we, before we go?

JOSIE: Oh yes, lovely!

> (GEORGE *does not move.*)

Well, what are you standing there for? What are you thinking about.

GEORGE: What am I thinking about? (*To cocktail cabinet for the wine.*) What am I thinking about? (*Pouring drinks.*) Do you realize, Josie, that that is a lover's question? 'What are you thinking about?' (*Hands her a drink.*)

JOSIE: Oh, you are daft. You make me laugh when you talk in riddles. Oh, well, cheers!

GEORGE: Cheers. It'll be tonight, Josephine. (*Drinks.*)

JOSIE: Whatever are you talking about? You are in a funny mood, I must say. Let's have some music while we finish our drinks. (*She goes to radiogram.*) We don't want to get there too early, do we?

GEORGE: All the best people arrive late.

JOSIE: (*Looking through records*) What shall we have? There's 'Mambo Man', 'Jambo Mambo', or 'Marmalade Mambo'.

GEORGE: Oh, let's have something to soothe my rather shabby soul, Josie.

JOSIE: Go on, you haven't got one. What about this then? (*She puts on Mantovani.*)

GEORGE: (*Screwing up his face.*) Heaven.
(*They begin dancing.*)
Sheer heaven.
(*After a moment.*)

JOSIE: Bit boring isn't it – the music I mean.

GEORGE: The preliminaries always are, Josie, my girl. But they make anticipation all the more exciting. Are you ever excited by anticipation?

JOSIE: No, not really. Only when I see fellows like Len Cook, he's lovely.

GEORGE: That's not anticipation, Josie, that's lust, plain lust. Although it never is really plain. Do you know what lust is, Josie?

JOSIE: Of course I do, silly.

GEORGE: Lust, the harshest detergent of them all, the expense of spirit in a waste of shame. Or as Jean Paul Sartre put it – sex.

JOSIE: We were only talking about sex a little while ago. Boring, I think.

GEORGE: Do you? Shall we go?

JOSIE: All right.

(*They move into the hall. At the foot of the stairs,* GEORGE *stops her.*)

GEORGE: Have you ever been kissed, Josie?

JOSIE: Hundreds of times.

GEORGE: Like this?

(*He kisses her fiercely. The lounge door opens and they do not see* PERCY *standing there.* RUTH *comes in through french windows, switches out main lights, leaving just a glow in the sitting-room.* PERCY *remains silhouetted against the light from the lounge as* RUTH *sits in armchair.*)

JOSIE: George – don't George, there's somebody coming!

GEORGE: I've never tried the etchings line – (*leading her up the stairs*) – let's see if it really works.

JOSIE: But George –

GEORGE: Come and see my etchings.

(*They are now halfway up stairs.*)

JOSIE: What are you –

(GEORGE *smothers her with another kiss.*)

GEORGE: Silly girl.

JOSIE: But, George, what will Mum say?

(*They are swallowed up in darkness.* PERCY *moves towards the foot of the stairs and looks up. Then he moves into the sitting-room and looks down at* RUTH *for a moment. She is suddenly aware of him.*)

RUTH: Why, Percy, how long have you been there?

PERCY: Long enough, I think. Quite long enough.

(*Quick curtain.*)

ACT THREE

SCENE ONE

Autumn. One french window is open. GEORGE *is lying on the settee in his shirt sleeves. His jacket is hung on the back of one of the chairs. There are some loose leaves of manuscript scattered by the side of the settee. After a moment,* GEORGE *shivers, gets up, and puts on his jacket.* MRS E. *comes downstairs into the sitting-room with a breakfast tray.*

MRS E.: Are you feeling any better, dear. You need not have got up at all, you know. (*She puts tray on table.*) Silly boy – the window open too. (*Crossing to window.*) You'll catch your death. The chrysanths have gone off. Chrysanths always remind me of Father. (*Stands at the window. Shuts window.*) Oh, dear, the clocks go back tonight. Awful, isn't it. (*Picks up tray.*) You didn't eat much breakfast, dear. (*Into kitchen.*) Your bed's made and your room is done if you want to go up any time. Nearly twelve – (*in from the kitchen*) the others will be back soon. Sure you're all right, dear? Everyone's a bit down in the dumps these days. It must be the winter coming on. Not that I mind it really. It's the awful in-between that gets me down. How's the writing going? All right?

GEORGE: Oh, not too bad, Mrs Elliot, thanks. Feeling a bit whacked at the moment though.

MRS E.: Well, you mustn't overdo it, you know. I'll get in some nice cakes for your tea.

GEORGE: Please don't do that, Mrs Elliot dear, you know I don't eat them.

MRS E.: All right, dear, just as you like. (*Going to him.*) I'm ever so sorry about the money, dear. Something will turn up soon I expect – don't worry, dear. Raymond's money didn't go as far as we thought it might, did it? Still, never mind. As long as I've got a shilling or two, I'll see that you're all right. Now I really must go and get some shopping done. I hate Saturdays – the crowds are awful. (*Crosses into hall, and puts on coat.*)

(*The doorbell rings.*)

Oh, that'll be the milkman. Now where's my bag? (*She picks it up from the hallstand, and goes to the front door.*) Oh yes, yes, he does. Won't you come in?

(MRS E. *stands back to admit a tall, official looking man. He carries a briefcase.*)

MAN: Thank you.

(*They go through the hall towards the sitting-room.*)

MRS E.: I'd better show you the way. He's not feeling so good today. Still, it'll be a nice break for him, having someone to chat to. (*In sitting-room.*) George, dear, someone to see you. Well, I'll leave you to it, if you don't mind. (*Exit through front door.*)

MAN: You are Mr George Dillon?

GEORGE: That's right.

MAN: I'm from the National Assistance Board.

GEORGE: Oh yes, I wondered when you were coming. Please sit down.

MAN: Thank you. (*He does so. Then opens briefcase, and extracts papers, file, etc., and fountain pen from jacket. He studies papers for a moment.*) Hmm. Now, with regard to your claim for assistance – you are Mr George Dillon?

GEORGE: I thought we'd cleared that up just now.

MAN: (*Making notes*) And you are residing at this address, paying rent of thirty shillings a week?

GEORGE: Right.

MAN: What does that entail the use of? A bedroom, and general run of the house, I take it?

GEORGE: Yes.

MAN: May I trouble you for your rent book?

GEORGE: Well, as a matter of fact, I haven't got one. Not right now, that is. I could get you one, if it's really necessary.

MAN: You understand we have to examine your rent book, Mr Dillon, in order to ascertain the correctness of your statement regarding the thirty shillings which you claim is being paid out by you in the way of rent each week.

GEORGE: Yes, of course.

MAN: So would you please make sure you are in possession of one, the next time I call.

GEORGE: Does that mean that I'll have to wait until then before I get any money?

(PERCY *comes in at the front door*.)

MAN: I'm afraid I can't answer that at the moment, Mr Dillon. Now, let me see. You are, by profession, an actor?

GEORGE: Yes, I am – by profession.

MAN: Have you any idea when you are likely to be working again?

GEORGE: It's rather difficult to say.

MAN: In the near future, would it be?

GEORGE: That phone might ring at this moment with something for me. Or it may not ring for months. It might not even ring at all.

MAN: You seem to have chosen a very precarious profession, Mr Dillon.

GEORGE: This money means rather a lot at the moment. I need – something – to show, you see –

MAN: Isn't there something else you could do, in the meantime perhaps?

GEORGE: Do you think I haven't tried? Incidentally, I am rather anxious that no one in the house should know about this –

MAN: Yes, of course.

(PERCY *enters sitting-room, and sits down*.)

MAN: Yes. I see. Well, Mr Dillon, I can only hand in my

report as I see things, and see what happens. The board is very hesitant about – paying out money to strong, healthy men.

GEORGE: Of course. Is there anything else? (*Looking at* PERCY. *The Assistance* MAN *is not quite sure what to do*.)

MAN: There's just the little matter of your last job. When was that?

GEORGE: Oh, about three months ago – television.

PERCY: Accch! You don't call that a job, do you? You could hardly see it was him. *We* knew it was him all right – but you had to be sharp to catch him.

MAN: Well, that'll be all I think, Mr Dillon. (*Rising*.) You won't forget your rent book, will you?

PERCY: Rent book. Rent book! He hasn't got one! Shouldn't think he's ever paid any!

GEORGE: He knows that, you idiot. Well, I'll show you to the door, shall I?

(GEORGE *shows him into the hall. They get to the foot of the stairs, and the* MAN *turns*.)

MAN: (*Officialdom relaxing*) You know, you people are a funny lot. I don't understand you. Look what you do to yourselves. And all for what? What do you get out of it? It beats me. Now take me and my wife. We don't have any worries. I've got my job during the day – secure, pension at the end of it. Mrs Webb is at home, looking after the kiddies – she knows there'll be a pay-packet every Friday. And in the evenings, we sit at home together, or sometimes we'll go out. But we're happy. There's quite a lot to it, you know. (*Quite kindly*.) What could be better? I ask you? No, you think it over, son. You think it over.

(*He goes out of the front door.* JOSIE *comes downstairs in her dressing-gown*.)

JOSIE: (*Quietly*) Ruth home yet?

GEORGE: No. Not yet.

JOSIE: Know where she is?

GEORGE: She's at the doctor's.

JOSIE: Doctor's? What for?

GEORGE: For me. (*Crossing to sitting-room.*)

JOSIE: For you? Thought you didn't believe in doctors.

GEORGE: (*Turns*) I don't. She's picking something up for me.

JOSIE: (*Going to him*) I should have thought you could have done that rather well yourself. What's she picking up for you?

GEORGE: What's called a report. You know? Making no progress, but he mustn't try so hard. Unpromising.

JOSIE: Oh, I see. (*Crossing through into kitchen.*) Think I'll have some hot milk.

(GEORGE *goes into the sitting-room after her, and picks up the scattered leaves of his manuscript.*)

PERCY: Well, young man – you're at it again I see.

GEORGE: Yes. I'm afraid I'm not getting very far with it though.

PERCY: I don't mean that. I mean you're busy fleecing money from someone else again.

GEORGE: What the hell are you talking about?

PERCY: Not content with taking the money we bring home, you're even trying to get hold of the money we pay in income tax. You're getting it all ways, aren't you, George?

GEORGE: I certainly am! Look here, Percy, you'd better be careful what you say –

PERCY: And I think you'd better be careful what *you* say. Telling a government official barefaced lies like that! That's a case – (*leaning forward with infinite relish*) – for the assizes, that is!

GEORGE: All right, I admit it. But Mrs Elliot knows that she'll get back every penny, and more, for looking after me as she has.

PERCY: Accch! I don't believe it. Anyway, you don't think she'll be very pleased when she finds out where it comes from, do you? Assistance Board! To think of us having someone like that at the door. What'll people think of that? I know all about you my lad. I've checked up on you at my firm – you owe bills all over the place. Don't be surprised if you don't have the police after you soon – for debt. *Debt!* (*Thrilling with horror.*) Imagine that! Police coming to my house – to me that's never owed a farthing to anybody in all his life.

(*Doorbell rings, followed by violent knocking.*)

PERCY: And it wouldn't surprise me if that was them already. I know a copper's knock when I hear it.

(*Exit quickly into kitchen. GEORGE sinks into armchair, exhausted. Doorbell and knocking again. Pause. BARNEY EVANS comes in through the front door. He is wearing a rather old Crombie overcoat, an expensive but crumpled suit, thick horn-rimmed glasses, and a rakish brown Homburg hat. He is nearly fifty, and has never had a doubt about anything in all that time.*)

BARNEY: Anyone there? Anyone at home? I say?

GEORGE: In here. Come in here.

BARNEY: Where? (*To sitting-room.*) In here? Oh yes. Good. Sorry to butt in on you like this. The fact is –

(*GEORGE rises.*)

Oh yes, you must be who I am looking for.

GEORGE: Oh? Sit down, will you?

BARNEY: No, no, no – I can't stop a minute. I found I was passing your door, so I thought I'd just pop in for a few words. I haven't a London office any longer – just for a moment, you see. I'm just on my way to Brighton, as a matter of fact.

GEORGE: For the weekend?

BARNEY: Business and pleasure. (*Thoughtfully.*) Business – mostly. Look, I'll come straight to the point, Mr –

GEORGE: Dillon, George Dillon.

BARNEY: (*Producing a script from his pocket*) Oh yes. It's on here. George Dillon. Been in the business long?

GEORGE: Well – a few –

BARNEY: Thought so. Didn't ever play the Palace, Westport, did you?

GEORGE: No, I didn't.

BARNEY: Face seemed familiar. Well, now – to get down to it –

GEORGE: Is that my script you've got there?

BARNEY: That's right.

GEORGE: How on earth did you get hold of it?

BARNEY: Andy gave it to me.

GEORGE: Andy?

BARNEY: André Tetlock. You know him, don't you?

GEORGE: Oh – the Trident. Is he a friend of yours then?

BARNEY: Andy? I knew him when he was a chorus boy at the old Tivoli. You wouldn't remember that. Why, it was me put him back on his feet after that bit of trouble. You know that, don't you?

GEORGE: Yes?

BARNEY: He hadn't even got a set of underwear – I had to get that for him. Silly fellow! (*Sucks in his breath deprecatingly.*) Still, he's all right now. That was my idea – that bar, you know. Oh, he did it up himself, mind you – Andy's very clever with his hands. But it was my idea. And now that bar's packed every night. Can't get within a mile of the place. He doesn't have to worry whether he puts on a show or not. Get some odd types there, of course, but you know Andy – so everybody's happy. And as long as he can find enough authors willing to back their own plays with hard cash, *he* won't go without his bottle of gin, believe me. (*Produces a packet of cheroots.*) Got a match? I take it you *don't* have any capital of your own?

GEORGE: Right.

BARNEY: Yes, he said you'd told him you hadn't any money to put up yourself.

GEORGE: (*Lighting his cheroot for him*) I rang him about it weeks ago. I remember he said he'd liked the play, but he'd passed it on to someone else.

BARNEY: Liked it! That's a good one. Andy doesn't *read* plays
– he just puts 'em on. Provided of course he can make
something out of it! Now, I've read this play of yours,
and I'm interested. Are you willing to listen to a
proposition?

GEORGE: Of course.

BARNEY: By the way, I'm Barney Evans. You've heard of me,
of course?

(GEORGE *hesitates, but* BARNEY *doesn't wait.*)
Now, Andy's a friend of mine. I've done a lot for him –
but he's only in the business in a very small way. Oh, he
does himself all right. But it's small stuff. You wouldn't
get anywhere much with him – You know that, of
course?

GEORGE: Yes.

BARNEY: I'm only interested in the big money. Small stuff's
not worth my while. I take it you *are* interested in
money?

GEORGE: Is that a rhetorical question?

BARNEY: Eh?

GEORGE: Yes, I am.

BARNEY: That's all right then. I don't want to waste my time.
This the first play you've written.

GEORGE: My seventh –

BARNEY: Dialogue's not bad, but these great long speeches –
that's a mistake. People want action, excitement. I know
– *you* think you're Bernard Shaw. But where's he today?
Eh? People won't listen to him. Anyway, politics are out
– you ought to know that. Now, take *My Skin is my
Enemy!* I've got that on the road at the moment. That
and *Slasher Girl!*

GEORGE: *My Skin is my* – Oh yes, it's about the colour-bar
problem, isn't it?

BARNEY: Well, yes – but you see it's first-class entertainment!
Played to £600 at Llandrindod Wells last week. Got the
returns in my pocket now. It's controversial, I grant you,

but it's the kind of thing people pay money to see. That's the kind of thing you want to write.

GEORGE: Still, I imagine you've got to be just a bit liberal-minded to back a play like that.

BARNEY: Eh?

GEORGE: I mean – putting on a play about coloured people.

BARNEY: Coloured people? I hate the bastards! You should talk to the author about them. He can't even be civil to them. No – I know young fellows like you. You're interested in ideals still. Idealists. Don't think I don't know. I was an idealist myself once. I could tell you a lot, only I haven't got time now. But, make no mistake – ideals didn't get me where I am.

GEORGE: No?

BARNEY: You spend your time dabbling in politics, and vote in some ragged-arsed bunch of nobodies, who can't hardly pronounce the Queen's English properly, and where are you? Where are you? Nowhere. Crushed down in the mob, indistinguishable from the masses. What's the good of that to a young man with talent?

GEORGE: I should have thought you had a vested interest in the masses.

BARNEY: Most certainly. I admit it. And that's why I believe in education. Education – it always shows, and it always counts. That's why I say let them who've got it run the whole show. We're not going to get anywhere with these foreigners once they see they're no longer dealing with gentlemen. They're always impressed by an English gentleman. Just because they've got no breeding themselves, they know how to recognize it in others when they see it. Oh, yes. I could tell you a lot you don't know. However, I am diverting from what I came about. (*He sprays his ash over the floor thoughtfully.*) To get back to this play of yours. I think it's got possibilities, but it needs rewriting. Act One and Two won't be so bad,

provided you cut out all the high-brow stuff, give it pace
– you know: dirty it up a bit, you see.

GEORGE: I see.

BARNEY: Third Act's construction is weak. I could help you
there – and I'd do it for quite a small consideration
because I think you've got something. You know that's a
very good idea – getting the girl in the family way.

GEORGE: You think so?

BARNEY: Never fails. Get someone in the family way in the
Third Act – you're halfway there. I suppose you saw *I
Was a Drug Fiend*?

GEORGE: No.

BARNEY: Didn't you really? No wonder you write like you do!
I thought everyone had seen that! That was my show too.
Why, we were playing to three and four thousand a week
on the twice-nightly circuit with that. That's the sort of
money you want to play to. Same thing in that: Third
Act – girl's in the family way. Course, in that play, her
elder sister goes out as a missionary and ends up dying
upside down on an ant hill in her birthday suit. I spent
six months in the South of France on what I made out of
that show.

(*Motor horn toots outside.*)

Here, I'll have to be going. As I say, you rewrite it as
I tell you, maybe we can do business together and
make some money for both of us. I'll read it through
again, and drop you a line. In the meantime, I should
redraft the whole thing, bearing in mind what I said.
Right.

GEORGE: I'll have to think about it. The fact is – I'm not
feeling up to much at the moment. I'm completely broke
for one thing.

BARNEY: OK then. You'll be hearing from me. You take my
advice – string along with me. I know this business inside
and out. You forget about starving for Art's sake. That
won't keep you alive five minutes. You've got to be

ruthless. (*Moves into hall.*) Yes, there's no other word for it – absolutely ruthless.

(GEORGE *follows him.* BARNEY *picks up his hat from stand and knocks over the vase. He looks down at the pieces absentmindedly.*)

Oh, sorry. Now you take Hitler – the greatest man that ever lived! Don't care what anyone says – you can't get away from it. He had the right idea, you've got to be ruthless and it's the same in this business. Course he may have gone a bit too far sometimes.

GEORGE: Think so?

BARNEY: I do. I do think so, most definitely. Yes, he overreached himself, no getting away from it. That's where all great men make their mistake – they overreach themselves.

(*The car horn toots more insistently.*)

Hullo, blimey, she'll start smashing the windows in a minute.

(GEORGE *follows him as he hurries to door.*)

Well, you just remember what I said. Tell you what – I'll give you a ring on Monday. I'll be busy all the weekend. (*Opens door.*) By the way, that girl?

GEORGE: What girl?

BARNEY: The girl in your play – what do you call her?

GEORGE: Oh, you mean –

BARNEY: Build her up. Build her right up. She's – she's a prostitute *really* isn't she?

GEORGE: Well –

BARNEY: Of course she is! I've just had an idea – a new slant. Your title, what is it? (*He doesn't wait for a reply.*) Anyway, it won't bring anybody in. I've just thought of a smashing title. You know what we'll call it? '*Telephone Tart*, that's it! '*Telephone Tart.*' You string along with me, George, I'll see you're all right.

(BARNEY *exits.* JOSIE *looks in from kitchen.*)

JOSIE: (*Coming in with a glass of milk*) It's all right, he's gone.

(*Sits in armchair.*) Don't know what all the fuss was
about.

PERCY: Well, I hadn't shaved, you see. I should hate to let
George down in front of his friends – what few he *has*
got.

JOSIE: Oh, you are daft, Dad. You don't know what you're
talking about half the time.

(GEORGE *comes slowly into sitting-room.*)

JOSIE: Who was it, George? Teddy-bear coat and all!

GEORGE: (*Smiling wryly*) I suppose he's what you might call
the poor man's Binkie.

JOSIE: What? Whatever's that? What's that, George?

(RUTH *comes in front door into sitting-room.*)

GEORGE: Oh, never mind. It doesn't really matter. Hello,
Ruth.

RUTH: (*After a slight pause*) Hullo.

GEORGE: Well, did you go to the doctor's?

RUTH: Yes.

GEORGE: Well – (*laughing*) – don't stand there with the angel
of death on your shoulder – what did he say?

RUTH: George – just come in here, will you, for a minute.

(GEORGE *follows her into lounge.*)

JOSIE: Well, of all the – I like that, I must say! We're not
good enough to know what's going on! (*Rising and going
up to radiogram.*) I'm sure I don't want to hear what she
got to say to George. Them and their secrets.

(*She puts on Mambo record very loud.* JOSIE *then picks up a
magazine and glances at it viciously, her foot wagging
furiously. After a moment she gets up and goes over to the
window and looks out in the same manner.* PERCY *watches
her all the time. She catches him doing it.*)

Well, had your eyeful? (*She walks over-casually towards
the lounge door.*) Real heart-to-heart they're having, aren't
they?

(*Over to mirror as* RUTH *comes out of the lounge and goes
into the sitting-room and says something to* PERCY. MRS

ELLIOT *comes in at the front door, laden as usual. She goes into sitting-room and switches off the radiogram.*)

MRS E.: Whatever do you want that thing on like that for, Josie? I could hear it halfway down the street. I thought you weren't well?
(*Pause.*)

MRS E.: Why, what is it? What's the matter with you all? What is it, Ruth?

PERCY: (*In a voice like sandpaper*) George has got TB.

MRS E.: TB, George. I don't believe it. It isn't true. There must be some mistake –

RUTH: There's no mistake. It's quite true, Kate. The doctor will be coming up soon to let us know what the arrangements are.

MRS E.: Does this mean that he'll have to go away?
(RUTH *nods her head.*)
George – poor old George. (*She moves into hall and up the stairs.*) George dear, where are you? He won't like this at all, will he? George –
(PERCY *comes out of room to foot of stairs as* MRS E. *is halfway up.*)

PERCY: (*Calling up loudly*) You'll have to burn everything, you know! All his sheets, blankets. Everything will have to be burnt, you know!

JOSIE: Oh, my God. Auntie Ruth! What's going to happen? What about me?

RUTH: You?

JOSIE: Yes, that's what I want to know – what's going to happen to me?
(*Quick curtain.*)

SCENE TWO

Winter. MRS ELLIOT *is on stage alone. She is looking up the stairs. George's hat, coat and suitcase are standing in the hall. She is looking very anxious. She picks up the hat and coat, and hangs them up carefully on the hallstand. Then she goes back to the sitting-room. She goes over to the wedding group picture, and stares up at it. As she is doing this* PERCY *comes in at the front door. He takes off his hat and coat, hangs them up beside George's, and comes into the sitting-room.*

PERCY: So he's back then?

MRS E.: Yes.

PERCY: Where is he?

MRS E.: Upstairs – talking to Josie.

PERCY: Upstairs?

MRS E.: Yes. She wasn't feeling too good this morning, so I told her to stay in bed. I didn't want to take any chances. I think she was over-excited at the thought of George coming back.

PERCY: Excited, was she?

MRS E.: Of course she was. She's thought about nothing else for weeks.

PERCY: Well, well! She's in for a bit of a shock, isn't she?

MRS E.: Listen to me, Percy. I've told you – you're to keep out of this. It's nothing to do with you. The only two people it need concern at the moment are George and myself. Above all, I don't want one word of this to get to Josie's ear. We've no idea what might happen if she was to get a shock like that. And in her present condition. If you so much as open your mouth about it to her – you can pack your bags and go. You understand? Besides, we don't know yet that it's true – not for certain. We've only got your word for it, and we all know what a nasty mind you've got. It would please you to think something rotten of George. You've always been against him. You're jealous of him – that's why.

PERCY: Me? Jealous of him! That wreck!

MRS E.: He's a gentleman – which is something you'll never be.

PERCY: Oh, he is, is he? Perhaps that's why he can't even earn the price of a cup of tea!

MRS E.: That's all *you* know.

PERCY: And what does that mean, exactly?

MRS E.: Never you mind. But there's a lot you don't know about George. George will come out tops in the end – you wait.

PERCY: Seems more like there was a lot *all* of us didn't know about him.

MRS E.: You don't understand, Percy. And what's more, you never will. You think everyone's like yourself. George is an artist –

PERCY: And what's *that* supposed to mean?

MRS E.: He's sensitive, proud – he suffers deeply. Raymond was like that – you never liked him, and he was your own son. That boy's gone through a lot – he doesn't have to tell me that. I could tell the first time I ever spoke to him. I knew he was a good fellow, that all he wanted was a chance to bring a little pleasure to other people. I don't think that's so much of a crime, anyway. Oh, he's never said anything to me, but I've known what he's been going through all these months. When he's come back here in the evenings, when he couldn't get a job or any kind of encouragement at all, when people like you were sneering at him, and nobody wanted him. He didn't think I knew when he was feeling sick with disappointment. He didn't think I knew he was trying to pass it off, by making us laugh, and pretending that everything was going to be all right. And I've never been able to tell him because I can't express myself properly – not like he can. He's got a gift for it – that's why he's an artist. That's why he's different from us. But he'll have his own way, in the end, you mark my words. He'll show them all – and you. God always pays debts without money. I've got down on my knees at night, and prayed for that boy. I've prayed that he'll be well, and get on, and be happy – here – with us.

PERCY: With us?

MRS E.: If that's what he wants. And I believe it is. I know we're not the kind of people George is used to, and probably likes being with – he must have felt it sometimes. Not that he's ever said anything – he's too well brought up for that. He just accepts us for what we are. He's settled in here. And while he's been in that hospital all these weeks, he's known he's got somewhere to come back to. He's known that somebody wants him, anyway, and that's a great deal when you're laying there in bed, and you don't know properly whether you're going to live or die. To know that someone is counting the days until you come home.

PERCY: What's he look like?

MRS E.: A bit thin. But who wouldn't look thin on that hospital food? I'll soon feed him up.

PERCY: Did you manage to have a word with the doctor?

MRS E.: No, I didn't.

PERCY: Well, why not?

MRS E.: Because I wasn't going to ask the doctor a lot of questions behind George's back, that's why. He's back – that's all I care about, that's all I want to know at the moment. Things will work themselves out somehow. George won't let us down.

PERCY: Well, we shall soon see, shan't we? He's a long time up there, don't you think? And what's he going to do about his wife?

MRS E.: How do I know what he's going to do? Why can't you shut up about it! You've talked about nothing else for days now.

PERCY: You mean to say you didn't tackle him about it?

MRS E.: I didn't have an opportunity. I couldn't bring it up on the bus, could I? Besides, I couldn't start on him straight away. And as soon as we got back, he wanted to go up and see Josie, naturally.

PERCY: Well, you wait till he comes down. If you're afraid to tackle him about it, I'm not.

MRS E.: I meant what I said, you know. If you try and cause trouble in this house, you can go.

PERCY: I think it's disgusting. Carrying on in someone else's house – a married man at that! Do you know what? It's my belief that there was something between him and your sister Ruth – and that's why she decided to pack her bags, and go, all of a sudden.

MRS E.: Oh, don't be so childish, for heaven's sake, Percy. You've got sex on the brain. I must admit you could have knocked me down when Ruth told me she was going to find herself a room somewhere. I mean – it seemed a bit suspicious. She didn't even give a proper explanation. Just said that she felt she had to 'get out of it'. It seemed a funny thing to say, and especially after all these years. Of course, she always was a dark horse. But, as for her and George – it's ridiculous. Why, she's old enough to be his mother.

PERCY: (*As he goes to lounge*) Oh, you women – you go on and on.

(RUTH *appears at front door – unlocking it enters, leaving door open.* RUTH *enters sitting-room.*)

RUTH: (*Quietly*) Kate. Kate.

(GEORGE *comes downstairs – shuts front door. Then goes towards sitting-room – meets* RUTH *face to face in the doorway.*)

Hello George. Are you better?

GEORGE: You're not really going, are you?

RUTH: I was coming to collect my things this morning – but I couldn't.

GEORGE: In fact it's quite a coincidence meeting you.

RUTH: No. Not really. I suppose it was silly of me to come

when I knew you'd be back. I always seem to let myself in for farewells.

GEORGE: We both ought to be pretty good at them by now. (*Pause.*) Are you really leaving then?

RUTH: Not again, please. There's only a few minutes.

GEORGE: (*Very quietly*) What's going to happen to me?

RUTH: George – don't! Try and help a little. (*Pause.*)

GEORGE: Isn't it hell – loving people?

RUTH: Yes – hell.

GEORGE: Still sounds rather feeble when you say it though. Rather like 'shift me – I'm burning'. What are you going to do?

RUTH: I don't know. Maybe find some scruffy wretch with a thumb-nail sketch of a talent, and spend my time emptying bits of brown cigarette stubs from his saucer – generally cleaning up.

GEORGE: Did you ever look up your – friend? (*He lifts up the wrist-watch.*)

RUTH: Yes. I did. Soon after you came in here. But he wasn't at the same place any more. His landlord gave me his new address. Number something Eaton Square.

GEORGE: But of course, my dear – everyone lives in Eaton Square.

RUTH: Apparently, she's in publishing. She's just published his book last week. But I mustn't be unfair – she didn't write the reviews as well. They fairly raved. He's on top of the world.

GEORGE: You know I've been waiting for you to tell me that you're old enough to be my mother. Still, mothers don't walk out on their sons – or do they?

RUTH: How's Josie – have you seen her yet?

GEORGE: God! What a farce! What pure, screaming farce! (*He starts to laugh.*)

RUTH: For heaven's sake!

GEORGE: Sorry. I just thought of something. How to make

sure of your Third Act. Never fails! (*Roars with laughter.*)
Never fails! (*Subsides almost immediately.*) Don't panic.
I'll not get maudlin. I probably would start howling any
minute, only I'm afraid of getting the bird from my best
audience. (*He looks away from her, and adds in a strangled
voice, barely audible.*) Don't leave me on my own! (*But he
turns back quickly.*) You haven't mentioned my – success
– once.

RUTH: I didn't know whether you expected me to
congratulate you or not.

GEORGE: Second week of tour – I've got the returns here.
Look: Empire Theatre, Llandrindod Wells – week's
gross takings £647 18s 4d. Long-hair drama gets a haircut
from Mr Barney Evans!

RUTH: I simply can't bear to go on watching you any longer.

GEORGE: But don't you think it's all very comic? I seem to
remember some famous comedian saying once that he'd
never seen anything funny that wasn't terrible. So don't
think I'll mind if you laugh. I expect it. We should be
both good for a titter, anyway. That's why religion is so
damned deadly – it's not even good for a giggle. And
what's life without a good giggle, eh? That's what I
always say! Isn't that what you always say, Ruth?

RUTH: Let go of my hand. You're hurting me.

GEORGE: Well – isn't it? No. Perhaps it isn't. We never really
had the same sense of humour, after all.

RUTH: Please don't try to hurt yourself any more by trying to
hit back at me. I know how you feel. You're overcome
with failure. Eternal bloody failure.

GEORGE: But I'm not a failure, I'm a – success.

RUTH: Are you, George? (*She turns away.*)

GEORGE: Listen! I'll make you laugh yet, before you go. Just
a trip on the stage-cloth, and Lear teeters on, his crown
around his ears, his grubby tights full of moth-holes.
How they all long for those tights to fall down. What a
relief it would be! Oh, we should all use stronger elastic.

And the less sure we are of our pathetic little divine rights, the stronger the elastic we should use. You've seen the whole, shabby, solemn pretence now. This is where you came in. For God's sake go.

(*She turns to go.*)

No, wait. Shall I recite my epitaph to you? Yes, do recite your epitaph to me. Here lies the body of George Dillon, aged thirty-four – or thereabouts – who thought, who hoped, he was that mysterious, ridiculous being called an artist. He never allowed himself one day of peace. He worshipped the physical things of this world, and was betrayed by his own body. He loved also the things of the mind, but his own brain was a cripple from the waist down. He achieved nothing he set out to do. He made no one happy, no one looked up with excitement when he entered the room. He was always troubled with wind round his heart, but he loved no one successfully. He was a bit of a bore, and, frankly, rather useless. But the germs loved him.

(*He doesn't see* RUTH *as she goes out and up the stairs.*)

Even his sentimental epitaph is probably a pastiche of someone or other, but he doesn't quite know who. And, in the end, it doesn't really matter.

(*He turns, but* RUTH *has gone. Bell rings,* PERCY *opens door.*)

NORAH: (*Coming in*) Only me. Forgot my key again. Is George back yet? (*Into room.*) George! You are back!

GEORGE: Yes, Norah, I'm back again, with a face like the death of kings.

NORAH: (*Rushes to him*) Oh, George, you look fine! Doesn't he, Dad? I thought you'd look awful – but you look fine.

(*Kisses him as* MRS E. *comes in from kitchen.*)

GEORGE: Here – mind my ribs!

NORAH: Oh, we'll soon feed you up, won't we, Mum?

(*She takes him into the sitting-room*, PERCY *follows.*)

MRS E.: We certainly will. We're going to look after him from now on. He can sit in here all day and rest, and – keep himself happy. Can't you, George?

GEORGE: Rather.

MRS E.: He can lie down on the settee in the afternoons with his books and things, and – oh, I forgot! We got you a little homecoming present, didn't we, Norah?

NORAH: Shall I go up and get it?

MRS E.: If you like, dear, I don't know whether George feels up to opening presents. He must feel all in after that journey. I expect he'd like a bit of rest.

GEORGE: I'm all right. I'd like a cup of tea though.

MRS E.: It's all ready. And I'll get you something to eat in no time.

NORAH: All right, then. I'll go and get it. I'll just pop in and have a look at Josie. Have you seen her, George?

MRS E.: He's been in there ever since he came in, haven't you, George?

NORAH: (*Crossing to and up stairs*) She's been so excited at the thought of you coming back. She's talked about nothing else for days. (*She laughs.*) Isn't love grand!
(NORAH *exits.*)

MRS E.: It's true, George. She's been quite a changed girl since you went away. I'm afraid she did used to be a bit on the lazy side sometimes, but not now – you wouldn't know her. Why, Sunday we spent practically all evening getting your room ready and looking nice. And Norah's been the same. Why, she's even booked seats for a coach ride for all of us down to the seaside.

PERCY: Well? How are you feeling, George?

GEORGE: Sorry, Percy. I haven't had a chance to say hullo yet, have I? (*Offers his hand.*)

PERCY: (*Shakes perfunctorily*) How have they been treating you?

GEORGE: Oh, not too bad, thanks. But it's certainly good to be back. You've all given me such a welcome.

PERCY: It's quite a nice place down there, I believe.

GEORGE: It's all right.

PERCY: Nice country.

GEORGE: Oh, lovely.

PERCY: Isn't that near Tunbridge Wells?

GEORGE: Not far.

MRS E.: I don't suppose he wants to talk much now, Percy. Let him have a rest first. He's tired.

PERCY: They say that's a nice town.

GEORGE: It's pleasant enough.

PERCY: Ever been there, George?

GEORGE: What are you getting at?

PERCY: I think you *know* what I'm getting at.

GEORGE: (*To* MRS E.) What is it? You're upset about something, aren't you. I could tell something was wrong when you met me at the hospital. And all the way home on the bus.

PERCY: I suppose you didn't happen to be in Tunbridge Wells on June 22nd, 1943, did you?

(*Pause.*)

GEORGE: I see.

MRS E.: George – it's not true, is it? I was sure he'd made a mistake.

GEORGE: No, He hasn't made a mistake. I *was* married in Tunbridge Wells, and it was in 1943. The middle of June. It poured with rain. How did you find out?

PERCY: Through my firm, as a matter of fact. As you know, it's our job to check on people's credentials, etc., for hire purchase firms and the like. Well, last week, I found myself checking on a certain Ann Scott, on behalf of a building society. She's contemplating buying some big property in Chelsea. Good report – excellent banker's references and all that. Living in large house in upper-class district. And it seems her married name is Mrs George Dillon. Well? What have you got to say?

GEORGE: Well?

MRS E.: Oh, dear.

GEORGE: What do you want me to say?

MRS E.: I don't know, George. I'm so upset, I don't know where I am. I suppose it's not your fault, but –

GEORGE: But, my dear, I don't see what there is to be so upset about. This doesn't change anything.

MRS E.: But – but what about Josie?

GEORGE: Nothing is changed, I tell you. It's simply that neither my wife nor I have ever bothered about a divorce. She's had other things to think about, and I've never had the money. But it's all easily settled. There's nothing to worry about. I promise you.

MRS E.: You're not just saying this, George? I'd rather –

GEORGE: Of course not. I've come home, haven't I?

MRS E.: Yes, you have. You've come home, thank heaven.

GEORGE: You see, my wife never was anything. With Josie, it's different. I know exactly where I am.

MRS E.: She loves you, George. She really does.

GEORGE: Yes. I know.

PERCY: It said on my report that she's an actress, this wife of yours.

(PERCY *feels cheated, and is desperately looking round for something else.*)

GEORGE: Right.

PERCY: She must do pretty well at it then.

GEORGE: She does.

PERCY: Can't say I've ever heard the name.

GEORGE: On the contrary, you know her very well.

PERCY: What do you mean?

GEORGE: I mean that somebody must have slipped up rather badly in your report. They seem to have left out her stage name.

PERCY: Stage name?

GEORGE: We both thought 'Ann Scott' a bit commonplace.

PERCY: Who is she then?

GEORGE: Well, you've always told me that she's the only one

in your favourite television parlour game who's really any
good at all. In fact, you've said so many times.

PERCY: You don't mean – What? Not *her*!

GEORGE: Her.

PERCY: Well, I'll be . . .

GEORGE: Yes. It's always puzzled me why you should admire
her so much. Or anyone else for that matter.

MRS E.: But George – honestly, I don't know where I am.
Now that – well – now that you're a success, how do you
know that your wife won't want you back?

GEORGE: Somehow, I don't think that will influence her!

PERCY: What are you talking about? Now that he's a success?

MRS E.: (*Recovered and triumphant*) Well, I don't see why he
shouldn't know now, do you, George?

GEORGE: No, I don't see why not.

MRS E.: George has had his play put on. It's on tour at the
moment, and last week it made – tell him how much it
made, George.

GEORGE: £647 18s. 4d. (*Flourishing returns.*)

MRS E.: And he gets five per cent of that every week, so
perhaps that will shut you up a bit.

PERCY: (*Staring at returns*) Well! Fancy that! Why didn't
somebody tell me?

MRS E.: Why should they? Well, I mustn't stand here wasting
time. You must be hungry, George.
(*Phone rings.*)

MRS E.: Do answer that, Percy, will you? Wish Norah would
hurry up.
(PERCY *goes to phone.* NORAH *comes down stairs carrying
parcel into sitting-room.*)

NORAH: Josie says she won't be long, she's going to get up.

PERCY: What's that? Oh, yes, hang on a minute while I find
my pencil. All right – go ahead.

NORAH: Well, George, here we are – I can't wait to see his
face when he opens it, Mum.

GEORGE: Well –

MRS E.: No, wait till Josie comes down. She'll want to be with him when he opens it.

NORAH: Oh, blow that. She's got all the time in the world with him now. If he won't open it, I will.

PERCY: Yes. Yes. I've got that. Who? What? What name? Right. Good-bye.

MRS E.: All right then. I don't suppose she'll mind. Go on, George, open it.

(GEORGE *starts opening the parcel*.)

PERCY: (*Coming in*) That was for you, George. A telegram.

GEORGE: Oh, who from?

PERCY: Somebody called Barney. I've got it written down here.

GEORGE: Read it out, will you? I'm busy at the moment.

PERCY: It says 'Playing capacity business. May this be the first of many smash hits together. Welcome home – Barney.'

MRS E.: Well, wasn't that nice of him?

GEORGE: Yes, good old Barney. Now, what have we here? (*Stands back to reveal a portable typewriter*.) Well! Look at that!

MRS E.: I hope you like it, George.

GEORGE: Like it! I should think I do! I think it must be the nicest present I've had. What can I say? (*He kisses them both*.) Thank you both. Thank you for everything.

MRS E.: That's all right, George. Believe me, all my prayers have been answered. Mr Colwyn-Stuart prayed for you too, every week you were away. All I want is for us all to be happy. Come along now, sit down, while I get the supper. Give him a chair, Percy, you look all in, dear.

PERCY: Oh, sorry. Here you are.

NORAH: It'll be nice, having George for a brother-in-law.

GEORGE: Yes, of course it will, Norah. It's about time you got married yourself, isn't it?

MRS E.: She almost has been –

NORAH: – Twice.

GEORGE: I'm sorry.

MRS E.: The last one was an American.

NORAH: Yes. The last time I saw him, we were going to get a bus to Richmond. He just simply said suddenly: 'Well, so long, honey, it's been nice knowing you' and got on a bus going in the opposite direction. It's swimming on the telly tonight. I think I'll go and watch it, if you'll excuse me.

(*She goes into lounge. Slight pause.*)

MRS E.: Well, I don't know. What with one thing and another! That's right, George, dear. Just you relax from now on. And you let him alone, Percy. I've always believed in you, George. Always. I knew he'd come out tops.

(MRS ELLIOT *goes into kitchen.* GEORGE *leans back, tired.* PERCY *turns on radio. Jazz – 'If you can't give me a dollar, give me a lousy dime.'*)

PERCY: Not too loud for you, George?

GEORGE: No – fine.

(*Pause.*)

PERCY: I can't get over it you know.

GEORGE: What?

PERCY: Your wife, I mean. Big star like that. Surprised she couldn't have helped you on a bit all this time. Still, you're doing all right yourself now, by the look of it. Turned out to be Bernard Shaw, after all, eh? I suppose you'll by writing some more plays when you start feeling better again?

GEORGE: I dare say.

PERCY: I see. Same sort of thing?

(RUTH *comes down slowly with suitcase.*)

GEORGE: Yes. Same sort of thing.

PERCY: Well, that's good, isn't it? What was the name of that theatre again?

GEORGE: The Empire Theatre, Llandrindod Wells.

(*The sound of* JOSIE's *voice singing comes from upstairs. From the lounge, the telly is playing music.*)

PERCY: Well, I don't think it would do any harm if we all
have a little drink on this. (*To cocktail cabinet.*) If we're
going to start living in style, we may as well get into the
way of using this, eh?
(*He opens the cocktail cabinet, revealing all its hidden glory.*
RUTH *exits through front door.*)
PERCY: Now, where are we. (*Staring into cabinet.*)
MRS E.: That's right. Let's have a little drink.
GEORGE: (*In a flat, empty voice*) Yes, let's have a little drink –
to celebrate.
PERCY: Music too, would not be inappropriate. (*Putting on
record.*)
GEORGE: Music too, would not be inappropriate.
(JOSIE *sings, off.*)
PERCY: Well, we can't leave the blushing bride upstairs all on
her own, can we? I'll give her a yell, shall I, George?
(*He goes out, calling upstairs,* GEORGE *goes to the door. He
looks trapped and looks around the room and the objects in it;
he notices the birds on the wall.*)
GEORGE: Those bloody birds!
(*Enter* MRS ELLIOT. *He stares at her as if for the first time,
then his face breaks into a mechanical smile.*)
Come on, Mum, let's dance!
(*They dance together for a few moments. Slow curtain.*)

THE WORLD OF
PAUL SLICKEY

No one has ever dedicated a string quartet to a donkey although books have been dedicated to critics. I dedicate this play to the liars and self-deceivers; to those who daily deal out treachery; to those who handle their professions as instruments of debasement; to those who, for a salary cheque and less, successfully betray my country; and those who will do it for no inducement at all. In this bleak time when such men have never had it so good, this entertainment is dedicated to their boredom, their incomprehension, their distaste. It would be a sad error to raise a smile from them. A donkey with ears that could listen would no longer be a donkey; but the day may come when he is left behind because the other animals have learnt to hear.

The first performance in Great Britain of *The World of Paul Slickey* was given at the Pavilion Theatre, Bournemouth, on 14 April 1959. It was directed by the author. The music was by Christopher Whelen, the choreography by Kenneth MacMillan and the décor by Hugh Casson. The cast was as follows:

COPY-BOYS	David Harding
	Julian Bolt
JO, *the secretary*	Irene Hamilton
JACK OAKHAM,	
alias PAUL SLICKEY	Dennis Lotis
COMMON MAN	Ken Robson
1ST NAVAL MAN	Ben Aris
2ND NAVAL MAN	Geoffrey Webb
DEIRDRE RAWLEY	Maureen Quinney
LADY MORTLAKE	Marie Lohr
TREWIN	Aidan Turner
MICHAEL RAWLEY	Jack Watling
MRS GILTEDGE-WHYTE	Janet Hamilton-Smith
GILLIAN GILTEDGE-WHYTE	Janet Gray
LADY MORTLAKE	Harry Welchman
LESLEY OAKHAM	Adrienne Corri
FATHER EVILGREENE	Philip Locke
GUIDE	Geoffrey Webb
1ST GIRL	Norma Dunbar
2ND GIRL	Pam Miller
3RD GIRL	Anna Sharkey
1ST MAN	Ken Robson
LADY PHOTOGRAPHER	Stella Claire
PHOTOGRAPHER	Charles Schuller
JOURNALIST	Geoffrey Webb
WENDOVER	Ben Aris
GEORGE	Tony Sympson
TERRY MAROON	Roy Sone

Geoffrey Webb	Stella Claire
Ben Aris	Patricia Ashworth
Julian Bolt	Norma Dunbar
David Harding	Pam Miller
Ken Robson	Anna Sharkey
Charles Schuller	Jane Shore

TIME: THE PRESENT

The entire action of the play takes place between the office of Paul Slickey, Gossip Columnist for *The Daily Racket*, and Mortlake Hall, a stately home somewhere in England.

MUSICAL NUMBERS

ACT ONE

Don't think you can fool a Guy like me JACK AND DANCERS
We'll be in the Desert and alone JACK AND DEIRDRE
It's a consideration we'd do well to bear in mind MICHAEL
Bring back the Axe MRS GILTEDGE-WHYTE
The Mechanics of Success GUIDE AND JOURNALISTS
Tell me later JACK
The Income Tax Man LESLEY AND MICHAEL
Them JACK AND DANCERS

ACT TWO

On Ice JO AND DANCERS
I want to hear about beautiful things MRS GILTEDGE-WHYTE
You can't get away with it FATHER EVILGREENE AND DANCERS
A Woman at the Weekend LESLEY, JACK, DEIRDRE
AND MICHAEL
I'm hers TERRY
REPRISE: *I want to hear about beautiful things*
MRS GILTEDGE-WHYTE
If I could be JACK, JO AND DANCERS

ACT ONE

SCENE ONE

The curtain goes up and a cloth covered in large keyholes is revealed, through which can be seen parts of the Paul Slickey office and JO *sitting at his desk U.L.*

SIX LADY JOURNALISTS *and* SIX MEN JOURNALISTS *come on in front of the cloth and dance with newspapers.*

They end the dance and go through one of the keyholes R. which is cut out. The last dancer curtseys, and goes through, the cloth goes away and the lights come up on the Offices of The Daily Racket, *early Saturday morning.*

Upstage, C., is a huge cloth representing a sheet of newsprint. In large letters all over is printed 'Paul Slickey'. The silhouette appears on the centre cloth of the man who is responsible for the Paul Slickey column. He wears a heavy, light-coloured overcoat, dark hat and bright brown shoes. When he is not embracing a GIRL *— he uses a cigarette-holder. He turns and we see his profile for the first time. As we hear his voice, a linotype operator clatters out his words and pictures and words appear on the column as the silhouette walks away.*

VOICE: There were no moral fervours in London last night
(COPY-BOY *crosses from down R. to office desks where the dancers are sitting, and places galley-proofs on desks.*)
But it was good to welcome several glamorous examples of passionate bankruptcy in all kinds of places.
(*There is a chord from the orchestra.*)
Last night's events . . .
(*Orchestra chord. Photograph projected on to screen showing three typical Guards officers in civvies.*)
Last night's events . . .

(*Orchestra chord. Photograph of a regal lady in tiara bowing graciously from a Rolls Royce.*)

Last night's events . . .

(*Orchestra chord. Photograph of a bad-tempered-looking Bishop in gaiters, pushing aside a small boy.*)

Last night's events . . .

(*Orchestra chords. Three pigs at a party.*)

Last night's events were certainly a colourful milestone in the National Drive for organized triviality.

(*The projection fades out. Up R. a* TELEPHONIST *chants:* 'Daily Racket . . . Who? . . . Just a moment.' *The phone rings in Slickey's office and* JO *picks it up.*)

JO: Who? . . . Jack Oakham . . . (*Stands.*) Oh, it's you, sir. I'm afraid Mr Oakham isn't here just at the moment . . . Yes, sir, I will . . . The moment he gets back. (*She puts the phone back and reads from copy, standing downstage of the desk.*) 'As I walked away from the pageantry, the happy crowds, the faces of those loyal subjects, I stopped inside a shop doorway to light my pipe. And suddenly to my surprise, I saw shining on my cheeks, a small column of tears. Dot, dot, dot, dot.' (*Sits on desk front.*) Well we've got one dot extra today. 'I puffed hard and walked back to Fleet Street in the evening sunshine with a gay heart. There are times when it is good to be an Englishman.'

(JACK OAKHAM, *alias* PAUL SLICKEY, *enters from behind the screen and hangs his hat on the hatstand.*)

Oh, you've arrived! (*Goes to him.*)

JACK: I'm just going.

JO: Finished your copy? (*Picks up copy.*) Where have you been?

JACK: Getting loaded.

JO: The great man rang for you.

JACK: He did?

JO: From Bermuda. (*Hangs Jack's coat on the stand.*)

JACK: So?

JO: (*Admiringly*) You boys are so tough in this racket!
(COPY-BOY *enters from down R. and stands waiting for
copy.* SECRETARY *hands it to him.*)
Here. They mustn't miss this one.
(*Exit* BOY *the same way.*)
Your wife left a message.

JACK: When?

JO: I don't remember. A few hours ago.

JACK: Oh, thank *you*.

JO: (*Kisses him*) She says she's got some important clients
from the Continent to see over the weekend, and will
you go down to your father-in-law's on your own.

JACK: She must be still mad with me. (*To desk chair.*)

JO: Don't tell me she's found out about you and that sister of
hers!

JACK: No, it's not that. At least I hope not. She's still mad
about that story I wrote about the Church
Commissioners having invested money in her brassière
company.

JO: Was it true?

JACK: What do you mean – true? Once you've said it in
print, it's difficult to make it sound like a downright lie.
You should know that by this time. It made a nice
couple of columns. I simply suggested that the Church's
one foundation might yet turn out to be an intimate
undergarment in ear-pink and mystery-blue. Her old
man was furious about it. Thank God, he doesn't know
it was me. (*Round to front of desk.*)

JO: You mean to say that your wife's family don't know that
you're Paul Slickey?

JACK: You know what her father and the Great Man feel
about each other. She'd cut my allowance if it came out.

JO: Your allowance? (*To* JACK.)

JACK: You know me, kid. I have to live big! (*Embraces her.*)

JO: But, darling, they offered you dramatic criticism on the
Globe. Why didn't you take that?

JACK: I take the theatre too seriously to be a dramatic critic.
Another thing – my old man was in the business, and I
know too much about it. It would shown in no time, and
I'd be out of a job again. Besides, you know I write
plays myself.

JO: Do you know a critic who doesn't?

JACK: That's what I mean. Too much concentrated
competition. Someday, people will find out what I'm
really worth. (*Quickly*.) Why I was just a kid when I
started. A kid out of the army when I won His Lordship's
journalism scholarship. I was tough, I'd read books – I
wanted to sleep with women! (*Kisses* JO *then returns to C*.) I
had chips on my shoulder, holes in my socks, and a hard-
hitting novel in my heart. I was a poor young reporter, and
as I stood around sloshing back other people's champagne
and eating their cold turkey and strawberries, I couldn't
forget the shabby raincoat I'd left at the door!
(DANCERS *start to gather round. A* GIRL *walks
provocatively past* JACK *and is glared at by* JO.)
Look at me now! Am I different? Have I changed? Am I
just as talented as when I started out?

> I'm just a guy called Paul Slickey, (*to downstage*)
> And the job that I do's pretty tricky,
> I'm twenty-eight years old
> And practically everybody, anybody, anything
> You can think of leaves me
> Quite, completely
> Newspaper neatly
> Quite, quite cold.
> Don't think you can fool a guy like me
> The best things in life are never free!
> Guys like us who are on the inside,
> Cannot be taken for a ride.
> We have professional ways and means
> Of getting in behind the scenes,

To put the screws on stars in jeans.
We don't need hidden television screens.
Don't think you can fool a guy like me. (*To L.*)
There's nothing that's not like ABC.
(*To R.*) Guys like us who are on the spot,
Can be relied to know what's not,
Nothing's so big we can't shrink it –
We'll blot your lot and printers'-ink it,
Whatever slop you want we'll see you drink it, (*To L.*)
We can't build your boat, but we'll make damn sure
   you sink it!

A shoddy little talent and a sawn-off imagination
Will never be allowed to go to waste,
While *we* have got our ear-holes to the heartbeat of the
   nation,
And our great big working finger on the moronic
   public taste.

So don't think you can fool a guy like me!
There's a woodworm in every family tree.
A princess or a premier can't ever come out rotten, (JO
   curtseys then goes to desk)
But an actor or a writer must be somehow ill-begotten!

In my cashmere coat and my seat at the Caprice,
The newest public wonder waits my merciful
  release.
ALL: He'll build them up in Edinburgh and Nice,
   Until he tells the public they must cease!
JACK: I'll deride, I'll be snide, have no heart, I'll be smart.
ALL: For this is the age of the common man!
  (*Enter the* COMMON MAN.)
ALL: He'll be always on the band wagon, never in the cart
   No one hates the simple little bastard like a newspaper
   can.

JACK: Who are you?

C. MAN: I'm the common man.

JACK: Whose age is this?

C. MAN: Mine.

JACK: Who looks after your interests, protects your freedom, upholds your glorious traditions and institutions?

C. MAN: You do.

JACK: Who investigates vice, denounces prominent homosexuals and Labour MPs who try to be Socialists, disturbs you about the divorce rate and the decline of your Christian heritage?

CHORUS: (*As each speaks his line, he comes downstage and stays there*)

Come off it you intellectuals!

British common sense will always prevail!

What on earth are they angry about!

We are the majority, we are the ones who matter!

Most people are jolly hopeful, thank goodness!

I believe in Britain!

Life is quite morbid enough as it is!

We are solid and so are you.

JACK: Remember our brave fighting ships.

(*Lights dim except for a spot on* TWO MEN *with naval caps and binoculars standing on desks R.*)

FIRST MAN: Thirty seconds to zero.

SECOND MAN: Well, Hawkesworth, this is it.

(*Pause.*)

FIRST MAN: Yes sir. (*Pause.*) What are you thinking, sir?

SECOND MAN: Thinking, Hawkesworth, thinking. I was just wondering if Celia had remembered to pay the boy's school fees in advance. Had a letter today. He's made the first fifteen.

FIRST MAN: Oh, really, sir? You must be pretty proud of him.

SECOND MAN: (*Thoughtfully*) Yes – I suppose I am. Decent kid. Funny the things you think about at a time like this.

FIRST MAN: Who do you fancy for the Cup Final, sir?

SECOND MAN: I've always been a Chelsea supporter myself.

FIRST MAN: I'd rather fancied Arsenal.

SECOND MAN: (*Thoughtfully*) Arsenal. Good old Arsenal. Well, maybe you're right. Hawkesworth.

FIRST MAN: Five, four, three, two, one, zero.

SECOND MAN: Number one and two! Fire!

(*There is the sound of a terrific explosion.*)

C. MAN: That's what I call entertainment.

JACK: And he's right, in his funny little heart he's right!

(JOURNALISTS *quietly exit.* JACK *and* JO *kiss in the centre.*)

TELEPHONIST: *Daily Racket* . . . Who? . . . Oh, just a moment.

(*Phone rings in the Slickey office.* JO *answers it.*)

JO: Slickey office. Oh yes, sir, just a moment. It's the great man for you.

(JACK *takes the receiver and sits on the desk.* JO *joins him and they kiss throughout the conversation.*)

VOICE: Oakham! Where have you been? Are you still working for me? I hear that Mortlake is ill again. He's only got a couple of days to make it. Get down there and see what's going on. It wouldn't surprise me if that old fraud were dead already and they were keeping it quiet! They've opened that place to the public at weekends haven't they? But I hear you've got connections with that idiot family – is that right? Well, get down there and come back with something good!

(JO *replaces the receiver, and they break away.*)

JO: What did he mean – he might be dead already?

JACK: Old man Mortlake gave away his entire estate five years ago to the family to avoid death duties. Well almost five years – five years all but about forty-eight hours. If he doesn't last out the weekend the Income Tax Man will move in and whip the lot like a fully recovered German.

(JO *lies on* JACK's *lap.*)

JO: It sounds like vintage Slickey. Go to it, boy!

JACK: Why can't someone else do it? Where's Joy?

JO: Paris.

JACK: Well, Sam then.

JO: You're a newspaperman, aren't you?

JACK: Well, Deirdre will be there. That's something I
suppose. (*Kisses* JO.)

   I'm just a guy called Paul Slickey,
(JO *sits up.*)
   And the job that I do's pretty tricky.
(JACK *stands on floor.* JO *fetches flower from desk, hat and
coat from stand and goes to* JACK.)
   I'm twenty-eight years old,
   And practically everybody, anybody, anything
(JACK *to C.*)
   You can think of leaves me
   Quite completely
   Newspaper neatly
(JO *puts the coat on* JACK's *shoulders.*)
   Quite, quite cold. (JACK *puts coat on.*)
   So don't think you can fool a guy like me.
(JO *puts carnation in his buttonhole.*)
   There's woodworm in every family tree.
(JO *presents* JACK *with his hat, and then goes off down L.*)
   A princess or a premier can't ever come out rotten,
   But an actor or a writer must be somehow ill-
      begotten.
   In my cashmere coat and my seat at the Caprice.
(*The keyhole cloth drops in behind* JACK *and the* COMMON
MAN.)
   The newest public wonder waits my merciful release.
   I'll build them up in Edinburgh and Nice,
   Until I tell the public they must cease.
   I'll deride, I'll be snide,
   Have no heart, I'll be smart,

For this is the age of the common man.
I'll be always on the band wagon, never in the cart,
No one hates the simple little bastard like a newspaper
    can.

(JACK *exits down R.*)

C. MAN: (*Produces a playbill from his pocket*) Where are we?
    Hallelujah Productions present in association with Gay
    Theatre Limited, Dame Penelope Smart and Sir Wilfrid
    Childs in *This Is Our World* by Beaumont Edner. Time:
    The Present. An early evening in April. Place: a
    bedroom in Mortlake Hall.
    (*Blackout. Music.*)

SCENE TWO

Mortlake Hall. The Marsden Room.
JACK *is sitting on a large bed. Beside him is* DEIRDRE RAWLEY.
She is wearing riding breeches and a slip. They embrace. DEIRDRE
stares up at him with soft eyes.

DEIRDRE: My darling – (*indicates clean sheets*) – I brought
    these – (*kisses him*) – to put on the bed. The visitors will
    be here very soon, gaping all over the place with their
    horrible guide books. It'll look very odd if they go into
    the Marsden Room and find the bed – well, unmade.
JACK: Isn't Cromwell supposed to have slept in it?
DEIRDRE: Yes, darling, but not last night. Have you got
    Michael's pyjamas there?
JACK: Here.
DEIRDRE: (*Clasping them to her*) Oh, isn't this sordid!
JACK: Yes, it is rather.
DEIRDRE: I'm sorry you find it sordid.
JACK: Um?
DEIRDRE: Nothing. I just hoped you'd say it wasn't sordid
    because we really love each other.

JACK: Well, that's perfectly true I suppose –

DEIRDRE: No, you're quite right. It is sordid.

JACK: (*Out of his depth*) Um!

DEIRDRE: Whether we love each other or not.

> (JACK *tries to think of something to say*.)

JACK: You didn't wake up Michael when you left?

DEIRDRE: Good lord no. Nothing wakes Michael. He just lies in bed all night, mumbling his beastly political speeches in his sleep. Oh, it's awful, I can't tell you!

JACK: Poor darling.

DEIRDRE: Do you know what he actually said to me the other night? He suddenly grabbed my shoulder in the middle of the night, and said, 'away with party labels and let us pull together'. Oh, darling what are we going to do?

JACK: (*Looking at sheets*) Make the bed I suppose. We've lain on our bed – and now we must make it.

DEIRDRE: Oh, Jack for heaven's sake – !

JACK: Sorry, darling.

DEIRDRE: It's just that these last few weeks have been so horrid what with having to be polite and casual with Lesley when she was here. I think she suspects.

JACK: I don't believe it.

DEIRDRE: What do you know about her! You're married to her.

JACK: I've known her like a rabbit knows an eagle.

DEIRDRE: (*Stands*) I think you're a little hard on her, darling. After all, she may be your wife, but she's my sister. I daresay she's been a little upset about daddy. Just like we all have.

JACK: He's all right now, isn't he?

DEIRDRE: The doctor says the crisis has passed, but one still can't be quite sure when he'll collapse again. Why, the slightest thing might –

JACK: I didn't realize you were all so fond of him.

DEIRDRE: Of course we're fond of him – and Mummy's been so terribly brave.

JACK: Yes, she's always been a brave soul.

DEIRDRE: She has. I remember how she was when they gave away India. But she's been even more wonderful this time. Why, sometimes she seems so serene. I've wondered if she's been aware of what is going on around her.

JACK: Kiss me.

(*They kiss on the bed.*)

DEIRDRE: Oh, my love, I am so afraid of it running out.

JACK: What?

DEIRDRE: Sex.

JACK: Running out? Like the coal mines, you mean.

DEIRDRE: No. I am afraid of it running out between us, you and me. I mean, suppose there really isn't anything else and it – runs out. What will happen? What will there be left for us?

JACK: We'll be in the desert and alone,
When we find our love has become overblown,
When the candle's lost its heat,
There'll be no market left for meat
We'll be in the desert and alone.

We'll be in the desert and alone,
We'll slip out of the cage and the bird will have flown,
When the springs on the bed start to rust,
There'll be nowhere to look for a crust,
We'll be in the desert and alone.

(*Kneels up.*)

The day is coming when mass diversions of the flesh will be launched like new washing powders by gigantic commercial empires in fierce competition with each other.

They'll take the 'I' and the 'Must' from our personal Lust for a voice at a microphone.

DEIRDRE: Personally, I always use 'slashit'! It doesn't merely satisfy, it actually kills desire.

> The scientists and bishops are out to make us lump it
> They'll make it much too hot for us to tackle any
>   muffin.

BOTH: We'll be in the desert and alone,
> Our song will be sung when our loins cease to groan,
> Double-crossing husbands with guilt-stricken stabs,
> Will stop fishing for trouble and making any grabs.
> Let passion go out of fashion!
> Let the groin give a last great groan.
> Let the lamb lie down with the lion
> This fulfils our grand design.
> We'll be in the desert,
> We'll be in the desert,
> We'll be in the desert and alone.

(*They kiss. Blackout.*)

SCENE THREE

The sitting-room.

DEIRDRE *is sitting on the sofa.* LADY MORTLAKE *enters through the french windows carrying an enormous bunch of flowers. She does very little else. She is in the long tradition of magnificently gracious ninnies so familiar to English play-goers. She is almost sixty and very, very handsome. She has passed through the recent 'valley of the shadow' as if it were Trafalgar Square on Armistice Night.*

LADY M.: Oh if only one didn't have to work for one's living!
> It's such a glorious day full of sunshine and flowers.

DEIRDRE: Hello, Mummy.

LADY M.: Hello, dear.

DEIRDRE: Mummy, why is it that whenever I see you, you seem to be coming in with an enormous armful of flowers?

LADY M.: Do I?

DEIRDRE: It's just that you look like one of those incomparable actresses who make incomparable entrances from the french windows, bring on half a florist's shop with them and then spend most of the play arranging them wittily and ignoring the plot.

LADY M.: I wonder if that's where I first got it from! I've never been very fond of flowers as you know. I think one learns so much from the theatre, don't you? One can watch people as they really are and behave. All doing those tiny little things that seem to be so inconsequential at first glance but which are really quite fundamental and *full* of significance.

DEIRDRE: Oh, Mummy, those bloody flowers! (*Desperately.*) Now you're going to arrange them, aren't you?

LADY M.: (*Blandly*) Why, Deirdre, is anything the matter? What dark rings you have around your eyes! Couldn't you sleep, dear? I mustn't let you hold me up this morning. I've just remembered – Mrs Giltedge-Whyte is coming here with that daughter of hers and she's sure to come early. That sort of woman always does.

DEIRDRE: Who is Mrs Giltedge-Whyte?

LADY M.: George! Where's George? Where's your uncle? Have you put him away yet?

DEIRDRE: Honestly, Mummy, I've had other things to do. Anyway I haven't seen him.

LADY M.: Well, we must find him. The visitors will be coming in very shortly and you know how he scares people away.

(TREWIN *enters. An embittered man.*)

Trewin, have you seen Mr George?

TREWIN: Not since breakfast, my lady.

LADY M.: Well, we must all look for him at once. Come along everybody!

(LADY M. *exits.*)

TREWIN: I believe he went down to the apple loft, madam.

He said he was going to write a letter to *The Times*.

DEIRDRE: Well, you'd better go down there and make sure that he's put away.

(*Enter* MICHAEL RAWLEY. *He is about thirty-five, a quintessential parliamentarian.*)

MICHAEL: Ah, Trewin, have you seen *The Times*?

TREWIN: I believe Mr George has it, sir.

DEIRDRE: He's probably made a paper hat out of it now.

MICHAEL: Well, see what you can do, Trewin.

TREWIN: Very good, sir.

(TREWIN *exits.*)

DEIRDRE: Do you know sometimes I am convinced that Trewin despises us. Do you think he's a Communist?

MICHAEL: I happen to know for a fact that Trewin has the highest possible respect and admiration for private enterprise. Why, he was a Trade Union Official for years. Until he was sent to Coventry by his workmates.

DEIRDRE: Poor Trewin, I had no idea!

MICHAEL: (*Encouraged*) He became an outcast. Even his children suffered at school.

DEIRDRE: Oh, no!

MICHAEL: Yes, the other children would call out after them in the streets.

DEIRDRE: Call out?

MICHAEL: Yes, you know the sort of thing.

DEIRDRE: No, what sort of thing. (*Passionately.*) Go on, I *want* to know!

MICHAEL: (*Hesitating*) Oh – vermin, boss crawlers, Tories, layabouts – pretty foul stuff like that.

DEIRDRE: Children can be so cruel.

MICHAEL: Trewin is like this house, Deirdre – solid! This has been a proud bastion of liberty for four hundred years. Its bulwarks are as sound as ever and I think we may safely say that the Mortlakes themselves have rendered a not unsignal service to their country in that time.

DEIRDRE: (*Seeing an onslaught coming*) Yes, all right, dear.

MICHAEL: Do you know that there has actually been a legal agitation to turn this place into the County Headquarters of the National Assistance Board?

DEIRDRE: Oh, to think that Daddy might have actually died this week and left us all on the rocks! I go quite cold every time I think of it. Just one more day to get through. That's all, and then we'll be safe.

MICHAEL: We have come a long way, my dear, but we are not yet out of the wood.

DEIRDRE: Oh, for some peace! I feel so very tired.

MICHAEL: You do look rather whacked.

DEIRDRE: What?

MICHAEL: Whacked. Perhaps you're not getting enough sleep.

DEIRDRE: (*On guard*) What makes you say that?

MICHAEL: I don't know really. After all, we always go to bed pretty early. Even more so just lately.

DEIRDRE: (*Near to hysteria by now*) Oh, my God, Michael – don't!

MICHAEL: (*Laying his hand on her shoulder*) I know how it is old girl. I really do. Stick it out at all costs, my dear, and I promise you we will win through somehow to the end.

DEIRDRE: Michael – can't you see I am crying?

MICHAEL: I know, my dear, you go ahead. Deirdre, just because I have been silent during the past few weeks it does not mean that I have been unaffected by what has been going on.

DEIRDRE: By what has been going on? You mean – you know what has been going on?

MICHAEL: Make no mistake. I am more than ready to take up the cudgels to defend what is mine.

DEIRDRE: Well I – I never thought you were so capable of feeling so strongly about – that.

MICHAEL: I can't think why, Deirdre. After all this time, you ought to know how strong my feelings are.

DEIRDRE: I'm quite taken aback, Michael. I am, really. You must admit you've never said very much to me about it – not even on our honeymoon.

MICHAEL: Nonsense. I distinctly remember discussing it practically every night. Why, I spoke of it only the other evening to the Chamber of Commerce.

DEIRDRE: The Chamber of Commerce! How could you?

MICHAEL: They were most enthusiastic I can assure you. I tell you this, Deirdre: if by chance this situation should call for desperate measures I shall not hesitate to use them. A man still has some rights left. I am prepared to go beyond the law if necessary – to the House of Lords. Thank goodness there are some representatives of the people left who have their genuine interests at heart!

DEIRDRE: Michael – before I have hysterics! *What* are you talking about?

MICHAEL: Why, the estate, of course. That's what we are discussing, isn't it?

(*Enter* TREWIN *carrying* The Times *shaped into a hat which he hands to* MICHAEL.)

TREWIN: *The Times*, sir.

MICHAEL: Thank you, Trewin.

TREWIN: I've placed your bicycle in the drive, sir. I've looked all over the house for Mr George, sir, but I can't find him anywhere.

MICHAEL: Good heavens, you don't think he's taking the money at the gates, do you? You'd better get down there at once.

(*Enter* LADY MORTLAKE.)

LADY M.: Ah, Trewin. I wish you would get someone to put that back door on. It's the first thing you notice when you come out of the North Gallery. It looks most unfortunate, especially as someone seems to have stored coal in the bathtub. People are only too anxious to jump to the wrong conclusion.

(*Exit* TREWIN.)

DEIRDRE: But surely no one could believe that – oh, how
could they!

MICHAEL: No, Mother's quite right. Let us say at least that it
is not an unjustifiable assumption.

DEIRDRE: Oh, my God! Michael do you ever *listen* to what
you're saying?

MICHAEL: Most certainly, my dear. No one pays more
scrupulous attention to the choice of words than I. The
English language and its proper usage is a matter for our
constant concern and vigilance. Oh, yes. It is a
consideration which we should all do well to bear in
mind.

It's a consideration we'd do well to bear in mind
You can play about with language in order to be
kind
The reason that we've always come through
flourishing
Is that English common sense is so astonishingly
nourishing.
Other nations less endowed
Go along with all the crowd
Using logic and statistics
When all they need is parliamentary linguistics.

It's a consideration we'd do well to bear in mind
Gladstone must have said it on the day that he
resigned
You only have to say in a lordly Oxford way without
thought or any gumption
That 'it's not an unjustifiable assumption'
Don't leave them any clues
While exploring avenues
And leaving stones unturned
If your words mean nothing, then your fingers won't
get burned.

  It's a consideration we'd do well to bear in mind
  We can safely say in a not unpompous way, blind
  Them with words! When there are things you can't
   mention.
  Say 'The Government is giving this matter its most
   grave and urgent attention'
  If they're concerned about the atom
  Simply hurl some clichés at 'em
  If a problem's in a pressing condition
  Give them words by the ton and the year – give them a
   Royal Commission.

LADY M.: Ah, they were always so useful. Freddie sat on one
once for nearly five years.

DEIRDRE: What was that about?

LADY M.: Something to do with the care and treatment of
children, I think. I know he didn't care for it. You know
how much he hates children.

MICHAEL:
  A good word nowadays is hard to find
  We have it on the highest authority
  That the present grievous anomaly
  Is unlikely to last
  We'll be caught up by the past
  Give me sound, top people's phrases
  To sing this country's praises
  I will tell you with authority
  And sensible sonority
  Angry words are being touted
  Ordinary decency is being flouted
  By an irresponsible and unrepresentative majority.

  It's a consideration we would all do well to bear in
   mind
  It is not unsensible to sound stupid to be kind
  To politicians words mean different things

You have to cheat on the roundabouts and swindle on
   the swings
When you've dropped your bombs first
And the other side has got the worst
Then your words must be strict
You're not at war, you – wait! – are in a state of armed
   conflict.
It's a consideration we'd do well to bear in mind.

This – is a consideration we would all do well to bear in
   mind
It is not unsensible to sound stupid to be kind
To politicians words mean different things
You have to cheat on the roundabouts and swindle on
   the swings
When you've dropped your bombs first
And the other side has got the worst
Then your words must be strict
You're not at war, you – wait! – are in a state of armed
   conflict.
It's a consideration we'd do well to bear in mind.

Well, the nation waits. Mustn't sit around. (*Kisses*
DEIRDRE.) See you later, Deirdre. And do try to take
things a little more calmly and clearly.

LADY M.: Take the laundry with you, will you.

MICHAEL: Of course. (*Picking up bag of laundry and* The
Times.) You see? A little intelligent discussion makes all
the difference. 'Bye now.

(MICHAEL *exits*.)

DEIRDRE: Mummy – do you think Michael is a bore?

LADY M.: I can't really say. I've never listened to him very
much. (*Perusing her correspondence*.) If only we could
afford to employ a secretary, even a temporary one.

DEIRDRE: I must say you're very brave to tackle it all on your
own, darling.

LADY M.: (*Smiling gently*) Ah, little do they know. No forty-four hour week for me. Deirdre, you seem jumpy this morning. Are you all right?

DEIRDRE: Oh, please don't make a fuss, Mummy. You know I can't bear a fuss.

LADY M.: This has been a terrible time for all of us. It's bound to take its toll. Thank heaven poor Freddie is his old self again. He wouldn't even let me help him down the stairs. He said he'd ring for Trewin.

DEIRDRE: I wish he wouldn't take such risks.

LADY M.: I think we can safely say that we have passed through our little valley of the shadow. I think Freddie had made up his mind that nothing was going to beat him.

DEIRDRE: How I wish I had his courage!

LADY M.: I know, dear, but very soon we shall be able to breathe like human beings again, which, after all, is what we really are, and then we can all go away for a nice long holiday. When I think of what this family has endured it makes me think back to that time just after the General Election in 1945.

DEIRDRE: There's no need to get morbid, Mummy. Besides all that's over and done with for good, thank heavens.

LADY M.: It isn't so easy for me to forget it, Deirdre.

DEIRDRE: Politics! God, I'm so bored with politics.

LADY M.: Well, after all, dear, you are married to a politician.

DEIRDRE: Mummy, I wish you wouldn't encourage Michael with his political career. I'd so much rather he did a job of work.

LADY M.: I suppose he could take a few directorships.

DEIRDRE: But darling, that wouldn't keep his *mind* occupied. Antonia's husband has got seventeen directorships and he hangs about the house all day making model boats. She says it's hell!

LADY M.: Naturally you're anxious for Michael to get

somewhere soon. Don't worry, he will soon enough. He's
already made an excellent start with the Young
Conservatives. They've been impressed by his initiative –
Lady Bartlett was only telling me the other day. Do you
know, they only had three tennis courts before he was
elected Chairman and then those awful hard ones at that?
And I do think you ought to remember that Michael has
been denied many of the advantages that fall to more
fortunate men.

DEIRDRE: I wouldn't call Eton, Oxford and the Guards
exactly liabilities.

LADY M.: Those things are hardly advantages, Deirdre – any
more than arms and legs are. Look at your father. I can't
tell you how badly he started off. Somehow whenever a
motion was being debated in the House he would
invariably speak against it and vote for it.
(*Enter* TREWIN.)

TREWIN: Mrs Giltedge-Whyte, my lady.
(*Enter* MRS GILTEDGE-WHYTE *and her daughter,*
GILLIAN. MRS GILTEDGE-WHYTE *is an attractive woman
in her forties.* GILLIAN *is about eighteen and rather bored.*)

LADY M.: How sensible of you to come early!
(TREWIN *exits upstairs.*)

MRS G.-W.: You really mustn't allow us to interrupt you,
Lady Mortlake. Gillian and I can go and join the visitors
looking around the house until lunch.

LADY M.: My correspondence – there's so much of it, I'm
afraid.

MRS G.-W.: Lady Bartlett tells me what sterling work you
have done for her pet charities.

LADY M.: I don't believe you've met Mrs Giltedge-Whyte,
Deirdre.

MRS G.-W.: How do you do?

DEIRDRE: How do you do?

MRS G.-W.: My daughter, Gillian –

GILLIAN: Hi!

LADY M.: Mrs Giltedge-Whyte wants me to arrange Gillian's coming-out for her.

MRS G.-W.: I am a firm believer in professionals in all things.

DEIRDRE: I believe it.

LADY M.: Well, are you looking forward to your first Season, my dear?

GILLIAN: Good Lord, no! Everyone says it's terribly boring. Still, I suppose there's no alternative really, is there?

LADY M.: I suppose it's not quite the thrill it used to be for a young girl.

MRS G.-W.: Ah! Before the war! Things will never be like that again, I'm afraid.

LADY M.: Some of us are doing our best.

GILLIAN: Do we have to pay half a crown to go round the rest of the house?

LADY M.: Only if you wish to, my dear. But you must wait until Freddie comes down. I know he'll be glad to meet you.

MRS G.-W.: I've been such a devoted admirer of your husband for many years. (*Sits.*) He has so many admirable qualities. He is a shining example to young people like Gillian here. As for these people with their envy and class hatred, hanging is too good for them. How drab and uniform they wish to make life nowadays! And now they are trying to do the same thing with death. (*Rises and crosses to piano.*) These silly people who want to do away with capital punishment are a case in point. For myself, I'm all for doing away with the rope but after all human life is sacred and we must not allow people like murderers to escape just retribution. Besides, I hope I'm a Christian.

> You may smile, my dear
> But wait until you hear
> Exactly what I feel
> This thing inside that's a part

Of my deepest, dearest heart.
(*Shes moves to C.*)
  Bring back the axe
  Listen to the facts
  The condemned man has died
  What could be more dignified
  Than his head on a plate
  In a deterrent state
  For a life to be ended
  In a manner so splendid
  Oh, why don't they bring back the axe.
(*Breaks L. to desk.*)
  Brings back the axe
  Listen to the facts
  Hanging's so sordid and mean
  The axe is so bright and so clean
  Executions become so much duller
  Oh, why don't they bring back some colour
  The Welfare State is so drab
  So give me his head on a slab
  Oh, why don't they bring back the axe.
(*Breaks upstage to C.*)
  Bring back the axe
  Listen to the facts
  I long for the roll of the drums
  As on to the scaffold he comes
  Some gentle-eyed muscular artisan
  Oh what a beautiful hunk of man
  Sex-maniacs and perverts would dread
  The British tradition of losing your head.
(*Comes back to piano.*)
  Bring back the axe
  Forget psychological quacks
  For some brute who ill-treats a dog
  Or a horsey, or pussy would flog
  I'd send a warm invitation

To his decapitation
We mustn't get soft but tough
Hanging is simply not good enough
So why don't they bring back the axe.

(*She flops her head and holds her arms at shoulder level. Then she crosses to the sofa and sits R.*)
The old ideals of duty and responsibility were so admirable, don't you think, Lady Mortlake?

LADY M.: Freddie's life has been a monument to them both. In fact, in recent years I believe that the purely spiritual values have become the only ones he prizes – or even recognizes.

(LORD MORTLAKE, *a bulky, shaky figure, obviously not very strong, and leaning heavily on* TREWIN, *starts to descend the stairs.*)
Ah, here comes Freddie now.

(LADY MORTLAKE *goes to stairs, and* MRS GILTEDGE-WHYTE *to upstage of the sofa.*)
Do be careful, Freddie. Hold on to him tightly, Trewin.

TREWIN: (*Panting*) Yes, my lady.

(LORD MORTLAKE *sees* MRS GILTEDGE-WHYTE *for the first time. He looks as if he has been shot.*)

LORD M.: Good God, Ethel!

(LORD MORTLAKE *begins to topple.* TREWIN *staggers under the overbearing strain, and* LORD MORTLAKE *falls heavily on the stairs. Blackout.*)

SCENE FOUR

In front of Mortlake Hall Gauze. Enter GUIDE *with tourists, journalists, etc.*

GUIDE: Hey, Bob, did you get any good pictures?
PHOTOGRAPHER: Sure.

SCHOOLGIRL: I'll be glad to get out of this lot.

GUIDE: Say, you really do look like a tourist.

FIRST GIRL: Let's get back to the office.

SECOND GIRL: Glad I don't live here.

GUIDE: If you are going to live in a place like that, you've got to think big.

THIRD GIRL: They say this place was built by the third Earl of Mortlake.

GUIDE: That's how you've got to be if you are going to be a success, that is.

WENDOVER: Who was the first Earl of Mortlake?

GUIDE: The first Earl of Mortlake's name was Cedric. (*He throws his hat off downstage R.*)

CHORUS: Cedric?

GUIDE: (*Coming C. Downstage*)
>Now Cedric's daddy was a chappie
>Who couldn't make a damsel happy,
>He'd hardly got his bride
>Safely tucked in by his side
>When he quickly thought it wiser
>To readjust his visor.
>Leaping from his bridal bed,
>He preferred the friendship of his squire instead.
>And leaving Cedric's virgin mum
>Set out for Jerusalem (*Moves R.*)
>Saying, 'No man wants some soppy maid
>When he can have himself a gay Crusade!'
(*The men imitate a horse rider.*)
>The years went by and Cedric's mum
>One night, feeling very glum,
>And wearing just her wedding ring
(*The 'Queen' fingers a ring on her finger.*)
>Sought the favours of the king.
>So little Cedric, by-and-by
>Became a gleam in the old king's eye.
>While his should-be-dad fought heathen Turks,

His mum received the Royal works.

(*The 'King' and 'Queen' go into a clinch downstage R.,*
covered from the front by girls.)

    Soon one medieval morn

    Little Cedric he was born,

(*'Cedric' appears downstage R.*)

    And as his dad was still away,

(*'Cedric' kneels.*)

    The king was prevailed upon to say:

    'For his daddy's honour's sake,

(*'King' knights 'Cedric'.*)

    I pronounce this bastard first Earl of Mortlake.

    He's an illegitimate little mess,

(*'Cedric' cries.*)

    But he's going to be a great success.'

(*The Mortlake Gauze flies away and the office is seen, with*
JACK *sitting at his desk and* JO *on it.*)

    If you don't want to be an unidentified mess

    You must make yourself Someone and be a success.

    You've got to understand the mechanics of success

    If you've meaning to express you must spell it like
        success.

    If you're going to impress you must pander to the
        Press,

    They'll want you to assess how much money you
        possess,

(GUIDE *crosses R. to 'Actress'.*)

    Don't feel distress if they malign your mistress,

    If they go to her address to photograph her in
        undress,

    You can forget her caress if you get your just redress,

    Fame's the best procuress, that's the Pattern of
        success,

    You've got to understand the mechanics of success.

JOURNALIST: Mr Wendover Williams sat back in his antique
    Charles the Tenth chair and remembered his humble

beginnings in a Nottingham rubber goods factory.
(WENDOVER *crosses his legs*.)
As he crossed his legs in his beautiful Savile Row suit, I
said to him: now that you are Somebody don't you feel you
are in danger of becoming a corrupt Nobody? Flicking the
ash of his personally monogrammed cigarette from his
twenty-five carat gold cigarette holder, he replied.

WENDOVER: Well, I must admit I began to wonder that
myself the other day when I bought my first five hundred
stocks in British Steel.

JOURNALIST: Already you feel that your values are changing?

WENDOVER: That's a weird question!

JOURNALIST: He stammered guiltily and called languidly for
another bottle of champagne.

WENDOVER: Hey, Mabel! Another light ale, please.
(MABEL *brings him a glass of ale*.)

JOURNALIST: And I put another question to the man who said
recently that the Tories were burglars, berks and
bloodlusters.

WENDOVER: Have a Woodbine? (*Brings out a packet*.)

JOURNALIST: Do you find, now that you have five hundred
shares in British Steel, that you are worried about
Nationalization?

WENDOVER: Should I worry?

JOURNALIST: What about your Socialist views now?

WENDOVER: If the Labour Party Nationalizes Steel, I'll be so
overcompensated I'll probably be better off than ever.
(WENDOVER *laughs, then drinks*.)

JOURNALIST: Mr Williams scowled savagely and said that as
long as he's got his money he didn't give a damn.

WENDOVER: Like a packet of crisps to go with that?
(MABEL *brings the crisps, and he tears the packet open and
eats with relish*.)

JOURNALIST: What, I said, as he tucked into his salmon at
eighteen shillings a pound, does your wife say about your
success?

WENDOVER: Well, I can't say we've ever discussed it much.

JOURNALIST: He said that he and his wife had not been on speaking terms for some time.

WENDOVER: Well, thanks for the sandwich. I must go home and get on with some work. 'Bye. Taxi! (*Takes his chair back upstage R.*)

JOURNALIST: And so, stepping into his gleaming Mercedes sports car, he left me – off to another gay round of parties. There, I thought, goes a success.

You've got to understand the mechanics of success,
(*He goes to* ACTRESS *on R.*)
> A mediocre young actress need not rely on her mattress,
> But if from acting she'll digress and stick to publicity finesse
> She can be as wet as watercress and still be a success.

(*To C.*) And you will say to the ultimate journalist, as he leans unsteadily against the bar of deceit, as he asks the questions that prevent real questions being asked, you will look up into his face and say: (*Kneels downstage C.*)

> Because of you, I am,
> Before, I never was, but now I exist,
> You drink, therefore I am.

(*He clasps* JO.)
> Every editor and every editress must be your dictator and dictatress
> Match your poor seductiveness against this goddam bitch success.

GUIDE:
> You may not have prowess but who the hell's to guess,

As long as somehow you progress, we'll give you
  happiness.
You've got to understand, you've got to understand,
You've got to understand the mechanics of success.
(*Dancers and* GUIDE *go off downstage L. and downstage R.*)

JO: Is that all? (*Rises.*)

JACK: Isn't it enough?

JO: The Honourable Penelope Cumming – well, I suppose
  she's always worth a few inches. (*Reading.*) 'Lady Poon-
  Tang, who is expecting her third baby early this summer
  . . . And a beautiful new face this season, Miss Poppy
  Tupper.' What about Deirdre Rawley?

JACK: How can I do that?

JO: If you don't, someone else will. And what about his
  lordship – old man Mortlake?

JACK: But I'm a guest –

JO: Does that usually stop you?

JACK: Not only that – I'm a relative.

JO: So?

JACK: (*Rises*) So there are such things as trust, loyalty, honest
  intentions.

JO: And?

JACK: There are excesses.

JO: There are?

JACK: There are times when you must –

JO: What?

JACK: Not exploit other people's misery. (*Sits on desk.*)

JO: I didn't notice you helping the woman in that
  factory blaze last month. We couldn't even
  publish the pictures you took. (*Moves downstage
  of desk.*)

JACK: It was a great story, wasn't it?

JO: Inhuman interest.

JACK: Endeavour isn't my line of country. You know as well
  as I do – it's just a gimmick.

JO: Then what about the Deirdre Rawley story?

JACK: You wouldn't do that to me? (*Sits on desk and cuddles up to* JO.)

JO: (*Putting arms round him*) What will you do for me?

JACK: Dinner at the Caprice?

JO: That place!

JACK: The Milroy?

JO: *You* know how to keep me quiet.

JACK: I'm married. (*Sits up.*)

JO: So is Deirdre Rawley. (*Rises.*)

JACK: Somewhere in all this chaos there must be some values I want to preserve.

JO: That's for the leader page: this united commonwealth family, our lifeline that must be preserved at the expense of British soldiers shot in the back three times a week, the treasure of family life, sexuality without sin, strengthening our ancient ties across the Atlantic, our supply of bombs and Coca-Cola to the troubled areas of the world, simple words but true, the beauty of the ceremonial, the essential spirituality of the rite!

JACK: There must be a place for me somewhere in all this!

JO: (*Sits and takes* JACK'*s head on her lap*) For both of us, darling. There's nothing in this world you can't get from me. Me and money. You do want that too, don't you? Don't you ever want to drink champagne you've paid for yourself? Don't you want to sit in the sun and write that play?

JACK: Are you kidding?

JO: Well – what about Lord Mortlake? What's the dope? Do you realize the old man's been ringing for you every ten minutes. He seems to feel that your painstaking literary style may not be finding its real outlet with a newspaper like us.

JACK: (*Sits up*) It's all right for him – playing about in the South of France with six telephones, a couple of film starlets and a cabinet minister.

JO: Don't worry, darling. (*Close to him.*) Stay with me. You can go back to Mortlake in the morning.

JACK: (*Pulls away so that* JO *falls on desk*) Why do people use their bodies as points of escape and not as objects of love?

JO: There! You'll write that hit one day. I know it. And then they'll be writing about you. (*Sits on edge of desk.*)

JACK: Imagine it – me in Paul Slickey's column. With Lady Penelope Cumming, and another beautiful new face this season, Miss Poppy Tupper. Am I as trivial as this? (*Moves to R. of desk.*)

JO: Great men are easily discredited.

JACK: Could I be great? (*Sits on desk.*)

JO: (*Softly*) I'll tell you later. I'm going to change. Don't go away.
(*Exits R.*)

JACK: You stand there to remind me
Wherever I look
You're always there behind me.
The Image with a smile so sweet
Of the thing I can't defeat.
Tell me later
Don't tell me now.
If I avoid those quiet eyes
I might learn how to be wise
So tell me later
Don't tell me now.

Our love has lost its shape.
It's an instrument
You run up to escape
The we of me
Is the longing to be free
Tell me later
Don't tell me now
Just wrap your arms around
My brain won't make a sound
But tell me later

Don't tell me now.
(*He moves downstage R.; the Keyhole cloth comes in behind him and he goes to the R. pros.*)
Why am I here?
What am I doing?
What am I thinking of?
I've got nothing but trouble brewing!
What am I living for?
I'm living from mouth to mouth
Going from your door to your door!

This matter of living
With its loving
Its pretention of giving
Its cream cheeks, its deception
Its whispered imperception
Tell me later
Don't tell me now
The lies we long to mutter
As you love me in my gutter
Tell me later,
Tell me later,
Don't tell me now.
Don't tell me now.
(*Blackout.*)

SCENE FIVE

Evening of the same day.
The stage is empty.
There is a sharp clanging, as the front doorbell rings. At the top window appears a stern little man of about sixty-five. He is dressed in eighteenth-century clothes and wears a rather rakish wig. He stops and listens intently. He chuckles, and comes downstairs. Hearing the sound of approaching voices from the hall, he hovers round the

open door, and then, as they get nearer he goes off, through the panel in the wall upstage R. TREWIN *enters with* LESLEY OAKHAM. *She is tall, very beautiful and superbly dressed.* MICHAEL *follows them.*

LESLEY: I was in the middle of a board meeting when Mother rang me . . . I couldn't get away sooner. How is he?
(*She starts to take her coat off and puts her bag on the sofa.* TREWIN *exits upstage L.*)

MICHAEL: Just about the same.

LESLEY: Who is with him now?

MICHAEL: Father Evilgreene.

LESLEY: Father Evilgreene?

MICHAEL: Good heavens, Lesley. You're looking pretty magnificent, if I may say so.

LESLEY: You may.

MICHAEL: May I – may I kiss you?
(*She inclines her head towards him and he kisses her gingerly.*)

LESLEY: Oh, do be careful, Michael!
(*She takes out a handmirror, peers at her face crossly.*)

MICHAEL: So sorry, my dear. It just seems so long since I saw you.

LESLEY: Does it? It's only five days. Pour me a drink. Who is this Father Evilgreene?

MICHAEL: (*Pours drinks at the piano*) Your father asked for him soon after he collapsed. Don't care much for the fellow myself. Looks altogether too cheerful for my taste. He's been up there since tea-time. Ate a whole trayful of fish-paste sandwiches and then sent down for some more. Astonishing appetite. Nothing of him either.

LESLEY: How long is there to go now?

MICHAEL: (*Crosses to* LESLEY *with the drinks*) Just a matter of hours, my dear. If we lose this race against time, I feel that we shall not only be betraying ourselves but the country itself and all it stands for.

LESLEY: I can't understand why you haven't got into Parliament yet, Michael. I certainly thought you would get into East Molesworth that last time. Wasn't it supposed to be a stronghold?

MICHAEL: It was. Couldn't understand it. I based almost my entire campaign on giving the H-bomb to the Germans. Half the town was destroyed in air raids during the war, so I thought they would have a particular interest in foreign policy. I'm afraid the electorate can be very irresponsible at times. You know, Lesley, I feel very strongly about all this, I can tell you. (*Sits on piano stool.*)

LESLEY: Who doesn't! I'm tired of all these miserable little people who want to take everything away from us. Something should be done about it. (*Crosses to* MICHAEL.)

I have a secret plan and because I love you
I should like to tell you all about it.
(*She pulls* MICHAEL's *arm back.*)
    This is what's happened to British aggression
    It's all concentrated on this one obsession.
(*She strangles* MICHAEL.)
    We want to screw, screw, screw the Income Tax Man,
(*She pulls him to C. and throws him on the floor.*)
    Screw him down as hard as ever we can,
    Take him, break him, scrape him, rape him,
(*She steps downstage over him.*)
    We're going to screw, screw, screw the Income Tax
        Man.

How can you describe him
He's weak and small
He is flabby and he's tall
He's hairy all over and his face is red
Just imagine him in bed, aa-aah.

(MICHAEL *rises and comes downstage.*)

MICHAEL:

    He's a canker in your ear.

LESLEY:

    How can you make him disappear?

MICHAEL:

    He's a sadistic, atavistic
    He's a cad, ask your dad.

LESLEY:

    He's contrary, he's a swishy,
    He's a disappointed lover.

MICHAEL:

    He's a man without a mother
    He's a schmo, he's a schmock.

LESLEY:

    His home life is disturbing
    He's irrevocably surburban.

   (*They face R.*)

BOTH: And think of him at school
    When he never played the fool.

LESLEY:

    When he played with little girls.

MICHAEL:

    I hope they pulled his little curls.

LESLEY:

    I'll bet he never made a noise.

MICHAEL:

    I'm sure he played with horrid toys.

LESLEY:

    And what about his wife,
    What about that poor bitch's life?

BOTH: We want to screw, screw, screw the Income Tax Man,
    Screw him down as hard as ever we can,
    Take him, break him, scrape him, rape him,
    We're going to screw, screw, screw the Income Tax
      Man.

LESLEY: (*To downstage R.*)

He is mintsy and he's chintzy.

MICHAEL: (*To downstage L.*)

He is prissy, he's a cissy.

LESLEY:

He is there, everywhere
Like a louse in your hair.

MICHAEL:

On your head,
In your bed,
In your ear, in your beer.

LESLEY:

While you're being inventive
He'll ruin your incentive.

MICHAEL:

He's longing to hear the sound
Of nineteen and six in the pound,
He's got bad breath.

LESLEY:

He's the new Black Death.

(*During the next few lines they point at the audience from L.
to R.*)

BOTH: He is watching, watching, watching every one of you,

The man we all want to screw,
Commissioner of Inland Revenue.

We want to screw, screw, screw the Income Tax Man,
(*To C.*)
Screw him down as hard as ever we can,
(*They face together.*)
Break his back, on the rack, sew him up in a sack,
Weight him down with irons,
Throw him to the lions
Before we end our Island story
Let's have our last bit of hope and glory

(LESLEY *curtseys.*)

On the day, on the wonderful day,
That we screw, screw, screw the Income Tax Man!
(*They run to sofa, collapse on to it and kiss. Then break apart.* MICHAEL *goes and sits again on the piano stool.*)

MICHAEL: Oh, I wish I knew what was going to happen to us all, Lesley. Seeing Jack here today doesn't make me feel any better. Between ourselves, I can't help feeling that he's on to us. Do you think it's possible?

LESLEY: That he knows about us? Quite. (*Rises and sits in Gothic chair.*) Jack has an odd feminine instinct about that sort of thing. He's extraordinarily passionate, you know. I think he must get it from his family. His mother is a charlady or something, I believe.

MICHAEL: Deirdre's rather the same.

LESLEY: It would be so like Jack to tread all over her with his great romantic boots on.

MICHAEL: Good heavens! (*Rises.*) You don't think that Jack and Deirdre –

LESLEY: All I know is that Jack has always suffered from excessive aspiration. There is a constant stain of endeavour underneath his emotional armpits. It throws off quite an unpleasant smell of sour ideals.

MICHAEL: Deirdre and Jack! I can't believe it. Why, I remember the very first day I met her. (*Crosses to sofa.*)

LESLEY: At the gymkhana, wasn't it?

MICHAEL: Yes, grand little horsewoman, Deirdre. And then at the Primrose League Conference late. Why, she seemed utterly sound through and through.

LESLEY: I think that's why I admire you, Michael. Even if your judgements aren't usually correct, you're so clear-sighted and level-headed.

MICHAEL: You don't think Deirdre would want a divorce, do you?

LESLEY: I've no idea. You said she was a romantic.

MICHAEL: But it's unthinkable.

LESLEY: Of course. I should never be able to talk to you in the Royal Enclosure.

MICHAEL: Good heavens, I hadn't thought of that! Lesley, what a penetrating intellect you have.

LESLEY: Simply free of bias and self-deception that's all.

MICHAEL: (*Goes to* LESLEY) My dear, if Deirdre did try to force me into a divorce, would you want to marry me?

LESLEY: I'm quite content with the present arrangement. Besides I don't really approve of divorce.

MICHAEL: I must say you'd be a magnificent asset to a man with a career like myself.

LESLEY: (*Rises downstage*) Now you are talking exactly like Jack. He always wanted me to be an asset to him in his career. You must realize, Michael, it is no longer a woman's job to make a hero of her man, but to be a hero unto herself.

MICHAEL: (*Aghast with admiration*) Ah, yes. Quite right, my dear, quite right. May I?
(*They embrace by the piano.*)
Good God, Lesley, you are a remarkable woman!
(*He kisses her again.*)

LESLEY: (*Calmly*) You're steaming my glasses.

MICHAEL: Damn your glasses!

LESLEY: Michael, really!

MICHAEL: (*Passionately*) Damn them, I say! Take them off!
(*She hesitates.*)
Take them off!

LESLEY: There are moments, Michael, when I wonder whether you are all man after all. (*She takes them off.*)

MICHAEL: By heaven, I wish I were! And you were all woman!

LESLEY: Impossible, I'm afraid.
(*They embrace again.*)
No, Michael, I couldn't marry you. Marriage is quite disgusting. For one thing it makes intimacy quite impossible. To say nothing of passion.

MICHAEL: Oh, my dear, you're so full of wit. (*Laughs.*)

LESLEY: I beg your pardon?

MICHAEL: What's that old tag? Someone's carved it on the door in the North Gallery. Ah, 'One would think from all this wit, that T. S. Eliot had written it.'

LESLEY: (*Coldly*) I think epigrams are so shoddy. Why are you staring, is my nose shiny or something?
(*She goes to her handbag, and powders her nose.*)

MICHAEL: Lesley – another thought has occurred to me. If a whisper of any scandal were to get to your father's ears, he'd move heaven and earth to change any financial arrangements he'd already made on our behalf. You realize that?

LESLEY: But surely if everything's legal, there's nothing that he can do about it at this stage?

MICHAEL: Legal be damned! He can soon get a lawyer to change that. My darling!
(*They embrace again, and a long shadow falls swiftly across the head of the stairs.*)

LESLEY: Sh!

MICHAEL: What is it?

LESLEY: There's someone on the stairs.
(*They both look up. The figure on the stairs is* FATHER EVILGREENE. *A tall, spare man with a short stubble of hair and ravaged cheekbones. The smouldering fires behind his eyes seem to have charred black-edged pits in his face. Being tall, he can look all around him without the necessity of ever having to look into anyone's face.* MICHAEL *and* LESLEY *break apart.*)

MICHAEL: Father Evilgreene! You startled us.
(FATHER EVILGREENE *shoots a long, quick glance round.*)

FATHER E.: I'm afraid *I* was lost in silent prayer.
(*Descending.*) I'm so sorry.

MICHAEL: Oh, I daresay we are a little on edge, you know. It's understandable in the circumstances.

FATHER E.: Quite.

MICHAEL: Ah – this is Mrs Oakham.

FATHER E.: Your wife's sister, isn't it? I remember you very well. (*He strokes her arm.*)

LESLEY: Do you? (*Breaks away and sits in the Gothic chair.*)

FATHER E.: Yes, very well indeed. I visited your father once before many years ago when he was going through a similar spiritual crisis. A very pretty little girl you were – yes, very pretty indeed. I believe you've made a highly successful career for yourself. What is it you do now?

LESLEY: Well, I dabble a little in show business – among other things I manage Terry Maroon.

FATHER E.: Terry Maroon? Ah yes, the – pop singer.

LESLEY: You've heard of him?

FATHER E.: Mrs Oakham, even I have heard of Terry Maroon. He seems to be a very pleasant young man. Most sincere too, I imagine.

LESLEY: Oh, he's sincere all right.

MICHAEL: She's also the managing director of the Blossoming Treasure Brassière Company.

FATHER E.: How interesting. (*Takes two long steps to LESLEY.*)

LESLEY: Oh, it is. We have placed the female bosom higher and rounder than ever before.

FATHER E.: My own efforts seem humble indeed compared with yours.

LESLEY: Not at all, Father. The Blossoming Treasure Brassière functions in exactly the same way. It does its work not by pressure, but by brilliant design.

(FATHER EVILGREENE *backs up into* MICHAEL, *who is startled*.)

MICHAEL: How is Lord Mortlake, Father?

FATHER E.: He will find his peace soon – one way or another. He is fighting very hard. In the meantime, I wonder if I might have a little food? No, don't bother, I know my way. (*Starts to exit upstage L.*)

LESLEY: I hope you've locked the wine cellar.

(FATHER EVILGREENE *turns, grins hideously, and goes.*)

MICHAEL: Lesley, that remark is in pretty bad taste.

LESLEY: Oh!

MICHAEL: One must be careful at all times not to hurt other people's feelings whatever may be your own private opinion. Only an extremely vulgar mind pokes fun at such things.

LESLEY: Of course, you're perfectly right. (*Advances seductively on* MICHAEL.)

MICHAEL: I didn't mean to sound harsh, my dear.
(*They embrace.*)
Lesley I – do you think we could –

LESLEY: If you wish.

MICHAEL: Oh!

LESLEY: We can go up to the Marsden Room.

MICHAEL: Yes, let's. (*Grabs her impulsively.*) Lesley!

LESLEY: Well?

MICHAEL: Whatever happens we must not go back to physical controls, rationing or restrictions.

LESLEY: Bring my coat with you.
(*She opens secret door – as she turns away* JACK *slips in through door, and into upstage R. arch*)

LESLEY: Hurry up.
(*A* PHOTOGRAPHER *appears at the head of the stairs.*)

MICHAEL: Oh, my God!

LESLEY: (*Pulling him after her*) Come on!
(*They exit through the secret door, which shuts behind them.*)

JACK: (*Re-entering and picking up telephone*) Give me Fleet Street, 10,000.
(*Blackout.*)

SCENE SIX

The Daily Racket. JO *is standing by Jack's desk,* JACK *by the hatstand. He looks troubled.*

JO: Hullo.

(*He doesn't answer her. She kisses him.*)

JACK: Well?

JO: Nothing. Perhaps I really enjoy being simply a variation of your usual performance. What have you been doing?

JACK: Performing, I suppose.

JO: You're in today's bulletin, by the way.

JACK: Oh!

(JO *goes up to the bulletin board and takes the bulletin down.*)

JO: Yes, you and Charlie Fudge come in for practically the lot. (*Reading.*) 'Congratulations to Charles Fudge on today's lead story. This really got over the terrible drama of an Iron Curtain intellectual's constant agony of mind and ever-present physical danger – without, incidentally, letting it be known that most of this stuff was told in complete confidence to Fudge and that this man's existence is now more in danger than ever.'

JACK: (*Takes the bulletin from her*) 'A touch of genius this, Charlie. Full marks for a piece of top-flight, political journalism told in real, human terms.'

JO: Good old Fudge!

JACK: Well, he's got a nose for it all right.

JO: He should get round to smelling himself sometime. (*She takes the bulletin from* JACK *and reads. Reading.*) 'Why nothing more on Mortlake? (*Moves to upstage of desk.*) Somebody will scoop us on this, if someone doesn't take it out and get stuck in!' What's the matter?

JACK: I'm just wondering why do I have to compete.

JO: You've got to.

JACK: Couldn't I be something else? (*Sits on desk.*)

JO: Why do you concern yourself with everybody else – let them do the worrying.

(*Exits R. The lights fade out except for a spot on* JACK. JACK *moves downstage R.*)

JACK: Why am I here?

What am I doing?
What am I thinking of?
I've got nothing but trouble brewing.
What am I living for?
I'm living from mouth to mouth
Going from your door to your door.
(*Music changes.*)
There must be something I can do,
Something to believe,
Something better, something matters,
There's someone to grieve,
Somewhere better, somewhere finer,
There must be something I can do!
(*The lights come up.*)
Ah, well! Who cares! Who cares!
Who the devil cares!

CHORUS: They do! (*Point out front.*)

JACK: Who do?

CHORUS: They do! (*Point out front.*)

JACK: They?

CHORUS: Them! (*Point out front.*)

JACK: Them? Who's them?

CHORUS: The ones we're not!

JACK: Who's that?

CHORUS: Him!

   (*From their centre they push out the* COMMON MAN. *He is reading* The Daily Racket.)

C. MAN: Pardon me! I'm not one of them, thank you very much. (*Exits downstage L.*)

JACK: Well, who is he?

   (*All accuse the audience.*)
      Them! It's them!
      It's not us, it's not you
      But it's them!

CHORUS:
      Them! Them! Them! Them!

JACK: This island of phlegm,
It's our staple apology,
Our apophthegm,
It's them! Them!

CHORUS:
Sh! Sh! Sh!
Sh! Sh! Sh!
We must think it, we must say it,
In our pubs we'll never nay it,
Don't try to write it,
You're never going to fight it!
(*Dance.*)

JACK: Them! Them! Them!
Sing a daily requiem,
They may be half unconscious
But it's not our problem
It's them! It's them! It's them!

CHORUS:
Sh! Sh! Sh! Sh! . . .
(*They go off L. in line.* JACK *is left alone in the centre of the stage, facing upstage, as the tabs fall.*)

ACT TWO

SCENE SEVEN

The offices of The Daily Racket. SECRETARY *and* SEVERAL
JOURNALISTS.
The sound of a linotype operator.

JO: (*On phone*) No – wait a minute. Jack – don't hang up yet.
The old man's going crazy for something from Mortlake.
And so am I, darling. What on earth are you doing down
there? What . . . Is she? Behaving like Lady Chatterley
on Ice? Well, she's your wife . . . Who's coming?
Deirdre? Oh, all right then. But you'd better ring back
with something soon . . . (*Hangs up. To* LADY
JOURNALIST.) Lady Chatterley on Ice? Perhaps I should
go down there and see what's going on.

LADY JOURN.: Why don't we all go down? I know Deirdre
awfully well. And, of course, I've known Lesley for
years.

JO: Ladies, ladies, think of your editions!
Edna Francis-Evans:
Write of politicians' wives
Important in your readers' lives.

Cornelia Tuesday:
Some crackling observations
On the US Air Force stations.

Belgravia Lumley:
What about this New Line?
Can't you say it's *not* divine?

And you – Ida Merrick:
When you write about the heart
Your wit is positively tart!

Ladies, ladies, think of your editions
Of a spanking line about boring social missions.

Edna Francis-Evans! Here!
Cornelia Tuesday! Here!
Belgravia Lumley! Here!
And you – Ida Merrick! Oh, here, I suppose.
Ladies, ladies, remember your best position.

JO *with* SIX SMART LADY JOURNALISTS:
Put it on ice!
On ice! On ice!
If it's cool
It's sure to be nice
If it's dreary
Pretty weary
The whole thing looks better on ice!

Put it on ice!
On ice! On ice!
If you're clever
It's cheap at the price
If you want to skate
On your fate
Put yourself bang on the ice!

Put it on ice!
On ice! On ice!
If you're bright
You can cut you a slice
Don't give yourself trouble
Let the others bubble
Keep your nose clean on the ice!

(MEN JOURNALISTS *enter downstage L. Ballet.*)

ALL: Put it on ice!
        On ice! On ice!
        Being hot's
        An unfashionable vice
        If you let off steam
        You're no maiden's dream.
JO: Why don't you get a licence for that
        Thing and walk it round the park!
ALL: Put the whole thing back on the ice!
    (*Passionate* MEN JOURANLISTS *dance with freezing* LADY
    JOURNALISTS.)
LADIES:
        Please do not sneeze
        We're in a deep freeze
        Just take our tips
        Those burning lips
        Give us the pips.

JO *with* SIX SMART LADY JOURNALISTS *and* MEN
JOURNALISTS:
MEN: Get in those bunks
        You icy chunks.
LADIES:
        Stand back you punks!

        Put it on ice!
        On ice! On ice!
        With the women
        Don't let's tell you twice
        When you write your column
        Be sparkling not solemn
        Pack yourself
        Wrap yourself
        Stack yourself
        Up to your freezing eye lashes in ice!
        In ice!

JO'S VERSE:
> Ladies, Ladies, think of your Editions!
>
> Edna Francis-Evans;
> Tell us what you think of men,
> How to give them hell – and when!
> Cornelia Tuesday;
> Help us out of sexual muddle,
> What's the newest way to kiss and
> Cuddle?
>
> Belgravia Lumley;
> Write something about Modern Art,
> Bitchy, brittle, awfully smart.
> And you – Ida Merrick;
> However things may worsen,
> You'll always be a Fun Person.
>
> Ladies, ladies, think of your
> Editions!
> Sink in your finger-nails, make
> Your incisions!

(*Cha-cha-cha Dance. Keyhole and blacks drop in during dance. Keyhole and blacks away.*)

SCENE EIGHT

Mortlake Hall.
MRS GILTEDGE-WHYTE *at desk and* GILLIAN *in Gothic chair.*

MRS G.-W.: If you're bored, Gillian, I'm sorry, but I'm afraid I really have no patience with you. I could have made all the arrangements for your coming-out with Lady Mortlake on my own quite easily.

GILLIAN: I just thought there might be a chance of meeting someone who could get me a job.

MRS G.-W.: As an actress? Honestly, Gillian, if I had thought you wanted to be an actress I would never have sent you to the Academy of Dramatic Art.

GILLIAN: Well, it doesn't seem much fun sitting about here waiting for the old boy to kick it off.

MRS G.-W.: Don't be unfeeling, Gillian. Besides, we don't know that Lord Mortlake is going to die at all. Oh, I think it's magnificent the way these old families are battling on. (*She rises.*) You see, Gillian, my dear, you can't destroy the really worthwhile things. Somehow they've a way of winning through in the end. No, I don't think the Mortlakes will let us down.

GILLIAN: I suppose it will be one in the eye for the Government if he does hang on.

MRS G.-W.: And they deserve it. They deserve much more.

GILLIAN: You do sound a bit barbaric sometimes.

MRS G.-W.: I'm afraid, like so many people, you're inclined to be sentimental about these things, Gillian. I've noticed it before. Ever since we had to eat your bunnies during the war.

GILLIAN: Oh, Mummy, don't!

(*Enter* GEORGE *still dressed in eighteenth-century costume through the secret panel.*)

MRS G.-W.: Oh! Good evening.

(GEORGE *nods.*)

I don't think we've been introduced.

(GEORGE *takes out a snuff box and taps it.*)

GEORGE: (*Offering box*) Snuff?

MRS G.-W.: No, thank you, I never take it.

GEORGE: Just as well. I haven't got any.

(*Exit* GEORGE *up stairs.*)

GILLIAN: Why do you suppose he dresses like that?

MRS G.-W.: Surely it's symbolic!

GILLIAN: He's strictly from Cubesville. (*She rises to piano.*) I wonder if they've got any records for that thing. Why, there's a whole stack of Terry Maroon's here. How marvellous!

(*A bent figure staggers into view at the top of the stairs. It is* LORD MORTLAKE. *He leans heavily against the staircase and glares down.*)

MRS G.-W.: Why, Lord Mortlake, what are you doing out of bed?

LORD M.: Are you still here?

MRS G.-W.: Is there anything we can do for you?

LORD M.: No, damn it. Help me down these stairs.

MRS G.-W.: But –

LORD M.: Oh, don't argue!

MRS G.-W.: Well, you really must be careful. Lady Mortlake would be most upset if she were to see you.

LORD M.: I'll bet. The whole crew of 'em too. Just give me a hand down and shut up. And tell that girl to go.

(GILLIAN *moves upstage to* MRS GILTEDGE-WHYTE.)

MRS G.-W.: This is my daughter Gillian.

LORD M.: Oh, is it?

MRS G.-W.: She's pretty, don't you think?

LORD M.: Too blasted pretty.

MRS G.-W.: Gillian, you'd better go into the library. You can take your Mr Maroon with you if you like.

GILLIAN: Oh, all right.

(*Exit upstage L. with records.*)

LORD M.: All right, all right. I'll sit here. (*Both sit on staircase.*) Now, Ethel, what are you doing here? What do you want?

MRS G.-W.: Why, I came to see you, Freddie. Aren't you pleased to see me after all these years?

LORD M.: Why can't you leave me to die in peace!

MRS G.-W.: You needn't worry, Freddie. I have no intention of telling anyone about us.

LORD M.: Thank heaven for that! I need hardly say that it was a great shock seeing you here this morning. I have to be so extremely careful. So many people look up to

me, Ethel. Not only my family, but people who matter –
the Press, the leaders of Church and State. It hasn't
been easy, believe me; but after all one must believe in
something. Otherwise there's nothing left except the
transient joys of personal pleasure. (*Eyeing her warily.*)

MRS G.-W.: How proud you look in your pyjamas, Freddie!
You never used to wear pyjamas. (*Puts her hand on his
knee, and he hastily removes it.*)

LORD M.: Why, only a few weeks ago I started an influential
movement to step up the stage censorship. There is
altogether too much laxity –

MRS G.-W.: But you've had your share of triumphs,
remember. There were those three publishers and that
obscene libel case.

LORD M.: (*Cheering up a little*) By George, yes! (*Rises.*) That
was an achievement of which British Justice can be
justly proud. We got 'em twelve months apiece.

MRS G.-W.: Such respectable men, too. (*Rises.*)

LORD M.: Marriages are breaking up all over the place.
Separations are commonplace. In life, in literature and
yes – in the drama – adultery is regarded as a jest and
divorce as a mere unimportant incident. (*Looking her up
and down again.*) There is far too much nonsense talked
in this quack kind of psychology.

MRS G.-W.: (*Putting her hand on his arm*) You're so right!
What we need is a return to common sense.

LORD M.: (*Admiringly*) Gad, Ethel, you haven't changed
much.

MRS G.-W.: Haven't I, Freddie?

LORD M.: As damned attractive as ever. That girl who was in
here just now – is she – ?

MRS G.-W.: Yes, Freddie, our daughter. (*To desk.*)

LORD M.: Good heavens, what a careless, pleasure-loving cad
I was.

MRS G.-W.: Not at all, you were most serious and after all it
was hardly your fault.

LORD M.: Of course it was my fault! (*To C.*) Whose fault do you think it was – the Lord Chamberlain's?

MRS G.-W.: (*To* LORD M.) What I meant was, that the young people nowadays have access to knowledge which was denied to us – knowledge which I believe they take advantage of quite freely.

LORD M.: Please don't mention it to me. (*Sits R. of sofa.*)

MRS G.-W.: Ah, Freddie, what a pity it is that more is not said of – (*sits on sofa*) – the inner and more beautiful side of marriage. Oh, it seems so strange to be sitting beside you again!

LORD M.: Ethel!

MRS G.-W.:

> I want to hear about beautiful things
> Beautiful things like love
> I want to hear about happy marriages
> Without complications and just baby carriages
> I want to fly to the moon
> And hear about June
> And dinners at Maxims and Claridges.
>
> I want to hear about beautiful things
> Beautiful things like love
> I don't want to hear of emotional wrecks
> Of people who practise peculiar sex
> I want my love to be pure
> My income secure
> I don't wish to wallow in a spiritual sewer.
>
> I want to hear about beautiful things
> Beautiful things like love
> I want to hear the sweet breeze in the trees
> I want to hear about the birds but leave out the bees.
> I don't care if you think it's absurd
> If there's never a dirty word
> I want to hear only nice things please.

I want to hear about beautiful things
Beautiful things like love
I don't want to know about fornication
But only of people who still keep their station
I want to fly on a cloud
And so to hell with the crowd
I'm content to know the word by inclination
I want to hear about beautiful things.

I want to hear about beautiful things
Beautiful things like love
I want to hear about happy marriages
Without complications and just baby carriages
I want to fly to the moon
And hear about June
And dinners at Maxims and Claridges.

(*They end up on sofa.*)

LORD M.: Ethel, what is it you want out of me? You're not trying to get me to change my will like Evilgreene?

MRS G.-W.: Is he indeed? In his favour?

LORD M.: More or less, I suppose.

MRS G.-W.: How can you trust such a man, Freddie? A stranger. What we need, Freddie, is a square deal – Gillian and myself, I mean.

LORD M.: Who? Ah, yes, Gillian. What does your husband think about Gillian?

MRS G.-W.: He adores her. Of course he thinks – oh, you've made him very happy, Freddie!

LORD M.: He must be about the only person I have made happy. You know, you're a good woman, Ethel – damn fine woman. I've always thought so. We'll have to see what we can do for you.

MRS G.-W.: I'm so glad you see my point, Freddie – now don't you think you'd better be getting back?

LORD M.: Yes, perhaps I had.

(*They rise.*)

MRS G.-W.: Now, you must let me help you.

LORD M.: No, it's all right. I feel better. Much better. You've made me feel better, Ethel.

MRS G.-W.: Have I really, Freddie? You don't know how glad I feel. Shall I help you back to bed?

LORD M.: Yes. Yes. If you would my dear. Looking at you now I feel a new man. Like I was twenty years ago.

MRS G.-W.: Dear, dear Freddie!

(*They embrace fiercely.*)

Sh! Someone's coming.

LORD M.: By George, Ethel, I'll show the lot of them.

(*He grabs her by the hand and they disappear up the stairs.* DEIRDRE *and* JACK *enter through the panel.*)

DEIRDRE: What about Michael and Lesley? Oh, I think it's disgusting. It isn't love at all, it's an assault course.

JACK: Do you think they saw us?

DEIRDRE: I shouldn't think they could see anyone. Not Michael, certainly. And in the Marsden Room too! Michael of all people – and I thought he was such a bore! How can people deceive you like that?

JACK: And Lesley, too. She seemed to be all woman up there with him. Lesley of all people! That superb creature who stares at you from the pages of glossy magazines. My wife – the new feminine ideal. A long slink of classical meanness. Up there carrying on like Lady Chatterley on Ice.

DEIRDRE: Do you think they're suffering?

JACK: Depends what you mean, I suppose.

DEIRDRE: Have they suffered like we have?

JACK: I doubt it. Not Lesley, anyway. She's as tough as a goat.

DEIRDRE: Michael's always been very fond of goats.

JACK: I'm sure Lesley won't want a divorce. If there was a way out I'd take it, believe me.

DEIRDRE: But Jack – darling – I am right, aren't I? We can't go on after what has happened.

(Enter GEORGE to top of stairs with fishing-rod. He is dressed in tweeds.)

JACK: Yes, you're quite right. Oh, what it must be to be a woman!

DEIRDRE: Oh, that's wonderful! When I think of the easy time you men have compared with the appalling emotional toil that we women –

(Enter MICHAEL and LESLEY upstage L.)

MICHAEL: I say, what's going on?

(JACK breaks upstage.)

DEIRDRE: *(Very cold)* Jack is complaining that he is worn out with the strain of being a man.

LESLEY: You do surprise me! *(Sits in Gothic chair and leafs through a* Vogue. *Enter GILLIAN upstage L. and goes to the desk still with the records.)*

GILLIAN: Do you mind if I play these records in here? That portable in the library sounds dreadful.

MICHAEL: Well, I shouldn't if I were you, my dear. We mustn't forget that his lordship is having a strenuous time of it up there.

(Enter LADY MORTLAKE upstage L. with FATHER EVILGREENE.)

LADY M.: I thought I'd never find a vase. Fortunately Father Evilgreene found one for me. He seems to know where everything is.

FATHER E.: It's time I returned to his lordship. I expect he will be needing me by now. Please excuse me.

(He hands vase to LADY MORTLAKE. He smiles at the air above the heads of the company and goes upstairs. DEIRDRE crosses and sits on the sofa beside MICHAEL.)

LADY M.: Ah, well, I'm quite sure Freddie wouldn't want us to sit around being depressed. Why don't we make up a little game of bridge? Would you like to play, Gillian?

GILLIAN: No, thank you.

GEORGE: *(Crossing over to JACK)* I happened to overhear what you said just now.

JACK: What?

GEORGE: You know – all that stuff about wishing you were a woman.

JACK: What about it?

GEORGE: (*Confidentially*) I have a friend in Harley Street who's made the most extraordinary advances in that kind of thing.

JACK: What kind of thing?

GEORGE: (*Rises.*) All a matter of injections, dear boy. You must come up to my little lab. Got a whole case of the stuff up there. Just a little stab and phtt! Nearly tried it myself once, but between you and me I've never cared much for the female body. But unsightly if you understand me. Can't be compared with – well – mangoes for instance. Ever tried 'em?

JACK: What?

GEORGE: Mangoes.

JACK: What are you talking about?

GEORGE: Oh, you've missed something, believe me. Makes my mouth water just to think of them. Lovely pickled, too. Oh, yes, you must come down with me to the stables sometime. (*To piano and sits on top of it.*)
(*Enter* TREWIN *upstage L.*)

TREWIN: (*To* LESLEY) A Mr Maroon is here asking for you, madam.

GILLIAN: Not Terry Maroon? (*Rises.*)

LESLEY: Oh, dear, I suppose he's come down all this way just for me to go through his new number with him. He's quite helpless on his own. Very well, Trewin, you'd better send him in.

LADY M.: Who is Mr Maroon?

JACK: Terry Maroon is Britain's number one singing star. The new male, tamed and delivered – (*Pointing to* LESLEY) – by the new female. He'll come in any moment brushing the floor with his knuckles. (*To* LESLEY.) Is he house-trained too?

(*Enter* TREWIN *with* TERRY MAROON. *Britain's number one singing star needs no description.*)

TREWIN: Mr Terry Maroon, madam.

TERRY: Hi, everybody!

(*There is a violent crash from upstairs. All turn and look up.*)

MICHAEL: My God!

DEIRDRE: Oh! It's the end!

JACK: (*To bottom of stairs*) What is it?

FATHER E.: (*At top window*) His lordship has locked himself in his room.

MICHAEL: We'll come up.

FATHER E.: No, stay where you are!

MRS G.-W.: (*Offstage*) Oh, Freddie!

(*There is a pause, then a mighty noise of splintering wood, a woman's scream and then silence. Presently* FATHER EVILGREENE *returns to the top of the stairs and looks down at them gravely. He nods his head, confirming their fears.*)

GEORGE: What an interesting way to end up – in bed with another man's wife!

(*Blackout.*)

SCENE NINE

FATHER EVILGREENE *with small requiem chorus and mourning ballet.*

Throughout his plain number the chorus respond with 'You Can't Get Away With It' in the appropriate places.

FATHER E.:

What shall be said to the hipsters when they cease to
flip and are silent?
When the false prophets sing no more and lie down
with their bankers for ever?

CHORUS:

> 'You Can't Get Away With It.'

FATHER E.:

> What shall be the crazy phrases on the brass plate at
> the end?
> Listen and tremble all you swinging chicks and broads.

CHORUS:

> 'You Can't Get Away With It.'

FATHER E.:

> When the last flip comes who shall be hip still?
> They who are hung up now shall not hang on when the
> time comes.
> It will surely bug you when there is no man to hug,
> and no tea to push. There shall be no Zen to the left
> of you nor throne to the right of you.

CHORUS:

> 'You Can't Get Away With It.'

FATHER E.:

> Death is a round hole which hath no place for squares.
> Then you will go, man, truly you will go, and you will
> be bugged for ever.

CHORUS:

> 'You Can't Get Away With It.'

FATHER E.:

> For this is the swinging truth. If you dig all things, you
> shall reap no harvest.
> For this is the crazy truth. You can't get away with it.
> For this is the swinging truth. If you dig all things, you
> will reap nothing at the end.

> (*Mourning ballet, with the family, dancers and* JO.
> *Blackout.*)

LADY MORTLAKE *is seated at her desk, replying to her correspondence on black-edged notepaper. From the hall outside comes the
sound of* TERRY *softly singing his latest hit.* DEIRDRE *is leaning
against a chair, her back to the audience.*

DEIRDRE: I'm sorry, Mummy, but I'm afraid I just can't
   believe in a God any longer. When you find yourself
   called upon to pay tax at nineteen and sixpence in the
   pound, the idea of a Divine Providence suddenly seems
   rather laughable. And how much longer is Father
   Evilgreene going to stay here?
LADY M.: Oh, he's leaving to take up some appointment
   tomorrow.
DEIRDRE: I'm sure he put Daddy up to making that utterly
   stupid will.
LADY M.: I don't see why you should call it utterly stupid,
   Deirdre. It merely says that the income will be stopped,
   and diverted to a suitable charity of Father Evilgreene's
   choice –
DEIRDRE: We all know the name of that charity!
LADY M.: If either you or Lesley should divorce your
   husbands, or vice versa. I don't see how it can affect
   either of you. It's simply a moral precaution. I expect
   your father was anxious to protect you both. It's so like
   him. Poor, dear Freddie!
DEIRDRE: It seems to me that Daddy had a genius for
   finding reasons for not doing things.
LADY M.: Of course, dear. That is the very basis of all
   religions and no one understood it better than your
   father.
DEIRDRE: Oh, Mummy, how can you be so calm! What are
   you doing, anyway?
LADY M.: I am replying to Lady Bartlett's letter of
   sympathy. I have also told her that she can, of course,

still depend on my assistance with next month's hunt ball.

DEIRDRE: You're still going!

LADY M.: Most certainly. The everyday business of living must go on just the same, Deirdre – Freddie would have wished that.

DEIRDRE: It isn't as though we shall even be able to afford to hunt any more.

LADY M.: I think we have all learnt to rough it in the last few years, and it should stand us in good stead. Anyway, we need not give up hunting altogether. It's a democratic sport, above all things – we can still follow in the car. Oh, we'll manage somehow, my dear. Thank goodness Mrs Giltedge-Whyte has agreed to pay twice my usual fee for sponsoring young Gillian!

DEIRDRE: It's about the least she could do, in the circumstances.

LADY M.: You must curb that tongue of yours, Deirdre. Father Evilgreene assures me that when he went into your father's room, she was merely helping him back into bed.

DEIRDRE: 'Any charity of his choice'!

LADY M.: As both you and Lesley are quite happily married. I really don't see that there's any harm done.
(*Enter* JACK.)

DEIRDRE: Where have you been?

JACK: Oh, trying to work things out.

DEIRDRE: I know. So have I.

LADY M.: Well, I must leave you children to yourselves. I haven't seen George since the funeral. I do hope he isn't up to something. (*Exit.*)

DEIRDRE: But what are we going to do about it? We can't get married. For one thing, I know that Michael would never agree to a divorce. He's too much like Daddy for that. Besides, he's got his beastly career to consider, apart from the money.

JACK: Lesley wouldn't agree either. She's too mean to give up your dad's money, anyway.

DEIRDRE: How could Daddy be so cruel!

JACK: And when I think of all the money she's making out of that lout in there! Listen to him! (*Indicating the direction of* TERRY's *voice.*)

(*Enter* LESLEY *and* MICHAEL.)

LESLEY: I can't think why you should object. At least it saves you from having to buy your wife's clothes. And I have such expensive tastes. Most men would be delighted, I'm sure. Wouldn't you, Michael?

MICHAEL: Why yes, I suppose so.

JACK: Listen to that timid, emasculated male!

MICHAEL: Now look here, you be careful what you say!

JACK: We're all being slowly deflowered – deflowered by the female!

DEIRDRE: Deflowered! Honestly, Jack you do exaggerate!

JACK: Oh, no I don't.

MICHAEL: Come, my dear fellow, this is no way to talk to the ladies.

JACK: (*As* TERRY *reaches a crescendo.*) Do you hear that nasal blubbering about little flowers and watching new-born babies cry? Of loving you, and no one but you? Baby, you're all mine, all mine through all eternity? That so-called man in there is making two thousand pounds a week – thanks to my wife – for what? For emptying the slop buckets of modern love into a microphone, for crawling and cringing before the almighty tyranny of the bosom.

MICHAEL: I say . . .

JACK: . . . for moaning his snivelling hymns to the female figure.

DEIRDRE: Do you mean to say that you don't believe in – well, love, any more?

JACK: No, Deirdre – this has nothing to do with you and me.

DEIRDRE: Of course it has everything to do with you and me! Oh, Jack, how could you!

JACK: Oh, for heaven's sake, Deirdre, don't take all I say personally! (*As he shouts at her irritably, her face puckers slowly into tears.*) There's no reason why it should effect you and me. I'll tell you we'll work it out somehow.

DEIRDRE: How can we possibly work it out! I think I could die!

JACK: All this business has upset my system.

LESLEY: His masculine sensitivity he means.

DEIRDRE: My poor darling! Put your head in my lap.
(*He does so gratefully.*)
There! (*And she strokes his forehead tenderly.*)

LESLEY: You see – there are still some of the old-fashioned kind of women left around. Poor Jack thinks I'm cold, don't you, darling?

JACK: (*Viciously*) You're like the school lavatory seat in December!

MICHAEL: Oakham, only a cad would say a thing like that to a lady! Get up!

DEIRDRE: Leave him alone, you bully!

MICHAEL: Well, really!

DEIRDRE: (*Threateningly*) Do you want a black eye?

MICHAEL: Well, I'm dashed if I really know what this is all about. I'm just a plain, ordinary chap, as you all know, and it seems to me that we have a jolly ticklish situation here. Damn it all, Oakham, let's be frank. It's bad enough just one of us carrying on with the other's wife, but both of us doing it is pretty damned indecent. I'm not a prig, I hope, but I have to say that I'm shocked. Yes, shocked!

JACK: I suppose you don't want to marry my wife, by any chance?

MICHAEL: Lesley and I have discussed the matter, and we have both decided against it. Lesley feels that my own career would clash with hers, and I respect her point of view. After all, she is a highly accomplished woman, and we must recognize the fact that woman – ah – is taking a new place in our rapidly changing society. We men will have to review our position, and – ah – bring it into line with present-day developments.

DEIRDRE: I shall have to do him soon.

MICHAEL: As far as this question . . .

(*Enter* GEORGE, *carrying a small leather bag. He stares at the company, particularly at* JACK *with his head still in* DEIRDRE's *lap. He starts to go up the stairs.*)

GEORGE: (*To* LESLEY) Shan't be long.

LESLEY: All right, George.

(*Exit* GEORGE.)

I believe there may be a solution to all this.

DEIRDRE: Meaning?

LESLEY: Michael and I have just seen something very remarkable, haven't we, Michael?

MICHAEL: What? Oh yes, indeed. Most extraordinary!

LESLEY: George has just taken us down to the stables.

DEIRDRE: Well?

LESLEY: It seems that George is really on to something pretty important. So important that it takes one's breath away.

DEIRDRE: What is it, for heaven's sake?

LESLEY: You know Robert?

JACK: The hunter? I know that vicious devil all right!

LESLEY: Well, the vicious devil is as gentle as a lamb, and from now on, it looks as though we'll have to call him Roberta.

DEIRDRE: Roberta? What *do* you mean?

LESLEY: I mean that old Robert has become a rather flirtatious mare, and that your mare, Christine, has become a particularly overpowering stallion.

DEIRDRE: I don't believe it!

JACK: Well, I do. George is capable of anything. He should be in Ealing Films.

LESLEY: Quite briefly, they have both changed their sex. Isn't
that correct, Michael?

MICHAEL: Yes, it's quite correct, Deirdre. I couldn't believe
my eyes – but there it was.

DEIRDRE: But how did it happen?

JACK: Was it this injection he was talking about?

LESLEY: It was. And we both watched him administer it.

MICHAEL: No question of trickery, I assure you. I don't think
I'm easily taken in by these things, and I watched very
closely indeed.

LESLEY: It was staggering.

MICHAEL: Bit embarrassing, too.

LESLEY: Staggering and most exciting!

JACK: But how did they react? Wasn't there any discomfort?

LESLEY: None at all. Whole thing took a matter of minutes. I
tell you, it's revolutionary! Just think of it! After all, it
had to come sooner or later. We all know that the line
dividing male and female is little more than a vague
shadow.

DEIRDRE: Personally, I've always found it rather obvious. Am
I being terribly old-fashioned?

LESLEY: Now George has got enough of his stuff up in that
little room of his to enter all this year's Derby runners for
the Oaks as well.

DEIRDRE: Poor Christine! Well, I think it's disgusting.

LESLEY: Do you? I'm sure Jack doesn't agree with you.

JACK: What are you getting at?

LESLEY: I should have thought it was plain. If men have
become sloppy, boneless and emasculated, it's their own
fault entirely.

MICHAEL: I say, it is a bit strong, old girl! I never thought for
a moment that you felt like that about us chaps. I mean,
then – well, why did you –

LESLEY: Have an affair with you, Michael? Because, my dear,
I still have a great many instincts of the purely biological
female.

MICHAEL: Ah – yes. Quite.

DEIRDRE: I want to know what you are leading up to.

LESLEY: Simply this. Firstly, we are all, I think, what might be described fairly accurately as maladjusted.

MICHAEL: Good heavens! You don't mean that we're not – normal!

LESLEY: You're a politician, Michael, and what you want, therefore, is power. And power, political power, like everything else, is passing into the hands of the women. Look to the future, Michael. Don't fight new battles with an old weapon! If you want to make certain of being a success in politics, there is only one realistic solution: become a woman!

MICHAEL: Lesley! You don't mean change our sex!

LESLEY: Certainly.

MICHAEL: (*Appealing to the others*) I don't know what you think, but that seems a pretty insulting thing to say to a chap. Why, if another chap made a suggestion like that to me, I'd knock him down!

JACK: Quite right – punch him on the nose!

MICHAEL: I'm not a fool, you know – I've been in the Army!

LESLEY: Don't you see, Michael, if you and Jack were to change your sex, your marriages would be naturally annulled. You would be free to do as you like – and without losing any money by having to go through with a divorce.

MICHAEL: I suppose you make it sound pretty plausible, Lesley. I can only say this – I shall give it my earnest attention. I can't say any more than that at the moment.

LESLEY: You could make the change as often as you liked. You could be a woman all the week, and a man at the weekends, for instance.

DEIRDRE: No, if he marries me, he won't!

JACK: Or a woman at the weekend and a man all the week. A –

woman at the weekend and a man all the week

Two days as Madame Pompadour and five as an
    Ancient Greek.

You could swop your pretty bras

For a moustache with handlebars

And be a woman at the weekend and a man all the
    week.

ALL: A woman at the weekend and a man all the week.

JACK *and* LESLEY:

    We could start the most exciting and exclusive clique.

MICHAEL *and* DEIRDRE:

    If we're too tired when to go to bed

    We could change our trews instead

    And be a woman at the weekend and a man all the
        week.

ALL: A woman at the weekend and a man all the week.

DEIRDRE:

    The thought of putting horrid shaving lotion on my
        cheek

    Of giving up my perfume by Dior

    For some stuff called 'Saddle Sore',

    I think it's positively ghastly – all this sexual hide and
        seek!

  (*To* JACK.)

    I suppose *you* like the idea?

JACK:

    What?

DEIRDRE:

    Well, of being a woman at the weekend

ALL: . . . and a man all the week!

LESLEY:

    Broad shouldered and belligerent

JACK *and* MICHAEL:

    With curves and furs and Cadillacs to keep us meek.

LESLEY *and* DEIRDRE:

    You would never have the fag

Of dressing up in drag
You'd be a woman at the weekend.

JACK *and* MICHAEL:
   . . . and a man all the week!

ALL: A woman at the weekend and a man all the week
We'd all know what's what – we'd have had our
   weekly peek
From our heads to our toes
We'd give seven different shows
As a woman at the weekend and a man all the week!
All the week! All the week!

(*They end up with* JACK *and* MICHAEL *sitting on the sofa,*
DEIRDRE *perched on its downstage arm, and* LESLEY *sitting
in the Gothic chair.*)

LESLEY: Well, what do you say?

JACK: And what about you?

LESLEY: Me?

JACK: (*Goes to* LESLEY) Yes, you. Are you as anxious as I am
to discontinue our association?

LESLEY: (*Goes to sofa*) Well, darling, you must admit it is
getting rather dreary, isn't it?

JACK: Look, I'll tell you what I'll do. I'll agree to this. (*Goes
to stairs.*)

MICHAEL: What!

DEIRDRE: (*Runs over to* JACK, *then downstage to chair*) You're
mad! Darling, think of your manhood!

JACK: I have. But I'll do it under one condition.

LESLEY: (*Goes to stairs*) And that is!

JACK: That if I go upstairs to George's room, you'll come up
and have a jab of the old hypodermic at the same time.
Different mixture, of course.

LESLEY: I see.

JACK: Well, what do you say? Aren't you raring to let that
inner man of yours get going?

LESLEY: I must admit it would be rather a relief. Very well,
I'll try it.

JACK: When?

LESLEY: Whenever you like.

JACK: Right – let's go. We can swop clothes in my room.

DEIRDRE: Jack, don't! I don't trust it! I think the whole thing is phoney.

JACK: Now don't worry, darling.
(*The embrace, downstage of the Gothic chair.*)
Everything's going to be all right.

DEIRDRE: (*Running her hands over his chest*) But when I think of it! Oh, it's awful! You can't do this to me, Jack. Why, we shan't be able to –

JACK: Sh! Deirdre, darling. I've made up my mind. I'm doing this for us. I'm tired of this miserable stupid life we've been leading. At last, there's a way out.

DEIRDRE: (*Feeling under his shirt*) Oh, he won't even have lovely hair on his chest any more! Jack! If you love me, you won't do this!

JACK: Darling, it's because I love you that I'm doing it. Everything will be all right, I promise you.
(*He kisses her.*)

DEIRDRE: But I'd even bought socks for your birthday! What can I do with them?

JACK: Give them to Lesley. (*Goes to stairs.*) I tell you what you can do – ring FLE 10,000. Well, Michael, have you made up your mind yet?

MICHAEL: I – er – don't think I am prepared to make a statement just at present. Bit overwhelmed, you know. I shall wait and watch – ah – further developments before I commit myself to any course of policy. This has made me uneasy. Yes, very uneasy. Well, good luck, old chap.
(*They shake hands on the stairs, and* DEIRDRE *collapses into tears.*)

MICHAEL: (*To* LESLEY) Good luck, old girl!

LESLEY: Thank you, Michael.

MICHAEL: (*Eyes her delightful figure doubtfully*) Sure you're doing the right thing, old girl!

(*She nods and smiles, then turns to* JACK, *and they run upstairs together, leaving* MICHAEL *to flap and* DEIRDRE *to wail on the sofa.*)

DEIRDRE: (*Pounding the sofa*) How could he do this to me!

MICHAEL: Try not to take it too much to heart, my dear.

DEIRDRE: (*Hysterical*) Oh, Michael, do try not to be such a fool! It wouldn't matter if you were to change *your* sex!
(*She crosses to the door upstage L., as* TERRY *and* GILLIAN *enter, hand-in-hand.*)
Nobody would care. Oh, I shall never forgive him!
(*Pushing them aside.*) Oh, get out of my way! (*Exits through upstage L. arch.*)

TERRY: Is she upset about something? (*Goes to C.*)

MICHAEL: Ah-yes. I'm afraid she is rather.

TERRY: Anything I can do to help?

MICHAEL: I think not, thank you.

TERRY: After all, that's what we're here for, isn't it?

MICHAEL: I beg your pardon?

TERRY: Why, helping each other along life's way.

MICHAEL: Yes. I suppose you're right.

TERRY: If you bring a little smile along, you can't go wrong.
(*He and* GILLIAN *rub their cheeks together.*)

MICHAEL: Well, if you will excuse me . . .

TERRY: We're not driving you out, are we?

MICHAEL: Not at all. I must go for a walk, that's all. I have rather a difficult problem on my mind.

TERRY: OK, Mike. You go for your walk. And maybe when you come back, you'd like to talk about it.

MICHAEL: Thank you very much.

TERRY: After all, if we can share our troubles – that's right, isn't it, darling?

GILLIAN: Yes, darling.
(*They kiss lingeringly, their foreheads touching, still holding hands, and sit on the sofa.*)

MICHAEL: She may be right at that! She may be right!

(*He turns to go out, and bumps into* MRS GILTEDGE-
WHYTE *coming in through the arch upstage R.*)

MRS G.-W.: Ah, Mr Rawley. Have you seen my daughter,
Gillian?

MICHAEL: Please excuse me – I'm in a hurry. (*Exit upstage
R.*)

MRS G.-W.: Oh! (*Calls out after him.*) I advise you to be very
careful if you go down to the paddock. There are two
very peculiar horses down there. (*To herself.*) Well, I do
hope that they won't do him any injury, that's all.
(*Comes downstage, and suddenly sees* TERRY *and* GILLIAN
head to head.) Gillian! What are you doing? (*To sofa.*)

GILLIAN: I should have thought it was obvious, Mummy.
(TERRY *rises.*)
Terry and I are in love, Mummy.

MRS G.-W.: I see. Is this true, Mr Maroon?

GILLIAN: Now, please, Mummy, don't –

MRS G.-W.: Just a moment, Gillian. I am speaking to Mr
Maroon.

TERRY: Yes, Mrs Giltedge-Whyte. I guess it's true, all right.
Gillian and me really love each other.

GILLIAN: And we want to get married.

MRS G.-W.: I hope you haven't tried to seduce my daughter,
Mr Maroon!

GILLIAN: Oh, Mummy, you are the end! (*Flounces to L.*)

TERRY: (*Embarrassed*) Honestly, Mrs Giltedge-Whyte, such
an idea never entered my head. You see, I was brought
up to respect women, and I do, I really do. You know
something? I believe that the greatest thing in this world
of ours is the love between a man and a woman.
(*Overcome at this sentiment,* MRS GILTEDGE-WHYTE *feels
her way to the Gothic chair.*)

MRS G.-W.: Really? Is that why you sing as you do? (*Sits.*)

TERRY: But certainly. Why, you've just got to be sincere in
my business, Mrs Giltedge-Whyte. They'd spot it in a
moment if I wasn't. Why, when I sing to all those

millions of simple, ordinary little people – folks like you
and me, Mrs Giltedge-Whyte –

(MRS GILTEDGE-WHYTE *swallows bravely*.)

– they know I'm singing to each one of them personally,
and that's why they write to me and tell me their little
personal problems. You see, I speak a kind of language
that everyone can understand.

(*Enter* LESLEY *at the head of the stairs, dressed in Jack's
clothes, a transformed vision of emancipated masculinity,
and smoking a cigar.*)

LESLEY: Excuse me, but have any of you seen Mr Rawley?

MRS G.-W.: Why, yes. He went out there just a few minutes
ago, Mr – ?

LESLEY: Please excuse me. I'm afraid I can't introduce
myself just for a moment. (*Strides out through the upstage
arch.*)

GILLIAN: What an attractive man!

MRS G.-W.: He seemed like most young men nowadays to
me – rather effeminate. How different they were in Lord
Mortlake's time – and your father's of course. (*Turning
back to* TERRY.) You were saying?

TERRY: Well, I was just saying that I'll dedicate my life to
Gillian.

> I'll see that the stars shine in her eyes,
> I'll be certain her life will be one long surprise,
> And before I make a pass

(TREWIN *enters upstage L. with a practical hand
microphone on a silver salver, which he presents to* TERRY.)

> I'll tell her that the sun shines out of her face.
> This isn't any madam,
> I've known lots of girls before,
> And, frankly, I've had 'em.

> I'm hers, all hers,
> From here to eternity,

> I'll dedicate my life to my pretty little wife,
> And hand in hand,
> Through love's wonderland,
> I'll be hers.

(*Throughout this interchange he holds the microphone in front of whoever is talking.*)

MRS G.-W.: Quite! And do you feel you can offer Gillian the kind of life she's been accustomed to? After all –

TERRY: Oh! I'm not worthy of her. I realize that!

MRS G.-W.: Oh! You do?

TERRY: I look at her and I know I am just a piece of dirt – just a little old piece of dirt beneath her pretty feet.

MRS G.-W.: You certainly seem to be entering on the idea of marriage with the right attitude, Mr Maroon.

TERRY:
> I'm hers, all hers,
> In health and maternity.
> At night we'll get undressed
> In our lovely little nest,
> And in a year or two,
> We'll have a little kid like you,
> Which will be hers.
>
> Even when her hair's in curls,
> I won't sleep with other girls,
> I'm going to be true
> Because she'll look like you,

(*Points to* MRS GILTEDGE-WHYTE.)
> I'm hers, all hers,
> I don't want to belong to me,
> All my life it's my choice,

GILLIAN:
> Terry, darling!

TERRY:
> To be waked up by that voice,
> She'll drive me insane,

My sweet, gold ball-and-chain,
I'll be hers, hers,
My love, my high life,
My posh trouble-and-strife,
I'll be hers.

(*Takes a running jump off the sofa and lands kneeling downstage C.* TREWIN *re-enters from upstage L. with the salver and takes the microphone from* TERRY.)

TREWIN: (*Speaking into microphone*) Thank you, sir.

MRS G.-W.: Now, Mr – er?

TERRY: Call me Terry, please. All my fans do. (*Goes to* MRS GILTEDGE-WHYTE.)

MRS G.-W.: Er – Terry. Are you an American?

TERRY: Blimey – no! What made you think that?

MRS G.-W.: I find it rather difficult to follow you, that's all.

TERRY: Nice of you to think so, anyway. Thanks very much. It's the clothes, I guess.

(*Enter* JACK *at the head of the stairs, dressed in Lesley's clothes, and in what looks suspiciously like a wig.*)

JACK: Excuse me, but have you seen Deirdre? (*Taps* TERRY *playfully on the shoulder.*)

TERRY: Yeah. She went that way, Miss – (*Points off upstage L.*)

JACK: (*Exiting as quickly as he can*) Oh, thank you so much.

MRS G.-W.: Excuse me, but you are remarkably like Mr Oakham.

JACK: Yes, I'm his sister, Jack – Jacqueline! Please forgive me, I have to be running along now! (*Exit upstage L.*)

MRS G.-W.: It's all very extraordinary. I don't believe any of it.

TERRY: She's quite a smasher, isn't she?

MRS G.-W.: Who?

TERRY: This Jacqueline.

MRS G.-W.: I really couldn't say. Young girls nowadays are

so busy trying to look like men, with their short hair and tight trousers, it's almost impossible to judge them by the standards that were accepted when I was a girl. You were saying?

TERRY: (*To sofa*) Well, as for looking after Gillian, you needn't have any worries about that.

MRS G.-W.: Yes, yes! How much *do* you make?

TERRY: (*Sits on sofa.*) Well, there's a thousand pounds a week from record sales alone. With the rest, radio, TV, the halls – well, it ain't peanuts, Mrs Giltedge-Whyte.

MRS G.-W.: No, I'm sure it isn't.

TERRY: Of course, Mrs Oakham – she's my manager – she handles all the financial side. Do you know, she taught me how to sing?

MRS G.-W.: Did she? (*Crosses to sofa.*)

TERRY: Oh, yes. I was just the lift boy in her bra factory you see. Well, one day I was taking her up in the lift, and she hears me singing and there I was! And you know why she believed in me?

MRS G.-W.: I've no idea. (*Sits on sofa.*)

TERRY: Because I was sincere. Why, look at this suit I'm wearing. How much do you think it cost? No – go on, feel that material. How much do you think? Have a guess! No idea? Forty-eight quid! You don't think I get that being insincere? Believe me, Gillian will have the very best – you can bet your drawers on that! (*Goes to* GILLIAN.) And don't think I won't look after her old mum too. Look after my own mum – so why not Gillian's? Well, what do you say, Mum? (*Puts his arm round* GILLIAN.)

MRS G.-W.: Well, I must admit, Terry, that you have impressed me enormously with your sincerity. I can only say that it's a great pity there are not more young men with your serious, responsible attitude to life.

TERRY: Oh, I'm serious, all right. (*To* GILLIAN.) Aren't I, baby?

MRS G.-W.: I think you are something of a poet. Yes, you are a true poet of the age we live in, a guardian of the *status quo*, of morality, and yes, of religion, too.

TERRY: But honestly, Mum, how can I help it? Why, every time I hear a new-born baby cry –

GILLIAN: Oh, not now, darling.

MRS G.-W.: What a sweet boy you are! Quite charming. Yes, you can certainly have my blessing.

TERRY: Good old Mum! (*Hugging her.*)

GILLIAN: Mummy, you are sweet, really. I knew you'd just adore him! (*Hugs her.*)

MRS G.-W.: This means, of course, Gillian, that we shall have to cancel all the arrangements I made with Lady Mortlake. I must remember to stop that cheque, too. (*Enter* JACK *through the arch upstage L., panting.*) Why, what's the matter? Is somebody chasing you? (*He nods.*)

TERRY: Has somebody tried to molest you, miss?

JACK: I'm afraid so.

TERRY: OK. Where is he?

JACK: No, please don't bother. It doesn't matter. Oh! (*Suddenly the eager figure of* FATHER EVILGREENE *hurtles on in hot pursuit. He puts his hand out to* JACK *when he sees the others.*)

FATHER E.: Ah! This young lady and I were having a little theological discussion. I'm sorry if we disturbed you. (*To* JACK.) Coming, my dear?

MRS G.-W.: Just one moment, sir. I have been trying to place your face ever since I arrived. I believe you're an imposter. Are you not the Father Evilgreene who ran a disreputable school in Ponders End until you were exposed in the Sunday newspapers last year? (FATHER EVILGREENE *stares at her, and then makes a quick dash for the door. But* TERRY *is there first and knocks him down.*)

GILLIAN: Terry! I didn't know you were so strong!

TERRY: Don't worry, honey. He won't get away.

(*Enter* LESLEY *and* DEIRDRE, *arm-in-arm, from the arch upstage R.*)

JACK: Deirdre! There you are! I've been looking for you all over the place.

DEIRDRE: It's no good, Jack. It's all over between us. Besides, I've found Lesley now.

JACK: You found Lesley? You really went ahead with all this?

LESLEY: Of course, didn't you?

JACK: (*Pulling off his wig*) No, of course not. You mean you want that instead of me?

DEIRDRE: Exactly. We've found each other, haven't we, darling?

LESLEY: That's right.

(*They cross to piano.* GEORGE *appears at the window, with his trout bag, grinning.*)

GEORGE: Trout are rising this evening.

JACK: Shut up! This is your fault!

(*Enter* LADY MORTLAKE *through upstage R. arch with an enormous bunch of flowers.*)

LADY M.: Ah! Here we all are! Dear me, Father Evilgreene what are you doing down there? Not still praying? Well, now, I'm just wondering what I should do with these.

JACK: I can't believe it! I can't believe it! Oh, woman, you are the devil's doorway all right!

(MICHAEL *staggers in from the upstage R. arch, looking a mild wreck.*)

And what's the matter with you?

MICHAEL: That bloody horse! I can't tell you what it's done to me! Anyway, I've settled his little game once and for all. (*His voice breaks into a high squeak.*) George!

(*Enter* TREWIN *upstage L.*)

LADY M.: What is it, Trewin?

TREWIN: Some gentleman in an 'elicopter, my lady.

LADY M.: An 'elicopter? What's that?

TREWIN: It's landed on the front lawn, my lady. They say they're from *The Daily Racket* – Mr Paul Slickey's column.

JACK: (*Wildly*) By God, yes! Why don't we give the entire Paul Slickey office a shot. Bring your little black bag down here.

MICHAEL: Yes, I say, George!

(GEORGE *grins down at them and disappears.* JACK *dashes up the stairs after him.*)

George! Come back with that stuff! George! You little bastard!

(MICHAEL *crawls up after him.*)

MICHAEL: (*Feebly*) George! I say, George!

LADY M.: Do give Father Evilgreene a hand, Terry. He looks so miserable down there. And why don't you sing us one of your nice songs?

MRS G.-W.: Oh, yes, What a good idea!

(TERRY *ignores* FATHER EVILGREENE *who is still nursing his nose, and runs over to stairs.*)

TERRY: OK everybody! Let's go! (*To* MRS GILTEDGE-WHYTE.) After you, Mum.

(*She comes downstage and the Mortlake gauze drops in behind her.*)

MRS G.-W.:

> I want to hear about beautiful things,
> Beautiful things like love.
> I don't want to hear of emotional wrecks.
> Of people who practise peculiar sex.
> I want my love to be pure – my income secure,
> I don't want to wallow in a spiritual sewer.
>
> I want to hear about beautiful things
> Beautiful things like love.
> I want to hear about happy marriages
> Without complications and just baby carriages,
> I want to fly to the moon – and hear about June,

And dinners at Maxims and Claridges.
(*Exits downstage L. Blackout. Mortlake gauze goes away.*)

SCENE ELEVEN

The Daily Racket.
  JACK *at his desk in his shirtsleeves, alone.*

JACK: That's another one to bed!
  (*Enter* SECRETARY.)
JO: Did you call, darling?
JACK: No, but I'm afraid I would have done later.
  (*They embrace.*)
  What have we got in for tomorrow?
  (*She shows him his papers.*)
  People, more people! More flesh and blood, more
  human interest! More of the truth about the world in
  which we all live, the people, the ordinary people!
  (*He grabs her.*)
  My God! What a function we fulfil!
  What a service we dispense! Nothing too trivial or
  unimportant for us to package up for consumption at the
  breakfast table or on the eight-fifteen! Just think of our
  circulation figures, the multitudes who hunger and yet
  starve not! And why? Because of us, of us! This happy
  breed of men who give them what they want! (*Hurling
  papers in the air.*) These are our loaves and fishes! Come,
  come and pay your tuppence-halfpenny and let no man
  be turned away or unregarded! *We* have food for all.
  What's on tomorrow?
JO: Well, a new night club opened tonight. You might still
  catch a bit of it.
JACK: Good! I'm hungry. Give me my jacket. What else?
JO: In the morning there's a meeting of nuclear scientists
  who want to end war.

JACK: Communists and queers!

JO: Then at twelve o'clock there's a Press reception at the Dorchester to launch a new British film.

JACK: Whores and longhairs! Still, I'll be thirsty by then. Hand me my hat.

JO: Then there is an interview with Dominique Flanders, the distinguished poet and Nobel Prize winner. (*Fetches hat and rose.*)

JACK: That phoney!

JO: Then London Airport to meet Red Evans, the film star.

JACK: Think of all the money he must make! What's he got that's so special? Why do I have to go and meet his lousy plane and look at his beautiful hand-made shoes? Why is there no justice in this world?

JO: (*Putting his hat on his head*) Darling, that's not your department.

JACK: Sure. It's a racket. (*Kisses her.*) Just another racket.

(JOURNALISTS *enter.*)

JO: Match your poor seductiveness against this goddam
          bitch success.
       You may not have prowess but who's the hell to guess,
       As long as somehow you progress, we'll give you
          happiness.
       You've got to understand the mechanics of success.

JACK: (*Stands on desk*)
       If I could be an MP
       Part of Democracy,
       Whatever I said,
       You could take it as read,
       Whitehall gives the orders – it
       Wouldn't be me!
       If I could be a lifetime Peer,
       You'd have nothing to fear,
       I'd beat up the whores
       Keep them working indoors,
       For the sake of the kiddies we'd have

English veneer.

JO *and* JOURNALISTS:
You've got to understand the mechanics of success, *etc.*

JACK: If I could be a magistrate,
You'd have to be importunate,
With the police on all fours
It's their word – not yours!
If you're up before me – it would be
Unfortunate! (*Falls into dancer's arms.*)

If I could live in Downing Street,
On the telly I'd look a treat.
If Ike went to hell,
Then I'd go as well
And I'd bring you lot with me – and
We'd all lick his feet!

JO *and* JOURNALISTS:
You've got to understand the mechanics of success, *etc.*

JACK: If I could be a soldier man,
Shooting up black men whenever I can,
I won't fight real battles,
In case Randolph tattles,
I'm not only strong, I'm antediluvian!

If I could build a rocket base,
I'd be a copper and smash in your face.
I'd wield all officialdom's might
If you'd dare to interfere with our right
To blow all you bleeders to outer space.

JO *and* JOURNALISTS:
You've got to understand the mechanics of success, *etc.*

A REPORTER: (*Comes to* JACK) Who did you say you were?
(JACK *puts his hat on the reporter's head, his holder in his
mouth.* JO *puts Jack's coat on the reporter.* JACK *exits R.,
disgusted, while* JO *throws the rose down.*)

JO *and* JOURNALISTS:

If you're going to impress, you must pander to the
    Press,
They'll want you to assess how much money you
    possess.
You've got to understand the mechanics of success.
(*The Keyhole drops in behind the other 'Slickey'. He turns to
face the audience.*)

REPORTER:

I'm just a guy called Paul Slickey
And the job that I do's pretty tricky.
I'm twenty-eight years old.

(*The* COMPANY *come downstairs; the keyhole has flown
away. The principals all have boards which they show the
audience and then take their places in the line-up.*)

FULL COMPANY:

And practically everybody, anybody, anything you can
    think of
Leaves me quite completely
Newspaper neatly
Quite, quite cold.

Don't think you can fool a guy like him
The best things in life are never free
Guys like him who are on the inside
Cannot be taken for a ride,
He has professional ways and means
Of getting in behind the scenes
To put the screws on stars in jeans
They don't need hidden television screens.

He'll be always on the band wagon, never in the cart,
No one hates the simple little bastard
Like a newspaper can.

(*Long sustained chord. House tabs in.*)

DÉJÀVU

CLIFF: My feet hurt.
JIMMY: Try washing your socks.

Look Back in Anger

Keep thou my feet; I do not ask to see
The distant scene; one step enough for me.

I loved the garish day, and spite of fears
Pride ruled my will; remember not past years.

And with the morn those angel faces smile
Which I have loved long since and lost a while.

John Henry Newman

First performed on 8 May 1992 at the Thorndike Theatre, Leatherhead, and subsequently at the Comedy Theatre, London

J.P.	Peter Egan
CLIFF	Gareth Thomas
ALISON	Alison Johnston
HELENA	Eve Matheson
TEDDY	Himself
Directed by	Tony Palmer
Designed by	Geoffrey Scott
Produced by	Bill Kenwright

Approximate running time: 2 hrs. 25 mins.

AUTHOR'S NOTE

Look Back in Anger is bristling with stage directions, most of them embarrassingly unhelpful. I have tried to avoid them ever since. At that time, however, they were very necessary to an author if his intentions were to be approximated. Actors, indeed directors, demanded literal signposts, not only about motivation ('Why do I say this when I've just said the opposite?'), but where they should actually sit down. Those days are long gone ('Wryly. Moves left.'). But something must be said about J.P.'s speeches, especially the later ones. Sometimes, these achieve an almost stiff, calculated formality. This is quite intentional. They have the deliberateness of *recitative* and it may not be always easy to spot where the 'aria' begins. However, when these passages occur, they must be deft in delivery and as light as possible. J.P.'s particular artifice but casually knocked off. Read, memorize and discard.

Without wishing to place too many constraints on the interpretation of this part, it is nevertheless important to indicate what are tediously and popularly known as 'guidelines'. They can be observed without imposing too many restrictions on the actor's freedom of interpretation. The original character of J.P. was widely misunderstood, largely because of the emphasis on the element of 'anger' and the newspaper invention of 'angry young man'. The result of this vulgar misconception was often a strident and frequently dull performance. Wearisome theories about J.P.'s sadism, anti-feminism, even closet homosexuality are still peddled to gullible students by dubious and partisan 'academics'. They continue to proliferate and perpetuate themselves among those who should know better. J.P. is a comic character. He generates energy but, also, like, say, Malvolio or Falstaff, an inescapable melancholy. He is a man of gentle susceptibilities, constantly goaded by a brutal and coercive world. This core of character is best expressed, not only theatrically but truthfully, by a *mild* delivery. In other words, it is not necessary or advisable to express bitterness bitterly or anger angrily. Things should be delicately plucked out of the air not hurled like a protester's stones at the enemy. This was true of the original. It is even more appropriate to what might be thought of as *Look Back II*.

ACT ONE

The Midlands. The present. Sunday morning. Around mid-day.

The large kitchen of a country house of the kind sometimes advertised as 'a minor gentleman's residence'. The kitchen itself retains its original farmhouse appearance of a working place at the heart of the building, dedicated to the pursuits of a large, prosperous and robust family. It is possibly the oldest part of the house with the original stone flags from an earlier period gleaming, leading off to a large butler's pantry, rooms for hanging game and preparing other fruits of the countryside. A few ancient hooks hang down from the high ceiling and a huge Aga dominates one side of the stage. All this workmanlike air of practicality has been modified in the interests of comfort, without too much emphasis on glossy Country Living. *In the suburbs the result would probably be described as a 'dinette'. However, it has rather evolved as a sitting-room and kitchen, a place for talk and conviviality.*

A warm glow from the Aga niche gives out a comforting light from its engine-room-sparkle surface. A large, empty dog basket with its scatter of hairy blankets spilling out from it stands beside the stove, together with a sporting gun and cartridge belt. Upstage, large, floor-length windows look out to a distant park-like landscape with hills of pasture and forest beyond it. The right stage area is separated by a partition through which the actors can see and speak to each other. But the centre is the main working area, containing two large deep sinks, not too overwhelmed by smart kitchen embellishments of the magazine 'farmhouse' style. In short, a relaxing, not too functional place, certainly not 'high-tech', in which to gossip idly while peeling the potatoes or drawing a game bird.

The walls of its cupboards and discreet 'units' are covered with old postcards and quite cunningly lit. A few sporting prints and posters decorate other walls. A wooden, rough table, which serves both for dining and working, dominates the centre area, flanked by a couple of extremely bright and comfortable old armchairs. There is also a seasoned bench and rocking chair, a Windsor chair or two. On one wall hangs a large Victorian-style sampler with the words: THANK YOU FOR NOT SMOKING. *Nearby is another:* THOU GOD SEEST ME.

As the curtain rises, ALISON, *a girl of about twenty, is leaning over a well-used ironing board, upstage left. She wears a T-shirt with the legend:* I AM SCUM. *In the two armchairs, right and left respectively,* J.P. *and* CLIFF *are seated. All that we can see of them is two pairs of legs, sprawled way out beyond the spread of newspapers which hide the rest of them from sight. Beside them and between them is a table on which sits a scruffy teddy bear, also surrounded by a jungle of newspapers and weeklies.*

When we do eventually see them, we find that J.P. *is a grey-haired man of indeterminate age, casually and expensively dressed. Clouds of smoke fill the room from the pipe he is smoking.* CLIFF, *the same age, is similarly dressed, perhaps slightly less Jermyn Street.*

The only sound is the occasional thud of Alison's iron on the board. It is a chilly, grey February morning, with occasional shafts of sunlight piercing the room from the french windows.

J.P.: (*From behind newspaper*) What ho, Bernardo!
(*Pause. Presently,* J.P. *throws his paper down and looks around. Nothing happens. He waits, listens, stares at Cliff's upraised paper hiding his face, then leans forward.*)
What ho, Bernardo!
(*No one responds.* J.P. *pauses then picks up his paper and disappears behind it again. Silence.* ALISON *pauses, looks at the two armchairs, pushing back the hair from her face. She goes to a transistor radio beneath one of the cupboards stage left and turns it on. After a little expert fiddling, the machine responds with a loud blare of pop music. She glances across to the men, then turns the volume down to a level which most sane people would think quite loud, and returns to the ironing board, where she carries on at her task with a little more relish. There is no response from the other two*

occupants for a while. Then J.P. *lowers his paper and listens. Slowly and deliberately he gets up, goes over to the transistor and turns it off. He looks at* ALISON, *who smiles sourly and puts on headphones. Looking to* CLIFF *for a reaction, he returns to his chair, picks up his paper and disappears behind it once more. The room remains silent except for the clatter of Alison's iron. Presently, his papers are set down again as he relights his pipe. Smoke pours from it as he clamps it down into a steady burn and he returns cheerfully to behind his paper.* ALISON *begins coughing. Pause.* CLIFF *sets down his paper and stares at the papers from which heavy clouds are rising.* ALISON *coughs again.* CLIFF *looks as if he might be about to protest, then retreats again behind his own paper. Silence as before until* J.P. *puts down his paper even again, looking round him. Then:*) Why *do* I do this every Sunday? (*Pause.*) I keep thinking it's Friday.

CLIFF: Well, it's Sunday.

J.P.: *La paix du dimanche.*

CLIFF: What's that?

J.P.: Some cunning French play I expect. All bombast and logic and no balls.

CLIFF: You don't say. Did you know that . . .

J.P.: What?

CLIFF: Yesterday was St Valentine's Day.

J.P.: Oh, yes.

CLIFF: Nary a card on the mat for me, matie.

ALISON: I sent you one.

CLIFF: Oh, that's nice.

ALISON: Perhaps it'll come tomorrow.

CLIFF: That's very thoughtful, Alison.

J.P.: She's very thoughtful. Tardy perhaps.

CLIFF: Something to look forward to.

J.P.: Well, it's time you looked forward.

CLIFF: Shouldn't we all.

J.P.: I used to dread tomorrow. Now it's only today.

(*Sings softly:*)
> Woke up this mornin', hopin' the day wouldn't come
> Woke up this mornin', but it wouldn't go away.

CLIFF: Blind Lemon Porter again.

ALISON: Blind who?

J.P.: In bed last night, got the blues about today

CLIFF: That's Sunday for you.

J.P.: Woke up this mornin', so tired and young and grey.

CLIFF: Well, you do look *dated*, but still powerful, man, still powerful.

J.P.: Wait for the evening, still feelin' younger . . .
> Hopin' tomorrow . . .

CLIFF: . . . will go away.

J.P.: . . . won't be no worse than today . . .

CLIFF: Where's my Valentine?

J.P.: Teddy sent you one.

CLIFF: Unstamped no doubt.

J.P.: That crimson twilight won't chase the blues away.

CLIFF: No more crimson twilight, colonel. No more blues. Try soul.

J.P.: What's that?

CLIFF: Ask your daughter.

J.P.: Here! (*Picks up another paper.*) Yesterday. Among the ads for Community Creative Projects Directors, we find 'Prig's Own Paper' too. (*Picks up another paper.*) Here: six full pages. It's here somewhere, a pulsing little message of pretending unrequited, shameless love. Senior Race Officers . . . Yes. Ah. Piggy Poos sends Kissy Poos to Mummy Piggy Poos and Curly Wigglers to Twirly Piglets.

CLIFF: Snuffle Bum wants Cuddle Drawers ever so ever and always Kentish Town Snuggle Wumti-Tumkins.

J.P.: All graduates and Harvard men.

ALISON: Here's one opposite the Court Circular. Naughty Boy Wittgenstein must have Mummy Meanie Winkle. Always, always, always.

284

CLIFF: Twinkle Twinkle Teggy Twinkle
　　　How I love your Ursine Twinkle.

J.P.: That sounds like Teddy.

CLIFF: If it is, it's to himself.

J.P.: That figures, I suppose.

ALISON: Squirrel's Drey Rent Free always and everwill for
　　　scruffy old bears. Please keep my paws and I will warm
　　　yours evermore.

CLIFF: Oh – my own gorgeous gusset.

J.P.: That – is enough nausea.

CLIFF: I do so agree. Teddy's quite nauseated. Whimsy.

J.P.: Kentish Town's made of harder stuff than that.

CLIFF: Well, yes, it is rather hard to believe.

J.P.: Well, it isn't *explained*, is it?

CLIFF: Palpably. Wouldn't have gone down in our day.
　　　(*They resume papers.*)

J.P.: Grown-up persons. Most embarrassing.
　　　(*Pause.*)

CLIFF: Snuffle Bum, Cuddle Drawers.

ALISON: Ugh!

J.P.: Ugh.
　　　(*Pause.*)
　　　Pour me some more wine, Whittaker, will you?

CLIFF: Pour it yourself.

J.P.: You're the nearest.

CLIFF: You're the oldest.

J.P.: Quite.
　　　(CLIFF *pours him some more.* J.P. *sips it thoughtfully.*)
　　　I don't feel so hot.

CLIFF: Now that won't do.

J.P.: No.

CLIFF: You've had a bottle and a half to yourself.

J.P.: The wine is excellent. Reticent, most despised of
　　　virtues, but *au fond* . . .

CLIFF: . . . *au fond* . . .

J.P.: Cheeky, subversive and coarsely voluptuous.

CLIFF: So what is it, don't tell me, colonel, friend o' mine?

J.P.: Brain fag.

CLIFF: Oh yes. Rather appropriate for you.

ALISON: Yes. Fags on the brain.

CLIFF: Exactly. Fags. Cigarettes, tobacco smoke, sodomites, brain, atrophy.

CLIFF *and* ALISON: Brain fag!

(*They both laugh.*)

J.P.: Such a droll pair. The executive echelons of television were rough hewn for the likes of you, Whittaker. How wise you were to take my advice and go in for that director's course when the Town Hall Praesidium took away our street trader's licence all those years ago. (*To* ALISON.) He told the BBC he'd fallen off the back of a lorry, which they took to be an example of quirky Welsh wit, didn't they?

CLIFF: That's right, boyo.

J.P.: Boyo. Listen to the Shepherd's Bush woodnotes wild. For thirty-seven years I have listened to that wheedling half-back, Bible black, mother's Methodist pride warble. Are you going to talk like that for the rest of your life?

CLIFF: Well, I always have.

J.P.: I thought I'd got you out of it.

CLIFF: That was a most uncalled-for remark.

J.P.: You're right. *No* one called.

CLIFF: Teddy thinks it's uncalled for.

J.P.: Don't – don't hide behind Teddy. Nobody asked him (*to* TEDDY) did they? *I* know the inflexions, cautious, crafty and respectable. Do you know what his mother said when she returned from the put-upon pit wives' excursion to Florence on the coach?

CLIFF: Oh, God!

J.P.: 'Well, what did you think of the excursion to Florence, Mrs Lewis?' 'Oh, it was lovely. The coach ride was lovely. All the brown ale, the crisps and the singin'.' 'But what about Florence?' 'Florence?' 'Yes, Florence!'

'Oh, that. Well. I think. Well . . . A lot of thought's gone into it.'

CLIFF: You're being very condescending.

J.P.: Of course.

CLIFF: And predictable. And – sneering. Sneering and predictable.

J.P.: You used to be just agreeably offensive. His wife, poor dear Ellie, may the Good Lord in his everlasting chapel cheerfulness bless and keep her for taking this principality front-parlour mouse off my hands for so long.

CLIFF: (*To* ALISON) He does have a way with the Celtic cadence, doesn't he?

J.P.: Do you remember, you smart-arse media Welshperson?

CLIFF: In his clumsy fashion. Do you think Lord Sandy should have been an actor? A lot of people thought he was. Now, there's even a hint of *hiraeth*, pit-pony Porter, masquerading as a nature's thoroughbred.

J.P.: You never had style, nor invention, brain dead to spontaneity . . .

CLIFF: Mind you, he's half Welsh himself.

ALISON: I know.

CLIFF: Born in Monmouth. Now that used to be in England.

J.P.: Still is.

CLIFF: Well, the timetables on the platforms are in Welsh. Just peeved because he can't read 'em.

J.P.: Well, I know the Welsh for 'May I please have a packet of Daz?'

ALISON: What is it, then?

J.P.: (*Precisely*) *Am cwn amwrn dai llangollen barra kowse* – packet of Daz! – There!

ALISON: Keep the English out of Wales.

CLIFF: Damn right. What have *you* done for Wales?

J.P.: Why do you imagine dear old Offa stuck his dyke up the road. To keep you dark, hairy, pointy-hatted little buggers out. Old Ellie's kept you in your pleased little place all right.

CLIFF: (*To* ALISON) He makes it all up, you know. His
memory's over-revved. What is it, Lord Sandy?

J.P.: When you left me in our flat, lumbering me with our
flourishing, yes, flourishing sweet-stall.

CLIFF: Leaving – his girlfriend moved in is what he means.

J.P.: I said – which you won't remember – some respectable
little madam from Pinner or Guildford would gobble
him up in six months.

CLIFF: Brits Out!

J.P.: I am *not* a Brit. I am English.

CLIFF: God's most divine gift.

J.P.: You bet. Nor do I exist or have my being in any tribal
slum called the UK. No! It was Ellie who married *you*,
sent you out to the studios, and here you are, clean as a
Jermyn Street pin, all due to Ellie, not of Pinner or
Guildford but Abergavenny, wartime prison of Rudolf
Hess and neighbour to the founding saint of the
National Health.

CLIFF: That rock on which our nationhood is built.

J.P.: Do you know what Ellie said the other day?

CLIFF: I wish she were here now.

ALISON: So do I.

CLIFF: T. S. Eliot and Pam. That act never really got off the
ground.

J.P.: What are you on about?

CLIFF: Nothing, captain of my soul, nothing.

J.P.: Anyway, *she's* never heard of T. S. Eliot. They all did
Elton John for 'O' levels. Wasn't it?

ALISON: Virginia Woolf, actually.

J.P.: Who else?

ALISON: She doesn't like him really.

CLIFF: Who – Virginia Woolf?

ALISON: Ellie. Him.

CLIFF: I don't think that's true.

ALISON: You just won't admit it – any of you, after a
lifetime.

CLIFF: She's very fond of Lord Sandy.

ALISON: No, she's not. He upsets her.

CLIFF: No, he doesn't.

J.P.: (*American*) We have a little problem in communication as human beings but I'm sure you would agree that is one of the great dilemmas of our time. You and me, we have a communication problem in a number of areas, which are in urgent need of restructuring.

CLIFF: Meaning you don't like him either. Where does he get his resistible charm? His mother? I don't think so.

J.P.: She should be among us now. My mother? This world was fashioned for the likes of her. Alas, she passed away peacefully, watching *Coronation Street*, while the home help was helping herself to her handbag and a while before some thumb-brained sob sister dreamed up the miracle malady of hypothermia, an affliction unknown to her grandmother, who would as lief as died from a surfeit of lampreys.

CLIFF: Most unconcerned of you, I must say. (*To* ALISON.) We had a different lifestyle in those days.

J.P.: Like we didn't use dumb words like 'lifestyle'. The pursuit of which is confined to those incapable of any style whatsoever.

CLIFF: Like myself.

J.P.: Just so. What I did know was what I did *not* want to grow up to be was a member of the public.

CLIFF: And you never did.

ALISON: Or the human race.

CLIFF: A palpable hit. On the behalf of yoof. You could have been like this woman. (*Newspaper.*)

J.P.: What woman?

CLIFF: This lady doctor. She's the country's leading expert on anal dilation in abused children.

J.P.: Quite. Think of the avenues that might have been opened up to you.

CLIFF: Or closed. Mind you, she does have a funny squinty-eyed look.

J.P.: Scarcely surprising. I may not be an identifiable or believable member of the public but at least I don't put my postcode on my writing paper.

CLIFF: Oooh! There *was* a time when you'd have said 'notepaper'. Still I won't let on. Besides, Ellie says we *must* use the postcode.

J.P.: Yes, well, we mustn't mess up the system. Ellie's right. Do you know what else she said on her last visit?

CLIFF: Must you?

J.P.: I gave him, that misshapen object, that uppity Welsh nigger, the most exquisitely camp sweater last Christmas, the purest of white to play off his junk-clogged plebeian skin with an elegantly amusing motif –

CLIFF: Motif?

J.P.: He tried it on, and I must say it didn't look too bad, for the hobbled runty class-creature that he is. Went into Ellie to get her verdict and you know what she said? '*Lovely*, Cliff! Only thing is if you wear it, it'll get dirty.'

CLIFF: Well, it *was* too good to wear, it's true.

J.P.: Ah, the marriage of adventurous minds.
(*Pause.*)

ALISON: I don't see what's so amusing about that.
(*Pause.*)

CLIFF: What are you giving up for Lent?

J.P.: Um?

CLIFF: What are you giving up for Lent?
(*Slight pause.*)

J.P.: Ethnic culture. And you?

CLIFF: The Alternative Service Book.

J.P.: You don't go to church.

CLIFF: Alternative comedy. Alternative women. Gay. *Thé dansants*. It should be genuine deprivation.

J.P.: Very well. Donating to charity.

CLIFF: You don't.

J.P.: I used to . . . street barrel organists.

CLIFF: And you, Alison. What about you?

ALISON: The Prime Minister.

J.P.: And they say the young have no hope.

> (*They return to the newspapers.* J.P. *relights his pipe.*
> ALISON *grimaces as the clouds of smoke reach her. She
> waves at it in front of her face.*)

CLIFF: What do you suppose Teddy's giving up for Lent?

J.P.: Buggery.

CLIFF: Steady on, J.P. That's not a very Teddy sort of word.

J.P.: What *is* a Teddy sort of word?

CLIFF: Meaningful relationship, I suppose.

J.P.: Makes your eyes water, you mean?

CLIFF: You really shouldn't say things like that in front of him.

J.P.: Behind his back, whoops, sorry! That would be better?

CLIFF: You know how hurt he is by words.

J.P.: You mean the word 'buggery', but not the act?

CLIFF: Come on, Lord Sandy, you've more compassion in
you than that.

J.P.: What about sodomy?

CLIFF: There's no talking to him in this mood. He's not
really so unfeeling. Are you, you whimsical old softie?

J.P.: I'm only mildly curious. Is Teddy a sodomite or isn't
he?

CLIFF: He's one of God's creatures and is entitled to dignity
and respect from the likes of coarse ruffians like you.

J.P.: I've no disrespect for Teddy. He has all the charm of a
Lithuanian carpet seller. I just wonder why he must
wear his heart on his cock.

CLIFF: As you – even in your heartless bigotry – must know:
he doesn't have one.

J.P.: Perhaps that's why he's given it up? Buggery, I mean.

CLIFF: Must you be so hurtful?

J.P.: Pricks and moans don't break his bones but words will
hurt him ever? Don't you think it piquant –

CLIFF: Piquant! Oh, *yes*.

J.P.: Don't you think it piquant that a most devoutly illiterate generation should be so maidenly about the *form* of words?

CLIFF: He refuses to be humiliated by this glib stereotyping.

J.P.: Good for Ted.

CLIFF: It's reducing.

J.P.: Indeed. Reduce a stiff prick up the arse and, lo, no stereotype. Only the limp but meaningful truth. If it's so meaningful, why is he giving it up?

CLIFF: I didn't say he was giving it up. *You* did.

J.P.: Did I?

CLIFF: Yes. How do you know, anyway?

J.P.: I assumed.

CLIFF: Assumed! (*Almost losing his temper.*) Oh, great!

J.P.: That was why he's looking so bloody miserable. He's not getting it.

CLIFF: What?

J.P.: Buggered. Sorry, meaningful relationships.

CLIFF: He just objects to your unfeeling use of words.

J.P.: So I understand. He likes doing it but not hearing it.

CLIFF: Anyway, he's into safe sex.

J.P.: Safe sodomy? Like meatless steaks?

CLIFF: He's into Green. Why shouldn't he campaign for the Green way of life?

J.P.: Why not? Better to be Green than slouch unseen. Decaffeinated copulation.

CLIFF: He doesn't want penetration. Just stroking.

J.P.: Stroking. Like the Boat Race.

CLIFF: Like tender, loving, on-going relationships.

J.P.: I remember her.

CLIFF: Who?

J.P.: Penny.

CLIFF: Penny who?

J.P.: Penny Trayshun. Strong, muscular girl, full of merriment, built like a nutcracker. Like Poppy.

CLIFF: Poppy?

J.P.: Poppy Tupper.

ALISON: I'm going mad.

CLIFF: I'm getting confused.

J.P.: Demonstrably.

CLIFF: Let's drop Teddy and Lent, shall we?

ALISON: Hoo-bloody-ray.

J.P.: (*Presently, reading from the paper*) 'Speaking from his £200,000 bungalow, Roddy said: Debbie and me are in love and we want all the world to know it.' Did *you* know it?

CLIFF: I did actually.

J.P.: You do keep up with the world, don't you? 'I know people says I shouldn't have left my bride and young baby. And I'm thirty years older than she is . . .' Open another bottle of the '75, will you.

CLIFF: I'm too tired.

ALISON: I'll get it.

J.P.: Oh, thank you.

(ALISON *goes off.*)

'A spokesman for the Group said, Rod and Debbie are wildly in love. You only have to see them at the poolside, hammering away at it.'

CLIFF: Actually, someone in the village asked me the other day what you do for a living.

J.P.: Oh?

CLIFF: That nice woman with the strawberry mark in the ironmongers.

J.P.: And? What did you reply, dreamboat?

CLIFF: I just said, 'Oh, well, you'll know James by now, always a bit of an unsolved Jimmy Riddle.' 'Oh, a lot of people have got him taped, I expect,' she said. And she laughed.

J.P.: Well, next time tell her I'm better off ignored.

CLIFF: Oh, I think she'll do that.

J.P.: Good. I don't want to be summed up or identified.

When I ran a sweet-stall nobody believed *that*. Why
should they believe me now?

CLIFF: Why. Indeed?

(ALISON *returns with a bottle of wine*.)

J.P.: Oh, you found it.

ALISON: '75. (*She starts to open it*.)

J.P.: (*Faintly surprised*) Oh, very kind . . . I think even I
deserve a little better than to be explained.

(*Back to newspapers*.)

(*Presently*.) You never really got it going as a mouse, did
you?

CLIFF: No.

J.P.: Bit of a wash-out . . .

CLIFF: As a mouse – yes.

J.P.: You weren't really cut out for it.

CLIFF: Not really.

J.P.: Still – you had a go. That's the thing –

CLIFF: I wasn't convincing.

J.P.: Yet, you had recognizable mouse-like qualities. Alison,
the wife, thought so. We both did . . .

(ALISON *pours wine into his glass. He watches her*.)
And yet . . . I can think of people who have mouse-like
qualities who are able to exploit them with enormous
success, benefit and pleasure to everyone. (*To* ALISON.)
Thank you. Very nicely poured.

(ALISON *goes to fill Cliff's glass*.)

CLIFF: Oh, thank you, lovely.

J.P.: She poured that very nicely, don't you think?

CLIFF: She does everything nicely.

J.P.: You *were* embarrassing.

CLIFF: Deeply.

J.P.: Well, people used to get mighty hot over bears and
squirrels – if they were exposed to that needless whimsy.

CLIFF: Ah, whimsy. It was.

J.P.: What do you think, Alison?

ALISON: What's it matter what *I* think?

J.P.: You're the future, my dear bejeaned spokesperson,
     bristling with communication skills, and bearing down
     ever in the omnipresent.
ALISON: I think you both have a lifetime's inherited and
     laboriously perfected skill at talking untrammelled balls.
CLIFF: The fearless perception of yoof: that's what your
     daughter's got.
J.P.: She has. Give yourself a glass.
     (ALISON *pours one*.)
     Well, here's to us all. God bless this house and all
     within.
     (J.P. *puts his arm round* ALISON.)
     A glass of '75, the friendly sentinel of tobacco and loving
     company. What could be more agreeable? What we need
     is a song. Sing us a song, Alison. No, you don't sing or
     whistle, like your mother. Cliff? Well, I tell you what.
CLIFF: No, no more blues.
J.P.: As sung at champagne gatherings of pith and moment.
     (*He grabs pineapple from bowl on table, which he holds
     above his head. Dances and sings in the style of Carmen
     Miranda.*★)
          I don't give a shit for Nicaragua,
          I don't give a bugger for Brazil,
          I don't give a hoot for Heethiopiaa,
          I'm the one the nobs would like to kill.
     (J.P. *tries to dance with* ALISON.)
          I don't give a fart for Venezuela,
          I don't even know it on the map . . .
     (ALISON *breaks from him, back to the ironing board. He
     tastes his wine again.*)
     Actually, I believe some of the Venezuelan wines are
     quite drinkable.
CLIFF: Where did you pick up all these cheap tricks?

★An artist once endlessly impersonated by even the most humble drag queen.

J.P.: Self-taught, my dear. Self-taught.

(J.P. *sits down and returns to reading the paper*.)

CLIFF: I feel quite snoozy.

J.P.: Well, don't go to sleep.

CLIFF: I see they're still having trouble in Market Harborough.

J.P.: Oh yes? Buttered toast.

CLIFF: What?

J.P.: Buttered toast. A recent survey carried out by the Human Engineering and Social Technology Department of Chichester New Town University has produced an impressive body of evidence in its third report that the annual consumption of more than five hectares of white buttered toast per person may lead to a serious incidence of pre-marital incest, particularly among young people.

CLIFF: They do seem to have trouble, some of these young people. I blame it on the teachers.

J.P.: And the parents.

CLIFF: Man is born free but everywhere –

J.P.: Persons.

CLIFF: – are crying buckets of Bollinger.

J.P.: A non-poly-saturated diet must be imposed by the process of education and, if necessary, by statute and, ultimately, other means. A national campaign must explain to the public the causes and dangers of buttered toast and the horrifying spectacle of the incest crisis about to shatter our English obsession with class. It cannot be too strongly repeated for the benefit of those young people unable to read the instructions on a used condom, that it cannot be caught by sharing a National Health dildo, or any other infrastructure of a male-dominated political system or multiculture crisis situation.

CLIFF: Why has all this been kept from us for so long?

J.P.: Because, Whittaker, because our ancient freedoms and rights to expression are being slowly but inexorably strangled.

CLIFF: I thought it wasn't just my feet.
>   (*Pause.*)
J.P.: (*Suddenly*) A black feminist dike from Khartoum.
CLIFF: We *don't* wish to know that.
J.P.: A black feminist dike from Khartoum
>   Took a nancy-boy up to her room . . .
CLIFF: We've heard it before, Alison?
J.P.: Well, *I* haven't.
>   A black feminist dike from Khartoum
>   Took a nancy-boy up to her room.
>   Why doesn't this government *do* something about it?
>   Instead of raising up temples to the greater glory of
>   greed and the sanctification of profitability, the blasting
>   of the furry rights of helpless animals . . . Here! Dear
>   sir, as a severely handicapped and lifetime campaigner
>   for Fallen Sparrow Concern . . .
CLIFF: Fallen cuckoos for you, dear.
J.P.: Fallen Sparrow Concern, I feel I must protest most
>   vigorously against the unfeeling obsession and
>   glorification in your advertisements for the so-called
>   properties of Kattomeat. The money being spent on this
>   vile industry could go to providing a thousand kidney
>   machines and alleviate the sufferings of a million unsung
>   sparrows in the Third World. In this age of privatized
>   selfishness, is it not a scandal that some persons are
>   sobbing themselves to death in a sea of Perignon while
>   others huddle, Fidelio-like, and grieving beneath the
>   aching spaces of the river's span at Waterloo? A million
>   nesting boxes cry out. Take back your buttered toast
>   and – Give Me Yesterday.
CLIFF: The Château Concern '56, please, duckie, pass it over
>   here.
>   (J.P. *does so. Pause.*)
>   Did you know it was National Motivation Year?
J.P.: No.
>   (*Pause.*)

CLIFF: Apparently.

J.P.: Seems to have passed *us* by.

CLIFF: What?

> (CLIFF *begins to nod. Pause.*)

J.P.: Lots of things. Don't go to sleep.

CLIFF: Why not?

> (CLIFF *disappears behind the paper. Pause.*
>
> J.P. *looks at* ALISON *for a response. She is clearly absorbed in one of the Top Thirty or so.*
>
> CLIFF's *head has meanwhile gone forward on his chest. Just dropping off.* J.P. *above him then leans forward above Cliff's slumped newspaper.*)

J.P.: When you *wake* in the morning! –

CLIFF: (*Starts*) Stupid sod!

J.P.: (*Sings sweetly, slowly and very crisply, rather like Coward, to the tune of 'John Peel'*)

> When you wake in the morning . . .

CLIFF: I'm going to bed . . .

J.P.: Full of . . . fucks and joy . . .

> And . . . the wife's in prison . . .
>
> And your daughter's coy . . .
>
> (*Smiles at* ALISON.)
>
> What's the matter with . . .
>
> (*With emphasis*) The bottom . . . of your eldest boy . . .
>
> When you wake . . . with the horn in the
>
>> morning . . .
>
> (CLIFF *looks at him, still rather dazed. Recedes behind paper for comfort.* J.P. *sups his wine. He smiles benignly at* ALISON.)
>
> Songs for swinging sexists.

ALISON: Very nice.

J.P.: Well, you know, the Senior Citizens' Christmas outing. *They* like it. It cheers them up a bit. Me and Dorita find it gets them going.

CLIFF: Heigh ho.

ALISON: I was just thinking . . .

CLIFF: Now who sang that?

J.P.: My dear . . .

CLIFF: Webster.

J.P.: Oh yes. He could be amusing in those days.

CLIFF: Before success spoiled him.

J.P.: Success merely put the hollow crown on the hollow selfish shit he always was.

CLIFF: Wonder if he ever learned to play the banjo.

ALISON: Never mind.

J.P.: No, *please* . . . You were asking?

(ALISON *huddles back to her headphones.*)

ALISON: How did you really feel when your first wife left you?

J.P.: How did I feel? Cliff?

CLIFF: How do *I* know what you felt?

J.P.: *You* were a witness to that memorable scene.

CLIFF: Well, go on, tell your little daughter. She's asked you a question. How did you feel when your first wife left you?

J.P.: I felt . . . I thought . . . I shall never have to go to the ballet again . . .

(*They return to their papers.* J.P. *relights his pipe. It belches black and furiously around them.*)

You know what?

(*No response.*)

Well . . .

CLIFF: What?

J.P.: I *feel*. I feel: very Dayzhar Voo.

CLIFF: Yes?

J.P.: Yes.

(*Pause.*)

CLIFF: Dayzhar *what*?

J.P.: Dayzhar Voo.

CLIFF: Well, you always *were*, weren't you?

J.P.: Not really, people thought I was.

CLIFF: Get on. You were born *déjàvu*.

J.P.: Actually, you are quite wrong. As always and, impeccably, fashionably wrong, ignorant and deluded.

CLIFF: Now then, you should mind your rhetoric at your time of life. Sorry, Lord Sandy.

J.P.: Let me explain if I can penetrate the mists of your radical squalor. Our furry friend Teddy is *not déjàvu*, as you, and a million other clockwork cunts, would have it. Very simply because he is *not* something which you have 'already seen' – literal translation from a forever foreign tongue. Thus, *déjàvu*. The meaning of which is quite simply a deluded sense of recall, a *recherché* experience which could not possibly have taken place and most certainly not privy to the likes of canting pillocks like yourself.

CLIFF: My, that old White Tile Alma Mater did you proud, didn't it? Gave you a life-long grammar of aloofness.

J.P.: Indeed, but not, alas, the language.

(*Pause.*)

Do you remember the Bishop of Bromley?

CLIFF: Which one's that?

J.P.: Not the present one. The one who believed in God.

CLIFF: Oh yes. And the H-bomb. We rather liked him. Or did we?

J.P.: He was preferable to this one.

CLIFF: Oh yes. Here he is. Good God, do you see how old he is?

J.P.: No.

CLIFF: Forty-one.

J.P.: They're getting like the policemen.

CLIFF: What's *he* on about?

J.P.: The newly created Bishop of Bromley, the Right Rev. Ted Sprogg, yesterday lashed out at the backward elements in his diocese. Sitting in his newly opened cafeteria in the Cathedral Close, the Reverend Ted, seen here with his wife Meryl, will refuse to wear the outmoded mitre and ecclesiastical gear at his enthronement next month. Wearing jeans and an open-necked shirt, he spelled out the future in today's plain terms. The new bishop, author of the controversial *An Unemployed Teenager Speaks with Christ*, author also of *Christ, the Good European* and *Those Feet in Europe's Green and Pleasant Land*, told his enthusiastic assembled flock what they could expect.

CLIFF: I got quite fond of Mark One.

    (*Church bells start ringing*.)

J.P.: Gone with the perils of this night, that comfort which the world cannot give and that service which is perfect freedom.

    (CLIFF *puts down paper to listen to the bells*. ALISON *can't hear them*.)

CLIFF: Bloody bells . . .

J.P.: I like to *hear* them . . . (J.P. *gets up slowly, goes to the window, looks out, then opens it. They are immediately much louder*.) Ring in the larger heart . . . the kindlier hand . . . Ring out the darkness of the land.

CLIFF: Don't they know someone's going mad in here? That poor girl's in a draught.

J.P.: Endless changes can be rung.

CLIFF: Can't hear.

J.P.: On church bells of the English tongue.

CLIFF: Why don't you close the bloody window?

J.P.: (J.P. *closes the window*.) You know we sometimes said . . .

CLIFF: What?

J.P.: Said all our children would be Americans.

CLIFF: You may have done. I never went in for that kind of grandiloquent small talk.

J.P.: Pity about America. If only it had grown up. I was very fond of America.

CLIFF: They were very nice to you.

J.P.: Now it's the Australian Age. Antipodea or the Recidivists' Revenge.

CLIFF: Well, I suppose the lower middle classes had their kingdom coming to them. A three-piece suite is the same the world over, right way up or upside down.

J.P.: How wise you are, in your simple open-hearted way, mighty continent, strainful strine, dark and unlovely suburb of the loveless desert . . .

CLIFF: Kookaburras flying duck-like on our every wall.

J.P.: Enthusiasm not appreciated. Effete and Pommie. You can't *impress* an Aussie however you squeeze their sun-baked leathery hearts. O Lord, protect me from the Australian Hun.

CLIFF: Do you think God is an Australian?

J.P.: Most certainly. *And* a woman. Ah, there he is His Grace, the Right Rev. Ted Bromley, himself a native of Wogga Wogga, which, if you rate Sydney as the Byzantium *de nos jours* on your cultural Richter scale, is somewhere between the twin dioceses of Canberra and Milton Keynes. An interloper to his horny fingertips, The Rev. Ted now speaks with the tongue of the horrible Brit, a brutal breed he has helped create as a seething, colonial act of revenge. Why, your craven ursine friend there would give his best furry pair of fourteen-hole Doc Martens to find the favours of koalas like Noylene, Norene, Charlene and Chlorine, all ripped timely from that knuckle of abandonment, old Ockers rib.

CLIFF: He does exaggerate, don't you, whitey? Still, he's *happy* . . .

J.P.: Did you ever miss the old sweet-stall?

CLIFF: No.

J.P.: Neither did I.

CLIFF: It was better than working.
(*Pause.*)

CLIFF: Alison's looking a bit frail.

J.P.: Why? She's been asleep ever since she came down here. About eighteen hours.

CLIFF: She's tired –

J.P.: We're all tired. She doesn't have to bring all that bloody ironing with her, does she? I shall burn that ironing board. *I've* never used it. It's a *plot* . . . Teddy's very quiet.

CLIFF: Thinking, I expect.

J.P.: Oh?

CLIFF: He looks thoughtful.

ALISON: Maybe he's bored.

J.P.: Oh, you *can* hear.

CLIFF: He's too polite. And caring.

J.P.: If he's bored he can get up and go.

CLIFF: Oh, he still enjoys a joke. Just like the next bear.

J.P.: But not Teddyist jokes?

CLIFF: He's very vulnerable.

J.P.: Aren't we all? Thin-skinned, I think you mean. Like all dissemblers, he shrinks from hard words. Thinks he's cuddlesome, I suppose.

CLIFF: He is.

J.P.: So are lioncubs. But they like raw meat.

CLIFF: Teddy's aware that to survive he must become increasingly competitive.

J.P.: So he should.

ALISON: I thought bears were –
(J.P. *looks up sharply.*)

J.P.: What?

ALISON: Oh – Beautiful?

J.P.: Not the way you say it.

CLIFF: Bears *is* beautiful.

J.P.: Bears is often bullies.

CLIFF: So might you be if you were a persecuted minority.

J.P.: You mean rancorous and noisy?

CLIFF: Ah, colonel, you've no feelings.

J.P.: I have, but I don't present them as cuddlesome.

ALISON: Not in your case they aren't.

CLIFF: She's right there.

J.P.: Some have found me passing cuddlesome.

CLIFF: It's sickening to contemplate the way this country treats its Teddies.

J.P.: The ones who cry over Teddy never lived next to him.

CLIFF: This constant sanctification of greed.

J.P.: You bet – all I think about is where my next hot buttered toast is coming from.

CLIFF: Teddy doesn't believe he's truly boring.

J.P.: Only the truly mad believe they're sane. I'd say that bear could do with a spoonful of reticence in his morning honey.

CLIFF: You've never suffered the marginalization of being a bear. The harassment, the prejudice.

J.P.: Yes, I have. It's on the record.

CLIFF: Never unemployed.

J.P.: *I* got myself a sweet-stall, remember, dreamboat?

CLIFF: *You* never grew up with an outside toilet.

J.P.: The cold wind round a young bear's parts doesn't seem the worst wound life can inflict. Besides, if he'd troubled to read the neatly cut-up newspapers hung handily and ingeniously on the empty toilet roll, he might have overcome his snivelling illiteracy.

CLIFF: All right for you. *You* live in a big house.

J.P.: Yes, but I keep two rooms in a Sunderland back-to-back just so I don't lose contact with my working-class roots – and where I can give interviews to the press.

CLIFF: Teddy is going to take his case to the European Court of Human Rights.

J.P.: Teddy – is not, I'm sorry – human.

CLIFF: Oh yes? How do you *know*?

J.P.: I don't.

CLIFF: Exactly . . .

J.P.: How right you are.

CLIFF: I'm afraid so.

J.P.: It's taken me almost, well, indeed, a lifetime to realize that I am wrong about – well, everything.

CLIFF: About time, my dear friend. About time.

J.P.: Yes. None too soon.

CLIFF: No wonder Teddy's gone quiet.

J.P.: There should be a Sunday moratorium on Teddy's big mouth.

ALISON: Say that again.

J.P.: I wish he'd shift his comfortable big arse down to the cellar for me.

CLIFF: *He* doesn't want an alcohol problem.

J.P.: To him, anything pleasurable's a problem.

CLIFF: The trouble is –

J.P.: Make him shut up.

ALISON: Please, Cliff.

(*They both look at him.*)

CLIFF: Teddy's asked me to tell you –

J.P.: Well?

CLIFF: He wants to get out of all this and –

J.P.: What?

CLIFF: Start living in the real world of today.

J.P.: Does he? He always did have a whimsical streak.

(*Sings:*)

> Teddy'll work for de local guvmin,
> Teddies all work for de town hall boss,
> Tings dat make de anti-racist cross.
> Don't look up man!
> Don't look down.
> You don't dass made de black boss frown . . .

(J.P. *returns to his paper.* CLIFF *going on when the game is closed . . .*)

CLIFF: I suppose if he doesn't like it here he can always go back to where he first came from.

J.P.: Precisely. A list of caring agencies is kept on the dresser where even he can reach it. You too. In the china-squirrel bank. Any time. Go back to sleep. Damn!

CLIFF: What is it?

J.P.: I've lost the Bishop of Bromley. Have you got him?

CLIFF: No. Don't think so.

J.P.: You *must* have. (*Pause.*) You know what's wrong?

CLIFF: Tell us, anyway.

J.P.: These. (*Holds up a quality Sunday paper.*) When we couldn't afford them, we spun them out the whole Sabbath. Look at that: a week's deadweight of investigative insight – interviewing junk. Why are you so *slow*, Porter. Once you could waste your energies for a passing laugh. You could take on the excesses of tedium, but no longer. You haven't the time. Look to your trusty filleting knife. (*Begins deftly to 'fillet' the papers.*) Business section: certainly not. The *Spectator*: can damage your health. Appointments: no interest whatever. Sport: banished from this house at all times. (*He applies himself to the rest beside Teddy.*)

CLIFF: Hey, not the sport.

J.P.: Out, damned sport. Review of the Week. All of you. The *Oldie*?

CLIFF: Surely no one reads *that*?

J.P.: (*Shoulders a pile of papers and magazines.*) Out! All of you. (*Takes them to the window and throws them out.*) There! That's better! You'll feel the benefit of it, later!

CLIFF: Bit drastic, if you ask me.

J.P.: (*Indicating* ALISON) Have you met the boyfriend, Anfony? Yes. Yes, you have. *He's* in search of motivation. Very short of it. Offer him the smallest handy grappling iron up the mountain slope and his reply? (*Yob accent*) '*Well*, it's not wurf my while, is it?' Anfony's whiles are almost beyond price or ingenuity . . . Not unlike those little sonny Jims of yours, the beasts of Beadales, and, before it goes unsaid, mine own poor thing. Ah, but they like expensive things to slurp with their beefburgers, beans and chips. The only time those brooding lads ever acknowledge me at all when you bring them to my house for a little easeful conviviality is when I rattle the stick in the champagne

bucket. Over they lope, hop skip and grunt, their
knuckles brushing the floor. What does that elder son of
yours want to be when he grows up?

CLIFF: An adolescent.

J.P.: Ah, like his grandparents.

CLIFF: He's not so bad.

J.P.: No?

CLIFF: He just wants to believe in something.

J.P.: How admirable. Like my own young feller-me-lad.

CLIFF: I don't know about my lot but young Jimmy's up
against a lot of things that weren't around for us.

J.P.: You mean you and I were more fortunate?

CLIFF: Looks like it.

J.P.: The old sweet-stall was a lucky break?

CLIFF: You're pretending not to understand.

J.P.: Oh, I think I understand. I don't think your lads – or
mine – would have been so fanciful.

CLIFF: I thought you said you'd enjoyed it.

J.P.: It was what I believe young actresses call 'a challenge'.

CLIFF: They don't seem to be offered much hope.

J.P.: Hope comes from within, as you well know, my poor
old guilty goosey. Be proud. You have thrived, by virtue
of your modest talents, in a cold and poisonous world.
When hope goes, we freeze. No, they are not chilled,
not with despair, why should they be? Maybe it will
come but not now. There is too much noise, comfort
and distraction. For the likes of young Jimmy. How I
hate diminutives. My real friends stopped calling me
Jimmy long ago. Oh . . . I suppose more or less when
Alison left me. (*He regards his daughter broodingly*.) She
doesn't have to do that, you know.

CLIFF: What's that, honky?

J.P.: All that bloody ironing. She has dressed like a long-haul
truck driver since she was twelve and yet, whenever
she's here, she's perched up there like the young brides
of my childhood, smoothing away at the silks and

embroidered crêpe de Chine. It can't be for Anfony. Ironing a man's shirt, even as an act of absent-minded kindliness, would be a blasphemy against her sisterhood. Perhaps it's for her old chum and blood-sister Helena. (*To* ALISON.) Has she taken to dressing up as Mrs Danvers then? Your friend? Ms Helena? She would look somewhat fetching in bombazine and leg-of-mutton sleeves. That and a stout bunch of keys. Have you noticed how portly the miners have become? Like the bishops getting younger. You must have noticed, Alison. (ALISON *lifts her Walkman headset, frowning.*)

ALISON: What's that?

J.P.: You were in on all those appeals with colliers' wives when they were flipping concrete blocks like tiddly-winks on the heads of passing cab-drivers, scabbing lackeys of the greedy classes. Raising money for the kiddies' Christmas toys as I remember, wasn't it? How do you suppose old Lawrence D. H. would have borne down over the kiddies' poor little faces as they faced Christmas without their hi-tech toys and the two extra weeks in the Costa gone?
(ALISON *looks at him, turns to the window and looks at the billowing newspapers. We see the reverse of her T-shirt, on which is written:* J.P. RULES, OK.

J.P. *goes over to the ironing board. He and* ALISON *begin a ritual game of staring each other out. Whatever childhood habit and affection there may have once been in this is quickly dissipated. They resume their customary, mutual, baleful boredom.*)

J.P.: (*Quietly, thrusting magazine at her*) Do you know who that is?

ALISON: (*Barely glancing*) Yeah.

J.P.: You do!

ALISON: It's Jason.

J.P.: Jason? And her? What about her?

ALISON: Yeah.

J.P.: You mean – you really do know who they are?

ALISON: So?

J.P.: Both?

ALISON: Are you kidding? No, you're not.

J.P.: Good God . . . (*To* CLIFF.) You don't know who they are? Well, do you?

CLIFF: Just about. (*Looking*) Yes. Well, I do have children of that age.

J.P.: So do I . . . Remember my first wife's Brother Nigel?

CLIFF: Not really.

J.P.: Ah, the rewards of wordmanship. Well, Brother Nigel had a bit of a turtley old voice in the land when you and I were quite indifferent to bettering ourselves, getting on or making some meaning of our lives. Old Nigel was at it, doing all of these things. Back bencher, loyalty, late knighthood, mind you. Brother Nigel of Outer Space. Alison's dad finally left him some hundred and fifty thousand quid. London railways, Penang rubber, glories of the Edwardian Age. All helped with the house in Godalming and the fees for Marlborough. Any road, (*newspaper*) here's young Nigel the second. Guess what he's become? An MEP no less. Minister for European pricks. Or Most Empty Person. He delights in full-time wrangling over the permitted length of bananas and the permissible centimetres demanded for the comfort of imported tortoises. I said to the man at the gate of the twenty-first century. Open up. Let us in. And there's young Nigel Junior waiting to let us in. 1992 . . . You know where I went wrong?

CLIFF: You haven't really chucked the sports section?

J.P.: You don't want me to be a passive victim of your Sunday section abuse, do you? I did think, I suppose, that those with what you might call privilege, the inheritance of confidence, family, shares, partnerships and heirlooms, being put up for your father's club, bygone perks, I thought these little gifts distributed unjustly to the likes of Brother Nigel rendered him unteachable. But I was wrong. No, it was the people I'd thought of as being oppressed or ignored by Nigel or Alison, Nigel and Alison, who were unteachable. They were avid and malign. Like those Ministry of Food women who used to preside over their trestle tables in provincial town halls, allocating ration books, if they felt like it, puffed up with power and illiteracy. 'You'll have to fill in Form NF72. Why haven't you got one?' They were the post-war sappers for all the rolling army of fanatics that have followed them ever since. I don't think we used to know many fanatics, did we?

CLIFF: The Builders Arms was pretty famous.

J.P.: I don't mean lunatics. I mean fanatics. The lady from the department with her briefcase at your door, the one that came the other week, the one with, yes, statutory powers. Lunatics do not have statutory powers.

ALISON: Did your wife get any of it?

J.P.: (*Surprised*) What?

ALISON: Her father's money?

J.P.: The middle classes never tell you when they've made a killing, especially when it's inherited money. I imagine Brother Nigel saw Alison was all right, as he saw it – he having the responsibilities, wife and three kids to educate. She looked very sparkling to me last time I saw her – that place San Antonio's with a pack of nancy friends hot from some runaway gala for Aids Concern. I don't think her Mummy would have been too happy to see her fawned on by so many strutting sodomites in a public place. The old rhino might have roared a bit at that.

ALISON: I went to that gala. It was very special and moving.

J.P.: I hope so. I really do.

ALISON: Alison read wonderfully. She really did.

J.P.: Good.

ALISON: Why don't you just shut up?

CLIFF: Yes. You know nothing about it.

J.P.: Of course I don't. How could I abandon my habitual
    diffidence, that diffidence of all right-thinking men?
      I was seeking shelter from the weather,
      It was on a rainy April day.
      You remember how we got together,
      In a shop across the way.

CLIFF: You're pissed, J.P.

J.P.: After being caught with my umbrella,
      I stepped in to have a cup of tea,
      Just for fun I called the fortune-teller,
      What a lucky day for me.
    What were we talking about before I blundered off?

ALISON: The Edwardian Age.

J.P.: Well, not much to say about that. Oh yes, except that it
    never existed. The *on dit* is that there never were long
    days in the sun, the slim volumes of verse. If the linen
    was crisp, some laundry maid's cracked hands had paid
    the price for it. As for the smell of starch, it was quite
    possibly poisonous and nothing so special. No, not only
    did we, did I at least, footlingly regret the passing of
    other people's worlds, they were ones we'd just
    confected for our vulgar comfort.
    (*While* J.P.*'s saying this, he fiddles with a tape recorder and
    then continues with his song of almost sublime banality, 'In
    a Little Gypsy Tea Room'. It is a ballad of the period of his
    childhood: the thirties; sung most famously by Arthur
    Tracey, 'The Street Singer'. However, the daunting task for
    the actor is to sing this with an unmocking sweetness so that
    it may almost overcome the cloying nonsense of the ballad
    itself. For most, it will hurtle the spectator into cool
    embarrassment – like* ALISON. *Certainly a kamikaze test of
    the potency of cheap music.*)
      It was in a little gypsy tea room,
      I first laid eyes on you.
      When the gypsy came to read the tealeaves,

It made me feel quite gay,
When she said that someone in the tea room,
Would steal my heart away.
(*Pause.*)
Strange how impotent cheap music is. Do you suppose
there ever was such a thing as a gypsy tea room?

CLIFF: Never know . . .

J.P.: I can see the girl in it. I can certainly see myself.
(*Sings:*) 'You made a dream come true.'

CLIFF: 'It made me feel quite gay.' Pretty poor tea, I should
think.

J.P.: Oh, I don't know. Hot buttered toast, oozing with
cholesterol. Some dainty cakes. Of course, the Gypsy
Tea Room, if it existed, which it didn't, wasn't
Edwardian, so it wouldn't have been too robust, even in
the imagination. I think I'd have been a small boy in the
corner, watching the man and the girl come in from the
rain, thinking of myself as him.

CLIFF: Sounds a bit like a Kelvinside tea shop I went into
one morning for a baptie. Slower than McDonald's but
more romantic.

J.P.: Camp, you'd say?

CLIFF: McDonald's is scarcely camp. Just bright and beastly.
Sorry, Alison.

ALISON: For what?

CLIFF: Can you hear with all that pounding in your ears?

ALISON: I've listened to him talking all my life. No group
could entirely drown that.
(*J.P. gently removes the earphones from her head and puts
them on his own.*)

J.P.: What pretty ears, pink, pearly lobes. How I do
remember them between the tips of my fingers. (*Listens.*)
Something strong, something simple, something.
Something English.
(*He puts the set back on her head and goes over to a large
portable record player, turns it on. An immediate blast of*

rock 'n' roll sounds shakes the room. He has to shout to make himself heard.)

Are you going to your concert, your gig, tonight? With Anfony. Are you going to *wave*? Have you noticed, Mildred, how they wave, like fields of rape, have you watched, they sway, like multitudinous stalks, they wave, limp and twitching like bleary puppies. Watch me, wave, wave and sway, come, Whittaker, wave and sway. O wave new world, proud and sound, brave, young, fearless, numb and gormless, they wave, side to side, arms stretched up, worshipping, side to side, fixed on the choreographic grunt, so tangible in the fullness of its torpor. Nuremberg was never so fine, so fluent. They are young, their hard baby fists softly flailing at the air, remote, in their thrumping, plaintive battering unison, boning fields, landscapes of them, a prairie of Babel, waving and smashing, wading . . .

(*During all this he mimes the waving gestures of massed pop concerts, encouraging* CLIFF, *achieving what should be quite an inventive piece of fairly artful mockery. When all this has gone on long enough,* ALISON *picks up the ironing board and throws it at him. Pause. The ironing board has caught him a hefty blow and his hand goes up to his head. He stands, swaying slightly. Presently, and in a quiet confidential tone of relief, he speaks.*)

You know, I was always hoping that my first wife would do that. She never did. I would see people urging her on with their eyes, shrieking silently from within: 'Chuck the bloody ironing board at him.' She was too strong, too fortified, certainly against anything as inconsequential to her as myself, too wilely and wised-up to press any red buttons.

ALISON: Who do you think you bloody are?

J.P.: No one of any interest whatever.

ALISON: I think you're mad and utterly horrible.

J.P.: I don't know why you ever come back here. I've nothing to offer you.

ALISON: You bet. You've never had anything to offer *anyone*.

J.P.: Candour suits you. You should draw on it more often.

ALISON: I come to see my brother, not you.

J.P.: I think you'll find him hemmed in by supporters. Your friend, the Rev. Ron, at the head of them. Vandals are a protected species in the Church.

ALISON: Why did you ever marry that poor woman? Or my mother, for that matter?

J.P.: It did legitimize you. It seemed proper at the time.

ALISON: Don't be so fucking cheap. Why bother to *have* us?

J.P.: Not to perpetuate myself, I assure you.

ALISON: That's something anyway. And, thank God, you haven't.

J.P.: That's a lot of questions. I'm sure you don't want me to attempt to answer them.

ALISON: No fear.

(ALISON *starts collecting up her clothes, readjusting her Walkman and cutting herself off from any further contact.*)

J.P.: (*To* CLIFF) My old dog's dying you know.

CLIFF: I didn't know.

J.P.: Well, I didn't want to spread gloom and despondency. I sat with her all last night and this morning. I'd better go again.

ALISON: (*As he is about to pass her*) Go on. Talk to your bloody dog. She can't answer back.

(ALISON *fixes her earphones firmly back in place and 'waves' in mockery of J.P.'s earlier parody.*)

J.P.: Are you angry?

ALISON: What do you think?

J.P.: (*Softly*) I think not. Anger is not hatred, which is what I see in all your faces. Anger is slow, gentle, not vindictive or full of spite.

ALISON: Couldn't hear you, old cock. Nobody wants to hear *you*!

(ALISON *'waves' defiantly. Deliberately,* J.P. *removes her headphones, picks up the attached instrument, drops it to the floor and steps on it. It crackles and breaks.*)

ALISON: (*Presently*) Oh – well done, J.P.

J.P.: I do try not to behave like the people I most despise.

ALISON: You're pathetic . . .

J.P.: No doubt. But *I* shall rally. *You* will never grapple with defeat. I refuse to allow a noisome prig in jeans and no bra to make me lose my good humour for no good reason.

CLIFF: Noisome's a good word.

J.P.: I am not known as El Cheapo for nothing. (*He goes to the door.*)

> The name is Porter,
> My critics curse on.
> I am a better class of person,
> Mangy of fur; at no time chic,
> I dine in hellfire twice a week.

(*He goes out.*)

ALISON: 'El Cheapo' is right . . .

CLIFF: Well – Teddy liked it . . .

(*Pause.*)

CLIFF: I think Teddy's given up brooding over market forces. Just concentrating on trying to become a good European. Even feeling a little less guilty over his colonial past. Aren't you? Less guilty? His part in the slave trade, for instance. About a hundred and fifty years before his time but it bothers him. Wouldn't think he had a colonial past to look at him, would you? Well, that's his considered view of it. Isn't it? (CLIFF *gropes among the newspapers for a black, hairy object which turns out to be a dreadlock wig. He arranges it on Teddy's head.*) That degree course in African Studies and Caribbean Culture didn't cheer him up either. He will worry about people, especially if he doesn't know them. Don't you, Ted? You *worry* . . . That wig's a mistake. Do you think he secretly hates whitey?

ALISON: Teddy – can go fuck himself.

CLIFF: He already thinks he's in a no-win situation.

ALISON: You know what? You two are mad. Barking.

CLIFF: Teddy's not mad. Not he that is gone into England.

ALISON: Oh, do *shut* up, Cliff. When he's not here, *you* start to sound like my father.

CLIFF: Perhaps a little mad but no, not malign. Ted never had a role model, you see. Not even a world that never existed to regret.

ALISON: You've both talked this brand of babyish balls ever since I can remember.

CLIFF: You wrong-footed him pretty adroitly just now.

ALISON: Oh? I goaded him, *I* exposed the vicious oik struggling inside every carping old dodo like J.P. Longing for some petty recompense for a lifetime of useless snarling. No wonder he prefers dogs to people. He came into this world bitching and he'll go out the same way. Unloved, unlovable and unloving.

CLIFF: Teddy's quite fond of him.

ALISON: Then Teddy *is* mad. *And* malign.

CLIFF: Did you never like him ever? As a little girl? At all?

ALISON: No.

CLIFF: Well – you didn't see much of each other. Your mother saw to that.

ALISON: She wanted to protect me.

CLIFF: Against what?

ALISON: Someone so rabid hopeless. With such a second, third-rate, oh, mind.

CLIFF: Well, your mother does have an obsession with what her sort of friends call 'first-class minds'. I don't think J.P.'s second class. What British Rail call 'Standard' perhaps. Whereas your mother's lover, Professor Randy, First Class Mind, has found at an advancing age, and to his great astonishment, that he can no longer get it up. He's been inconsolable for weeks. Even your mother's attentions with mid-morning smoked salmon and her

best Wine Society claret in the evenings haven't brought
him comfort.

ALISON: There's nothing wrong in being brainy.

CLIFF: I met a girl once. In Cannes. I was sitting on the
terrace, having breakfast and reading *The Times*. She
was sitting at the next table, looking quite gorgeous at
that time of day. Suddenly, she looked up and said,
rather coldly I thought: 'What have you got for
seventeen down?' 'Seventeen what?' 'The crossword.
You've got it there.' Oh, I thought: There goes that one.
'I'm sorry: I don't do *The Times* crossword.' Her
beautiful lip curled, it really did. 'You don't? And how
do you exercise your mind?' No joy there, I thought.
Exercise my mind? By fucking intellectual girls like you.

ALISON: Why do you try so hard to be unpleasant? My
mother admires intellect. So what? So do I.

CLIFF: There's such a thing as decent intellect. Like dumb
insolence.

ALISON: She's accustomed to the company of clever men.
She comes from a clever family. Her parents, her
brothers.

CLIFF: Ah yes, barristers, judges.

ALISON: Yes, all right: diplomats, scholars, historians.

CLIFF: And the cleverness of strangers too. You wouldn't call
J.P.'s family clever. More silly to themselves, eh, Ted?
You must have your mother's intellect.

ALISON: (*Fierce*) What's he ever given me – forget *done* for
me? And *don't* say 'What's he ever done for Teddy?'
Sometimes I think you're worse than he is. At least he
seems to *enjoy* being a bully and a bigot – every now and
then.

CLIFF: J.P.? He's just an old dog. Now, I'd say your
mother's a bully.

ALISON: She isn't.

CLIFF: She sends you up here to report on him.

ALISON: Is that what he says?

CLIFF: Why else would you come up here so regularly? When you despise him.

ALISON: Oh, and you think young Jimmy comes up to spy as well?

CLIFF: I think your brother's too unconcerned to hitchhike two hundred miles to eavesdrop on his father. He comes up for free meals, twenty-four-hour sleeps, a hefty tip and, possibly, even some respite from your mummy. Dad's place is an all-right squat, and, if there's a great gig up the road in the big city, OK.

ALISON: You must think we're hard up.

CLIFF: You forget. I have children of my own.

ALISON: Well, he's sure not doing much about his son being jumped on by the police.

CLIFF: He's talked about nothing else since *I* came up.

ALISON: Oh yes. Jimmy may go to prison. And where's his father? Slumped over a filthy old blanket in his posh drawing room we're not allowed in, keening like a peasant over a cheesy old dog.

CLIFF: I think young Jimmy is happier where he is – with the Rev. Ron. Anyway, the dog does love him.

ALISON: Yeah. Like Teddy, I suppose.

CLIFF: I don't think he is quite sure. 'Occasionally held but never moved,' as they say. I've learned very little during the time I've seen you grow up, but one small thing has become clear to me, that, apart from the fact of realizing that one's parents may be corrupt or even wicked, your children may also be vindictive and even vengeful. Above all, as with your ironing-board pantomime, something stares you in the early-morning face: that those whom you no longer love can still inflict amazing pain.

ALISON: On *him*? Who?

CLIFF: Yourself. Your mother, young Jimmy even.

ALISON: He's never loved anyone. Not even himself and God knows that *does* make sense.

CLIFF: Forgive me, Alison. I *was* there. You weren't.

ALISON: Do you think my mother cares what happens to him?

CLIFF: Perhaps you're right. It's those bloody church bells. I always told him it was a mistake having a church tower next door to your runner beans. It was bad enough in the old days, when they made him angry. I dare say the Rev. Ron will silence all that with a strong rock beat soon enough. What message do they have for young people today? Decadence, shabby sentiment, yes, what J.P. calls 'the crimson twilight'. Those were our Sunday evenings. Bloody bells. Unheeded, élitist bells. But then I was brought up a Methodist. Leave him alone, Alison.

ALISON: With pleasure.

CLIFF: He may not have lightened up your life but he hasn't darkened it.

ALISON: And he won't.

(*Telephone rings offstage.* ALISON *and* CLIFF *both wait to see if it's answered. It stops.*)

Don't you think you can drop all this seedy male conspiracy for a bit? What's he going to do for his own son when he's in such trouble? That's what I've come to find out.

CLIFF: Nothing. I imagine.

ALISON: There you are.

CLIFF: Your mother didn't exactly hurtle back from her US lecture tour. Just a few gushy phone calls and a list of pushy lawyers who only appear for the grievously oppressed. Unlike the Rev. Ron who always barges to the front at a pile-up on the motorway like a funeral parlour executive. (CLIFF *grabs the local paper and reads:*) Here we are: 'The Rev. Ron Peplow stood bail for James Hugh Porter, aged twenty, of 17 Burne-Jones Villas, W11, who pleaded not guilty to seven charges of arson and malicious damage to church property.' There must be church property nearer home, around Burne-Jones

Villas? Why did he come all the way up here for a spot of the Saturday Night Vandals? Blah, blah. 'Porter's parents were not in court. The Rev. Ron, who *also* stood bail for his own son, Anthony, (*looks meaningfully at* ALISON) said outside the court, "Our society is looking for scapegoats for its spiritual and political failure." '

(*Enter* J.P. *He is carrying a Walkman-style machine.*)

' "This unhappy incident may spotlight and target in" ' – there's a telling phrase from a man of God – ' "target in on the complacent and uncaring forces that have produced our inner cities and their tragedy may now be about to be visited upon our more comfortable and enclosed little world." '

J.P.: These words, these disturbing incidents, prompt us to ask: 'How long have we been living in an unreal world?'

CLIFF: Or the world in real terms.

ALISON: Here we go.

(J.P. *hands her the Walkman.*)

J.P.: There. I was keeping one in reserve. In case of contingencies.

(ALISON *takes it and sets it down.*)

No, the Rev. Ron targeted in pretty smartly but our own editor sounded a rallying cry to the nation.

(*He takes the paper from* CLIFF.)

Where are we? 'The New Model Army Invades the Heart of England.' Young Jimmy – one of Cromwell's men! (*Reads, quick and smarmy:*) 'An act of barbarism has been perpetrated in our midst which makes us shudder for the future. We will only add that the two young men who face these allegations are both from comfortable middle-class homes. They have, thank God, the right to a full and fair trial. We say only this: that this was an outrage committed, not in the new purpose-built cities of the twenty-first century but in the kind of small and ancient towns we assumed were still outposts against the vandalism of modern urban life.'

CLIFF: The Inner City. It sounds like the Bishop of
Bromley's hard-hitting best-seller on spiritual agony.

J.P.: That's why his spokespersons like old Rev. Ron
invented it. They wouldn't know an inner city if it was
dropped on their heads like a collier's tiddly-wink.
Detroit, *there's* an inner city for you, damnable and
desolate within, while outside, when you come to its
limits, there's just the great swathe of highway America
ahead. That's why Americans never go for a walk.
There's nowhere to go on the way.

CLIFF: I think the last tram left Leeds about 1960.

J.P.: Oh? I didn't notice. (*To* ALISON.) That was your friend
Helena on the phone. She's visiting Jimmy at the Rev.
Ron's. But the place seems to be full up. I said she could
stay here.

ALISON: (*Astonished*) Did you?

J.P.: *She* seemed surprised.

ALISON: Your last meeting wasn't very pleasant.

J.P.: Oh, I think she enjoyed taking a few sisterly bites out
of my ankle. Is she still a vegetarian?

ALISON: Yes.

J.P.: You mean she eats fish?

ALISON: Yes.

J.P.: Ah yes. And chicken. There must be fifteen rooms in
this house. I never understand why all one's guests
huddle in the kitchen like prohibited immigrants.

ALISON: The dog's occupied the drawing room ever since I
arrived.

CLIFF: How is she?

J.P.: There are those who prefer the company of pythons and
grandchildren . . . She's gone.

CLIFF: I'm sorry.

J.P.: Teddy shall wear a black armband.

CLIFF: Oh God . . .

J.P.: (*To* ALISON) You can sit in there now if you wish. Still,
I think the old thing deserves a little toast.

(*He pours three glasses. Hands one to each of them. Holds up the empty bottle.*)

I think we'll have some more of that. Well. (*Almost barks.*) Well – easy come. Easy go! (*To* ALISON.) Off to your gig, then?

ALISON: I expect so.

J.P.: After coffee in the Rev. Ron's liturgical café? Well, I dare say an evening of Nuremberg Meatloafing will raise young Jim's persecuted spirit.

ALISON: At least it's not been tamed by dogs and snobby wines.

J.P.: Tamed? Tamed? Is that what you all think? (*To* CLIFF.) Is it?

CLIFF: Chained up, a bit more like it. I can't say I've exactly walked to heel . . . yet. (*To* ALISON.) You may be right about dogs. They do have this lurching instinct to please. It's there in all their little doggy sinew. Even unto death. Well, here's to her. No, you can't accuse J.P. of that. Performs in his fashion but never aims to please. Always had a friendly wag in there for most of us.

ALISON: It's not generally noticed.

CLIFF: You *might* say that about Teddy.

ALISON: I wouldn't say *anything* about fucking Teddy.

CLIFF: He doesn't approve of swearing.

J.P.: Who's paying for the tickets? Rev. Ron?

ALISON: I don't know.

J.P.: I understand they're snapped up at pretty snobby prices.

CLIFF: Alison, love, would you save my old feet? Get us some more of this? I reckon we'll be dining in tonight.

ALISON: Sure.

J.P.: Let's have the '65. We deserve it.

CLIFF: My feet don't. She's right about wine snobs.

J.P.: I know. The Nicaraguan '89 must be coming on nicely. Less taming.

ALISON: Right.

J.P.: Thank you.

(ALISON *goes out.*)

CLIFF: We'll have something exotic but simple to go with it. (*Crosses to a shelf lined with books.*) Let's have a look at all those chat-inducing books you never use.

J.P.: Tame. I should have thought smashing up churches was pretty tame. Nasty but tame. I think everyone was delighted to see the end of that crapulous lectern bird designed by friend Helena's mentor, Laugh-a-minute Lars Jasperson. Not a moment too soon.

CLIFF: (*Riffling through cookery books*) Or that huge Arts Council offering they both worked on.

J.P.: Oh. The one in the Winnie Mandela shopping precinct?

CLIFF: Dedicated to the spirit of Saint Gabriel.

J.P.: Gabriel, patron saint of postal, radio, telecommunications, telegraph and telephone, television operators. When I hear 'money for the arts', I reach for my Semtex plastic.

(CLIFF *has caught sight of himself in the mirror.*)

CLIFF: Mirror, mirror on de wall, who am de fairest of dem all?

(J.P. *casually takes out a leather-bound book from Alison's shoulder bag.*)

J.P.: (*Casually*) Snow White, you cocksucker.

CLIFF: Teddy thinks that's offensive.

J.P.: He mustn't expect cloying good taste in this establishment. If he's so downtrodden and loud-mouthed about it, he shouldn't be so wafer-skinned. (*Turning the leaves of the book*) I suppose illiterates believe in some protocol of words. And candour breaks it.

CLIFF: Who said that?

J.P.: I did. No one.

CLIFF: Well, I wouldn't repeat it.

J.P.: You're right. My taste is going the way of my
    judgement.
CLIFF: You've marked a hell of a lot of these dishes. Ah,
    Italian. That looks good.
J.P.: I don't want any Welsh pasta, thank you. A lot of
    thought's gone into that cuisine.
CLIFF: What's that you've got?
J.P.: Young Alison's diary.
CLIFF: Wouldn't you say that was her private property?
J.P.: The great Jeremy Taylor said, 'Never ask what a man
    carries covered so curiously, for it is enough that it is
    covered curiously. Every man hath in his own life sins
    enough, in his own mind trouble enough and in
    performance of his offices more than enough to entertain
    his own company.'
CLIFF: It's a nasty flaw in the minor masterpiece of your
    character.
    (J.P. *flips through the diary throughout his speech.*)
J.P.: Exactly. Curiosity after the affairs of others cannot be
    without envy, and an evil mind. No, delighted though I
    was about the lectern, it was the memorial to poor
    Cornet Shanks VC. There was his marbled sword,
    breastplate and plumed shako and campaign medals.
    And its inscription: 'Cornet Shanks, son of the Right
    Hon. Timothy Shanks of this parish and Castle Tremlett
    – on the 20th February 1857, in a skirmish near
    Umkala, Cornet Shanks particularly distinguished
    himself when his captain was wounded by gallantly
    leading on his troop and twice and thrice charging a
    body of infuriated fanatics, thus incurring fifteen
    wounds of which he afterwards died.' D'you know,
    those vandals actually took a sledgehammer to Cornet
    Shanks and smashed him to powder.
CLIFF: Put her book away. It's private.
J.P.: Ah, deep waters here, you think? As expected,
    concerning a most empty seabed down below. (*Snaps the*

diary shut.) Not much springtime in that little heart . . .

CLIFF: I see you've marked this one up. (*Reads*) 'I said I will take heed to my ways, that I offend not in my tongue. I will cup my mouth as it were a bridle.' Blimey, where's that?

J.P.: What?

CLIFF: Your bridle. 'While the ungodly is in my sight. I held my tongue and spake nothing. I kept silent, yea, even from good words.' When did we last hear a good word from you?

J.P.: Frequently. You didn't listen.
      (*Enter* ALISON *with bottle of wine.*)

CLIFF: 'Let me know mine end, and the number of my days; that I may be certified how long I have to live.'

ALISON: 'Certified' is right.

CLIFF: 'And verily every man living is altogether vanity.'

ALISON: Man.

CLIFF: Sorry. Person 'walketh in a vain shadow: he heapeth up riches and cannot tell who shall gather them. And now, Lord, what is my hope: truly my hope is ever in thee.'

J.P.: You've caught Cliff in a Psalm situation, seeking guidelines. It's the morbid Methodism in him.

CLIFF: (*Returning the book to its shelf*) Only you would keep Cranmer next to Elizabeth David.

J.P.: The kitchen has its meaningful mysteries also. (*Hands* ALISON *the diary.*) Yours, I believe.

ALISON: Helena's arrived. Should I tell her to go?

J.P.: Ah, reinforcements. The Gay Gorgons are gathering. By no means. I'm afraid we'll bore you out, but she might find the Nicaraguan '89 amusing. There are still some brave causes left. (*Takes the wine from her. He sings a few lines quietly of 'If You were the Only Girl in the World'.*) I think that's probably the best song ever written.

ALISON: You would.

CLIFF: Better than Schubert.

J.P.: Oh, yes.

CLIFF: Strauss, Mahler.

J.P.: Different. Tell me, do I take it that you are embarking on a brave new adventure?

ALISON: What do you mean?

J.P.: Becoming a one-parent family.

ALISON: It's none of your business.

J.P.: Quite. That was always a standby in the drama of my days. Last act: get the girl in the family way. It hardly poses the same dilemma now. I can't believe your heart was ever touched by something as flighty as a caprice. Still, sloth has its ways of striking back. Like young Jim and Cornet Shanks. I must go and reassure your friend that she is welcome in our vain shadow. (*Puts his fingers to his mouth.*) 'I will cup my mouth as it were a bridle.' Promise.

ALISON: I hope so.

(The following, like the end of the scene, stretches the dangerous element of parody, even farce, to breaking point. But perhaps here in particular, it must be controlled so that both CLIFF *and* ALISON *may repeatedly undercut J.P.'s more lyrical flights without diminishing him, still allowing him to remain intact. It requires a delicate delivery from the actors and, above all, the overriding force of irony, to carry him through the snares of ridicule. Eventually, however, it is heroic, an affirmation.)*

J.P.: You ask for hope that is in no one's gift. Certainly not mine. You wouldn't come to me.

ALISON: You're joking.

J.P.: Yes. Hope does not feign feeling it cannot have.

ALISON: Don't patronize me, *Dad*.

J.P.: It doesn't dissemble or explain what is unknowable.

ALISON: Don't bother.

J.P.: It is deaf to comfort and counselling.

ALISON: You *are* deaf.

J.P.: To those who believe their heart strings are not in place to be struck and broken . . .

ALISON: You're broken, broken and washed up.

J.P.: . . . but can be – restructured is the word – by experts and crack Samaritans.

ALISON: Good and past it. We've had anger. Now it's the line on hope.

J.P.: I may be mangy, Alison, mangy, disordered but tame, tame I am not.

ALISON: Sorry!

J.P.: It suffers degradation that seems oh, infinite. And *not* always silently.

ALISON: You can say that again.

J.P.: But forgivingly.

ALISON: Forgiving. You!

J.P.: It might turn out to be my only virtue.

ALISON: No sign of it yet.

J.P.: When I was a little older than you –

ALISON: A packet of fags, a plate of Yorkshire pudding and a pint of beer all for fourpence. Even Teddy's heard that.

J.P.: The Testament of the New, you might say, did seem to have the merest edge in my restricted life. But now the Old, vengeful and warlike, has clouded over, darker than night or death because it must be *lived*.

CLIFF: (*Yawning*) I don't have to spell it out, Alison.

ALISON: Please. Don't. It's of no interest to me.

CLIFF: J.P.'s fairly potty at present. Aren't you?

J.P.: Barking.

ALISON: He always was.

CLIFF: And pissed. But not biting. Just at his own lead. Aren't you, Lord Sandy? Old thing? Young, grey-haired dodo?

ALISON: He *is* worse. You know he is.

CLIFF: It's only madness. Only nowadays they call it stress. It's just old-fashioned madness like we always had. There's a new, virulent strain, that's all.

ALISON: I know. There's a lot of it about.

CLIFF: Listen to his tone of voice, observe his demeanour. Is that the image of a madman?

J.P.: I'll smack your legs in a minute.

ALISON: Don't *you* get caught.

CLIFF: Tell us one of your feeble jokes, sing us your boring little songs. If you must. No, don't.

J.P.: Hope falters but never fawns or crowds, stands in line or even *waves*. Even in dread and noise, *your* youthful noise, tame, timid and commonplace. It strains for a snatch of harmony.

CLIFF: Oh, doesn't 'e go on! Poor old dad.

J.P.: (*Quiet, smilingly*) All of which, my dear, is probably as unclear to you as it is to me as I say it. Barking. An old trumpet, played upon but not playing. Hearing but only in my head. But, coherence isn't all. Coherence, like the intellect of your mother's friends, conceals as much as is revealed to the lost like me who contemplate the wreckage. To be alone and not demand the light, *that* dear, one-parent-family Alison –

ALISON: Words. Stupid words.

J.P.: Language! – that only is goodness, gaiety, unapproved, unlegislated, unscaled, that is alone life, triumph, victory and dominion . . . (*To* CLIFF.) You know, Whittaker – I *am* foolish. I must remember to breathe when I speak.

(*Slow fade out.*)

ACT TWO

SCENE ONE

The same, later that day. CLIFF *and* J.P. *are both seated on either side of the table, centre. Below them, in the comfortable, unkitchen-like armchairs, are* ALISON *and* HELENA, *sprawled and immersed in the 'quality' newspapers.* J.P. *is reading a Murdoch tabloid with huge headlines, smoking his pipe with genuine enjoyment, and the lamp above the table creates a billiard-room cavern of smoke and light upon all their faces.*

HELENA *is a handsome girl, rather older than* ALISON, *muscular and speedy-looking, both in body and intelligence. Charm is a word she would abhor but she has an undoubted, natural magnetism which beckons imagination. The occasional blast of a sporting gun outside punctuates the earlier action.*

CLIFF, *wearing an apron, is still concentrated on the Book of Common Prayer. On the Aga are several saucepans, simmering gently, their steam mingling with the smoke from J.P.'s pipe.* HELENA, *downstage right from them, turns her face in mild irritation.*

J.P.: (*Presently*) Who would you rather sleep with?
    (*No response. He looks up.*)
    Who would you rather sleep with?
CLIFF: Please, James, not that.
J.P.: Who would you rather sleep with? Shirley Bassey or
    Margaret Drabble?*
CLIFF: Help!

---

*In the playing of the game Who Would You Rather? names may be substituted according to the prejudices and fashions of the day and locality.

J.P.: You've *got* to choose.

CLIFF: I don't. Oh, I don't think I could bear those Tiger Bay armpits.

J.P.: Bigot.

CLIFF: All right. Margaret Drabble. Nice, intellectual cuddle.

J.P.: Sexist.

CLIFF: (*To the girls*) You can't win this silly game.

J.P.: That's right. Who would you rather sleep with? Joan Collins or Joan Plowright?

CLIFF: Myrna Loy.

J.P.: That's not what you were asked. Meryl Streep or Snow White?

CLIFF: Snow White.

J.P.: You would. Fay Weldon or the Seven Dwarfs?

CLIFF: *Not* disadvantaged people?

J.P.: Edwina Currie or Ben Elton? Colonel Gadaffi or Yasser Arafat?

CLIFF: Well, I've heard of laying a tablecloth . . .

J.P.: Come on. Imagine you're a hostage.

CLIFF: Sometimes I think I am.

J.P.: Jane Fonda or –

CLIFF: Jane Fonda.

J.P.: You haven't heard the alternative. Jean Rook.

CLIFF: There. I was right. I don't see what this has to do with the global struggle between hate and love, greed and peace, oppressors and the oppressed.

ALISON: Who's Jean Rook?

CLIFF: There you are. You're mixing up categories. It should be for tragedy, comedy, history, pastoral, pastoral-comical, historical-pastoral –

J.P.: All right, here's one for all of you.

CLIFF: They're not interested.

J.P.: Who would you sleep with? Myra Hindley or Lord Longford?

CLIFF: Bad taste.

J.P.: Would I break faith with that? It's quite harmless.

CLIFF: You've upset Teddy.

J.P.: All right, girls. Some easy ones for you. Neil Kinnock or Barry Manilow? Very well. Jeffrey Archer or fragrantly, downwardly, thrustingly Mrs A?

CLIFF: All the best ones are dead. Anti-racist-pastoral, gay-right-surbanites, rapist-inner-citical . . .

J.P.: Bob Monkhouse – or Sir Peter Hall?

CLIFF: Bruce Forsyth or Quasimodo?

J.P.: Noddy or Little Black Sambo.

CLIFF: The Rev. Ron or the Bishop of Bromley?

J.P.: Too close too home.

CLIFF: Saatchi and Saatchi or Little and Large?

J.P.: Anyone called Kevin or Wayne.

CLIFF: Or Sharon or Tracey. I know: Harold Pinter *and* Antonia Fraser *or* the Beverly Sisters.

HELENA: I thought you didn't like games.

J.P.: I don't. Here's one for you, Helena.

CLIFF: Keep it.

J.P.: Melvyn Bragg or Bernie Grant?

HELENA: It's a rather cruel, pointless game.

CLIFF: He's not at his best today. Anyway, you're dead right. Here's another good one. (*Reading*.) 'He that begetteth a fool doeth it to his sorrow, and the father of a fool hath no joy.' Proverbs.

J.P.: A stiff prick hath no conscience – Thomas Aquinas. Put that bloody book away. It causes enough trouble.

CLIFF: You really shouldn't – that's another for Teddy's swear box. Time we dished up. Come on, boyo, what's got into you? Be useful instead of sitting there failing to come up with solutions. You've been quite good up to now. Decant the Château North–South divide. Get busy. It's all right, girls. Stay as you are. The Great Goddess Aga Person calls. Born to demand, to dominate.

(CLIFF *goes to the Aga*.) Do you think Teddy's got BO?

J.P.: Palpably. (*Sniffs.*) Ah, the unmistakable, underfunded ambience of the Royal Court. BO, pot and bargain breaks at the gay sweatshop. I'm reminded of the young constable who arrested my son. I asked him how he felt about policing demonstrations like the ones favoured by Alison and her brave little brother. He said: 'I don't mind the banners hurled at your eyeballs, even the tormenting of the horses. It's that trampling cloud of BO.'

(HELENA *has stepped up her attempts to fan away the smoke and steam within. She coughs.*)

CLIFF: That stinking old pipe.

J.P.: Shut up.

CLIFF: Why don't you do something? Poor Helena, look at her. She's choking.

J.P.: I'm sorry.

CLIFF: So you should be. We're just about to eat. Didn't you read the sign (*i.e.* THANK YOU FOR NOT SMOKING)?

J.P.: Yes. The hand of Teddy, I thought. Do you suppose that heaven's been designated a no-smoking area?

CLIFF: Well, it does sound like the General Synod's idea of the Good News. You'll have to knock that stinking thing out on them pearly gates before you're allowed through. Can't have all them little cherubim keeling over from passive smoking. Can't you see St Peter putting out his gnarled old fisherman's arm: 'Sorry, J.P. you can't bring that thing in here.'

J.P.: Indeed. Peter Prig's paradise. No élitist caviare to the sound of trumpets any more.

CLIFF: All that swept away ages ago. It'll be like the BBC. 'I'm afraid if you wish to smoke – '

J.P.: It'll have to be the other place. (*He starts to refill his pipe.*)

CLIFF: Picking up fag ends for eternity. Still, you'll meet a better class of person.

J.P.: A Lucifer to light my fag.

HELENA: What *do* you get out of it? Look at it. All that smugness and deliberation, the little knives, the petty ritual.

J.P.: You mean there's no longer ritual in heaven? Just committees and persons calling themselves chairs?

CLIFF: What do you suppose the French will do? After all, their chairs are feminine. Do what they always do, I suppose.

J.P.: They'll *all* speak English. German American. Australian. Chill-cooked English. (*To* HELENA.) There's spirituality in a pipe, rarely in love but occasionally in friendship.

CLIFF: Oh do shut up, J.P.

HELENA: You really are slipping, J.P., aren't you?

J.P.: Yes. It may not be the general experience but it's *mine*, however foolish it may seem to you, Helena. Half a century of convivial smoke.

HELENA: Convivial! Filthy, you mean?

J.P.: Yes, filthy and fetid, unhygienic, the swirling anticipation of people gathered together, the blue mist of Collins and the Hackney Empire . . .

HELENA: O God!

J.P.: Picking up your cues nicely. It must be the Chilean *rosé* I slipped into your chalice.

CLIFF: You tell him to shut up, Helena.

HELENA: Why?

CLIFF: You have authority.

J.P.: Her? Her kind like it best from their own class, not NCOs like your dear self.

CLIFF: Actually when I did my National Service, they told me I was prime officer material.

J.P.: Did they? What regiment was that? Jewish Rifles?

CLIFF: I was Leading Aircraftman – *as* you well know. He does.

J.P.: Very fetching you must have looked. All Brylcreem, acne and camp concert tutu. No wonder we were trounced at Suez.

333

CLIFF: (*Indicating the girls.*) They don't remember Suez.

J.P.: There he is – the spokesperson of illiteracy spread for generations from the staff rooms of our teacher training colleges. Swansea-terrace ignorant!

CLIFF: I was a prize graduate.

J.P.: You were. You are. A tribune of the British Playground.

CLIFF: I was before comprehensives. He knows that.

J.P.: You mean it went downhill *after* they chucked you out? That third-class degree didn't help so much in them days.

CLIFF: I didn't have a third-class degree. *He* only got a poor Second.

J.P.: It was the only acceptable and only stylish one. It combined natural modesty with a refusal to strive for commonplace ambitions. Only monkey-witted little strivers got Firsts. I'll bet your pupils all called you Cliff.

CLIFF: I was addressed as 'Mr Lewis'.

J.P.: Ah, not 'sir'?

CLIFF: I drew the line at that.

J.P.: While you were trying to deprive the little Zulus of their Stanley knives, or was it bicycle chains in them gentler days of free milk and the odd traumatic caning? No wonder you didn't last.

CLIFF: There's nothing wrong with the system.

J.P.: Apart from the results we have to live with – the New Scum, like Young James and his A level pass in joined-up writing.

CLIFF: Well, tell us a joke if you won't shut up. Best of all, shut up and give me a hand. What about the one about the Bishop and the pink blancmange?

J.P.: That only makes *me* laugh and *I* heard it when I was seven. Anyway, I don't tell jokes any more. Not in front of ladies. A good woman of the meagrest spirit or intelligence can destroy a joke between the eyes of a gnat

at a hundred paces. My first wife wasn't half a bad
marksperson.

HELENA: (*To* ALISON) Why do you come back to this
madhouse?

J.P.: The Rev. Ron doesn't have an ironing board. He thinks
they're a symbol of male dominance, like Our Father,
(*chanting*) which art in the Happy Non-Smoking Zone
beyond.

CLIFF: Come on, daddy blue-eyes, help me dish up.
(*They do so,* J.P. *pouring the wine first. The meal should be
simple but with a show of formality. Little quails. Bread,
cheese and salad.*)

CLIFF: Ah, the vegetarians. No fish or chicken, I'm afraid.

HELENA: Thank you.

CLIFF: There is a chicken's Auschwitz up the road. But J.P.
never uses it . . . The quails now, *they've* been shot so I
know you wouldn't fancy them.

HELENA: They do seem to have a happy Sunday, banging
away.

CLIFF: The brutal ways of country folk.

J.P.: First, there's the tactical softening up.

CLIFF: He's back on joke abuse. Sing us a song, if you must.
Must be nearly Mother's Day. What about (*sings*):
It's my mother's birthday today:
I'm on my way with a lovely bouquet.
That's very moving.

J.P.: 'No, darling, before you start the story, it *wasn't*
Christmas Eve it was Good Friday.' That's just a
preliminary rattle to your verve. Then, during the actual
telling, there are the follow-up blows on selected targets.
'Darling, I'm sorry to interrupt but I think Philippa's
glass is empty. Sorry, darling, do go on. It's very funny
when he tells it well.'

CLIFF: Right, come on, girls. Grub up!

J.P.: There you are! *He's* doing it.
(*The girls move to the table and sit down.*)

CLIFF: It only works well when he gets the mime right.

J.P.: Up she gets, refilling already brimming glasses, plumping cushions, thrusting unneeded ashtrays.

CLIFF: Like Alison at her dressing table.

J.P.: Piss off. Eventually, the end comes, just as the paltry little punchline hurtles into sight, all but intact. It comes, the cobra strike of her hand on the poker. And, yes, she pokes the fire, not as you and I poke it, but she explodes into the embers. There is a silence and she looks up in wifely bafflement. 'Oh, I'm sorry, darling. I thought you'd finished.' Your tiny quail of wit is blown from the sky.

HELENA: Perhaps the killer instinct for the Porter joke is just an aversion to a tired old routine of juggling with stereotypes?

J.P.: You've got it, Helena. Hasn't she?

HELENA: Like mothers-in-law.

J.P.: Listen, Helena, people strain, study, often at great public expense, to *become* stereotypes; to be home-buyers, high-up-there-flying executives, brief-case Boadiceas, tragic mums, anorexics. These roles are our right, made available to all. All members of the public, stereotypes all.

CLIFF: I'm a stereotype.

J.P.: You bet you are. Your wife Ellie certainly is. 'What made you choose that colour?'

CLIFF: I'm a very warm human person, rumbling with complexities.

J.P.: You're full of Celtic shit.

CLIFF: Teddy's a stereotype.

J.P.: He was *born* one. Born middle aged, creeping little cuddly conformist.

CLIFF: Bad parenting. Doesn't know what kind of stereotype he should refuse to be.

HELENA: (*To* J.P.) And you? Are you?

J.P.: Someone's working on it.

CLIFF: He's a hermit stereotype. Most unattractive.

HELENA: (*Lightly*) I've never heard two men sit around talking such bone-crunching balls.

CLIFF: Now then.

J.P.: There you are, Whittaker. I told you: I must learn to breathe when I speak.

HELENA: Am *I* a stereotype?

J.P.: No, Helena. I think you're an attractive, unusual, perceptive woman, nobody's fool and a bit anxious to prove it. You've just picked up some bad language, all the dumb pieties of the progressives, futurologists and illiterates you have been unprivileged enough to grow up among.

CLIFF: Come on, it'll get cold. Not a punchline in sight.

J.P.: (*Pouring wine*) You corrupt and you call it caring.

HELENA: Why *do* you reach for the Semtex when you hear the word 'culture'?

J.P.: (*Sharply*) I am saying that there may, only may, be an order of precedence of arts and skills, like marine navigation, astronomy, sonata form, cabinet and clock making, gothic revival, horse racing, tapestry, oratorio, *The Tempest* and Turner and between, let us say, not unfairly, limbo, break dancing and dreadlock, rapping and pugilism, soul food and music, calypso and oil drum, *Robinson Crusoe*, Sugar Ray Robinson. Well, so much for culture.

HELENA: You shit.

J.P.: Pass me one of the posh papers, will you? Gossip, that's what we want. Now there's a cultured art. Thank you, Helena. Ah. Do you know *I* invented 'Posh Papers'.

HELENA: You?

J.P.: *I* coined the phrase 'Posh Papers'.

HELENA: Fancy. You have your footnote in history after all.

J.P.: Oh, nobody knows. Oh yes, at the end of the day, they took it on board, seeking out the world's leaders and,

sensitive to world opinion, they targeted in on it: Posh
Papers.

HELENA: You identify it and, hey presto, it exists. Like a
new strain of flea.

J.P.: I give to airy nothing a habitation and a name.

HELENA: Can you do it to people?

J.P.: Not really. Unless I can crack their motive. The quail is
excellent, Whittaker.

CLIFF: Thank you, sir.

J.P.: Don't you think, Alison?

HELENA: The vegetables are terrific.

CLIFF: I was a vegetarian for a while. *He* was too. Gave it up
same time as the banjo.

J.P.: Life is terrible and death is worse. We are unconnected
to the past, and hopeless about the future. Let me put
this idle little dinner-table doodle to you, Helena.

HELENA: Well?

J.P.: If a man says life is hell, he is thinking, 'God doesn't
love me any more.' His wife, hearing this, says, 'My
husband, doesn't love me any more.' His best friend
thinks –

CLIFF: 'Poor old bugger. He never *was* very lovable.'

J.P.: The wife says to her husband, '*You* don't love me any
more.' To which the man replies, 'I do love you. Of
course I do. All I said was: Life is hell.' To which the
woman replies, 'You wouldn't say that if you loved me.'

CLIFF: El Cheapo Teddy Award, I think, don't you, Helena?

J.P.: It doesn't require a response. I'm accustomed to the
banging of uptipped seats.

HELENA: I've often wondered, what *did* you read at that
White Tile University? What *was* it?

J.P.: Well, I tell you, Helena, it was what you might call the
Explanation Schools. I learned what marked a poet
down as 'minor', what made a masterpiece flawed,
observed the course of the class struggle as structured in
the *Beano* and the *Dandy* and why a university graduate

should be running a sweet-stall. Discuss. Where were we? Oh yes, culture. (*Grabs a dictionary from among the cookery books.*) Panacea, Polytechnic, Pusillanimous.

CLIFF: What does that mean?

J.P.: What?

CLIFF: Pusillanimous.

J.P.: How do *I* know? It's not a word I'd ever use. Wrong volume. A to M. Albigensian, Buggery, Chauvinist, blimey, aggressive patriotism. Here we are, Culture: 'enlightenment or refinement arising from artistic values and pursuit of excellence'. 'Acquainting ourselves with the best that has been known and said' – Matthew Arnold. Here's Auntie Wordsworth: 'Where *grace* of culture has been utterly unknown.' Poor old bugger. *He* got it all wrong.

CLIFF: Well, not very multicultural, Grasmere, in them days. All that tranquillity sounds fair hell.

J.P.: Wordsworth! Never faced up to the exciting potential of the Industrial Revolution.

CLIFF: Steam, coal, iron, cotton. No apprehension of the satanic mills, the envy of the world, just cloud-capped hills and dozy daffodils, ventureless, privileged, private world.

J.P.: Hell. If a man says life is hell –

CLIFF: Pass *me* the poker, Alison.

J.P.: If a man says life is hell to an American, he replies. What?

CLIFF: Does it matter?

J.P.: 'You've got a problem.' If he says it to a Frenchman, he replies, 'En français, this means nothing.' To a Welshman, life is hell?

CLIFF: 'But not in Wales.'

J.P.: To an Irishman –

CLIFF: 'Brits Out.'

J.P.: To Dr Dreadlocks: 'It's the legacy of colonialism.' To a socialist: 'It's cruel, uncaring Thatcherism.'

CLIFF: The Tory says: 'Privatize it.'

J.P.: And the feminist? Helena?

HELENA: Pass *me* the poker, Alison.

J.P.: 'The tyranny of men.'

CLIFF: Can we have the France–Wales match on, captain?

J.P.: No.

HELENA: You know what you two sound like? A pair of lovers. Befuddled old lovers.

J.P.: Yes, it was always a commonplace assumption. Especially among women and Americanos. I think Ellie gave it a lot of thought, don't you?

CLIFF: She never mentioned it. (*To* HELENA) He was always very camp, mind you. When nobody knew what that was.

HELENA: And were you?

CLIFF: Lovers?

J.P.: Good heavens, no. He's far too plain. Aren't you, dreamboat?

CLIFF: But very kissable.

J.P.: Oh yes – Miss Tongue Sandwich. Like a beery labrador.

CLIFF: Teddy's more of a dry kisser.

HELENA: Oh, not Teddy.

CLIFF: Yes, you really must stop being so camp. It's dated and it never really suited your vapid personality. Besides, you bring odium on the gay community.

J.P.: Fuck the gay community.

CLIFF: Now then!

J.P.: A sensitive writer from Arden
 Sucked thespians off in his garden
 Said: I can't get enough
 Of this heavenly stuff
 While Thatcherite tyrannies harden.
(*Gulps.*) . . . Pardon.

CLIFF: You're all washed up, Gaylord, you know that?

J.P.: For this craven Welsh wisdom much thanks.

HELENA: Your friend's right.

J.P.: Are you ganging up on me?

CLIFF: Yes.

J.P.: Well, that's all right. Complaining is *not* endearing. We
must take what comes. Rise above it.

> Young gays undergoing analysis
> Say: Straights just *don't know* what malice is
> And with anal dilation appalling the nation
> They cling to their stiffening fallacies.

I *shall* try to improve. Promise. (*He raises his glass.*)

CLIFF: Excellent. (*To* HELENA.) You've had a chastening
effect on him.

J.P.: My complaints are but the cries of severed enthusiasms.
To think that when I lay in the Anderson shelter,
suffering the abuses of the Hun, from the suburban
ashes of ration books and sweetie coupons would rise
Teddy's new almighty army, the unstoppable LMC.

HELENA: (*To* CLIFF) What's LMC?

CLIFF: Lower middle class. The likes of him. Born not in a
trunk but in a three-piece suite. Not a picture on the
walls nor a book in sight. Poor Jim, James laid waste by
junk, junk persons, children, junk ending all. All he can
do is pretend it isn't happening. No 1992 round the
corner. A lifetime before the race to run. Look forward,
beyond yourself. Don't look down, but above all, not
back. Turn again, Porter. You shall thrice be Lord
Lower Middle Classes.

J.P.: You don't seem to have done much looking back at this
quail.

CLIFF: Job Porter's complaint.

J.P.: I'm sorry, but it's barely warm.

CLIFF: It's the Great Goddess Aga.

J.P.: It's Alison's mother. My first wife's. Not *hers*. Though
it could be. It's numero uno. Come to haunt. It's her
mouldering rhino spirit. (*Bangs Aga with poker.*) Are you
in there? Can you hear me, Mother?

CLIFF: No swearing. Not in front of ladies.

J.P.: I shouldn't think they'd care to be called that.

CLIFF: Or I shall go back to London. You never used to swear.

J.P.: No.

CLIFF: Not even when you were angry.

J.P.: I *was* quoting, actually.

CLIFF: It's a bit desperate when you start plagiarizing yourself.

ALISON: Hear, hear.

J.P.: I'd say massive reputations were built on it.

CLIFF: Be positive, innovative, invent.

J.P.: Be original? Not much market there, Whittaker. Like modesty.

CLIFF: Think of something.

HELENA: No more limericks, please.

J.P.: Ah, the poor sonnets of irreverence. We need a new vocabulary of swearing. Fresh words.

CLIFF: You should have stayed down among the three-piece suites. You'd have been happier. And called your daughter Beverley, Belinda or Sharon.

J.P.: Alison was in worst taste.

HELENA: Why *did* you call her Alison?

J.P.: Actually her mother was behind it. It made her feel generous about the failure of my first marriage. She does thrive on feeling sorry for people. You've met her.

HELENA: She *does* greet you always as if you've just suffered a bereavement.

J.P.: Quite. Or are about to.

HELENA: (*Feeling disloyal*) Sorry, Alison.

ALISON: (*Shrugs*) It's just Mummy's way. She's only wanting to help.

J.P.: Who needs her – (*To* HELENA.) What gossip have I got for you? A lot's happened since you were here last. Apart from young Jim's attempted arson and wholesale destruction, but he's really an outsider. I only learnt last

week that the local verger wears ladies' underclothes.
His wife runs the post office. Apparently, these things
on the line are not hers but his. I did think they're
rather large. Everyone's amazed that Mrs Nichols didn't
win first prize for the best home-made fruit cake for the
fifth time running. I must say, so am I. If you stay for
tea you can have some. Not like news from Chile or
Czechoslovakia but it gives me something to think
about. Lots of sex round here. A little violence.
Drunkenness, yes. The pubs seem to stay open all hours
and the police crowd outside them like the SAS
watching Norma Major. There's a certain amount of
growing concern about poor Captain Shanks.

HELENA: Fancy.

J.P.: They're getting up a fund to put him back together
again. Gave 'em a fiver. I may not be hot on brave
causes but I know a more-or-less good one.

HELENA: You think so? It seems to me you've never made an
honest decision in your life.

J.P.: Honest indecision –

HELENA: Feebleness.

J.P.: Complaining may not be admirable but it's better than
sanctimony.

HELENA: Ah, the old dog's lost all the teeth it ever had.
Regretting things it never had or never were. Spitting
scorn on your wives who've both left you and now on
your children, who are just about to. Have you never
thought about what *you've* done or, rather, haven't
done?

J.P.: Little else. But you're right.

HELENA: I wish you'd stop agreeing with me.

J.P.: How beautiful you are when you're angry.

CLIFF: Oh, El Cheapo.

J.P.: Mistake. I'd given up paying compliments to ladies.
The wateriest smile. I idly admired the frock of one of
Alison's friends the other day and she looked as if she

was off howling to the rape centre. But you must admit, Helena's looking splendid. Like a cat with a bird in its mouth.

HELENA: Thank you.

J.P.: As you know, I don't much care for cats.

HELENA: No. Slobbering, grateful old dogs.

J.P.: Like all selfish creatures, cats have no manners. Do you know the most odious word in the English language?

HELENA: I can think of two. Both proper nouns.

J.P.: Foreplay. Foreplay. A word of most feminine extraction. Cloying, charmless and rapacious . . . (*To* CLIFF.) You know, Whittaker, not only must I learn to breathe when I speak, I *must* watch my inflexions. They are beginning to *plunge* horribly. We inhabit a world of dying inflexions, dragging down everything with them. Listen to young Jimmy. That *down*ward fall of the voice. Alison's not so bad. Downwardly, boringly. Cliff's Welsh at least rises in complacency. But you, Helena, your voice rises like a kite on the heath. It has the drift of irony, vigour and courage. God, imagine waking up with the sound of the Midwest or Birmingham in your ears, or the tones of Debbie or Kevin on your pillow. (*In falling inflexion.*)

What a piece of work is a man, how noble in reason, how infinite in faculties, in form and moving how express and admirable, in action how like an angel, in apprehension how like a god.

Shall I put you through now, caller? There go your high spirits if you ever had any, down, down.

CLIFF: It's getting late. I think I'll get the lamp. Mustn't get morbid.

J.P.: For every light on Broadway lies a broken heart.

CLIFF: Yes. Money doesn't buy happiness. And we've none of that.

J.P.: Ah, yes, the crimson twilight. It comes around quite soon. Don't go yet.

(*A car horn.*)

What's this then? A motor. (*Goes to the window.*) 'Tis but the Reverend Ron. I say, the Synod *has* done well by him. That's his second motor in a year. Well, he must be *mobile*. The inner city is a large parish, even though *we* don't inhabit it. He's getting out . . . left the liturgical cafeteria to look after itself. He's got one of those snappy little shirt dog-collars.

HELENA: Would you say you were a Christian?

J.P.: Not necessarily, Helena. Do you know there are people who have 'poet' inscribed in their passport? It does seem a trifle presumptuous. To call yourself a poet and sodomite is one thing, but *poet*. James Porter, poet, Christian and broadcaster. No, I think not. What do you suppose he's doing here, in the crimson twilight?

ALISON: He's come to pick up Jimmy's things.

J.P.: Ah yes, there he is with his AA book and the Good News Bible in the glove box no doubt, with last year's red nose and comic hat in aid of mob philanthropy.
(ALISON *leaves to go upstairs.*)
And there's young Jimmy, to coin one of Teddy's phrases, keeping a low profile. Why did he bother to come at all, all pale and ill-used in the vicar's passenger seat? Is *that* the face of a generation whose aspiration and enthusiasms *I* have crushed?

HELENA: Yes.

J.P.: You should read our parish magazine and see what's going on at England's heart.

HELENA: Should I?

J.P.: Its hard-hitting editor is none other than our fearless young abductor, the Rev. Ron. And here he is, on the front page, beside the Chancel Roof Appeal, featuring our very own axe-happy iconoclast, young James, as the subject of this month's 'Ron Speaks with Christ' column. 'I should have liked to take as my talking point young James Porter, a personal friend of mine and a popular figure in our parish. However, Jim, as you all know, is at present in a spot of public bother, and I am unable to discuss his situation while the matter is *sub judice*. But it does allow me to bring to your attention the plight of similar young people all over our nation. Folk who are daily being driven to violence, acts of destruction and degradation, by evil forces and often through no fault of their own making; that's telling 'em. Well, it's past remedy, I'd say, wouldn't you? I'd say yoof custody was preferable to chat-along-a-Ron. Rather face the spears of Captain Shanks's deadly dervish than the plain pop chat of the parson. In the face of such Christian things, Madam, I have become very Saracen.

> My name is Jimmy Fucked-up Porter
> It started with the Colonel's daughter.
> A stranger still I stand afraid
> Alone and in a world I never made. –

(*Doorbell rings. Long pause.*)

J.P.: I'll go.

(*Sings verse of 'It's My Mother's Birthday Today . . .',* 'With Laughing Irish Eyes'.)

> My heart is singing a happy refrain
> Blue skies are smiling above.

(*As he goes off singing.*)

> I'm going home to my mother again
> Off to the one that I love.

(*Exit. Off:*)

> It's my mother's birthday today
> I'm on my way with a lovely bouquet . . .

CLIFF: Sorry about dinner.

HELENA: It was fine. Thank you.

(ALISON *arrives back with packed suitcase.*)

CLIFF: Well, *everyone* seems to be leaving.

ALISON: Yes.

CLIFF: You staying with Ron too?

ALISON: Till Jimmy's case comes up.

CLIFF: Pity he didn't blow up that People's Mother and Children abortion in the shopping centre. J.P.'s quite right for once. You can't have much respect for the people if you think that's what they deserve.

HELENA: Are you off too?

CLIFF: Tomorrow. The real world calls. Pressing, urgent problems have to be faced, lived with, not just endured.

HELENA: He'll be on his own.

CLIFF: He's accustomed to that, I'd say.

HELENA: Well, he'll have Teddy.

CLIFF: Hope he doesn't invite Ron in. He's one of those people who are funny in their absence. Their presence is only tolerable. Think I'll light the lamp. Pity old Hugh's not over here.

HELENA: The famous friend who lives in California?

CLIFF: J.P. often rings him; late at night. Always good company, our Hugh.

HELENA: He's not exactly *famous*, is he?

CLIFF: To a few hundred people I suppose he is. Famous but unsuccessful. Somehow, he manages to carry on. A subject of interminable speculation and bafflement. He's very gifted but no one is quite sure what the gift might be. He's a kind of fireball of intelligent tastelessness. J.P. is *still* perplexed at his leaving England. But there was no place for him here. I've not see him for years. He's adopted a quite ludicrous American accent, I hear. Sad thing is, Hugh was never in London more than twenty-four hours. The captain had to dash up to town if he wanted to see him before Hugh became stricken with the idea that the country that spawned him may have insidiously poisoned him or defiled him in his hotel bedroom. He got out all those years ago, leaving J.P. to face the advancing Birnam Wood of three-piece suites and Hugh's mocking voice saying, 'What did you expect?'

(*He strikes a match, about to light the oil lamp, when a shadowy figure appears in the wrong part of the kitchen. It emerges swiftly into sight, wearing a black balaclava, a raincoat and pointing a sporting rifle. They look at it for a few seconds, then the flame from the match burns* CLIFF's *finger and he retreats from the lamp. The figure points the rifle slowly and deliberately at him, raises it, aims it and looks about to fire. Then it throws the rifle at* CLIFF, *who catches it somehow. The figure whips off the balaclava. It is* J.P., *who sings immediately:*)

J.P.: There's a little devil dancin'
    In your laughing Irish eyes . . .*
    (*When* CLIFF *has recovered from his undoubted shock after a few moments he looks down at the rifle and approaches* J.P. *in genuine anger.*)

CLIFF: You imbecile! You absurd obscene imbecile! You pillock Porter! You nearly gave me a heart attack. You did! You really did.

J.P.: Of course, I didn't. You wouldn't be fooled by a cheap trick like that. The girls weren't, were you?

CLIFF: How do you know they weren't? How could you be sure? Talk about El Cheapo. It's not even an unfunny joke to me.

J.P.: Nonsense.
    (*He continues to sing in the exaggerated style of an old Irish tenor.* CLIFF *is still not quite recovered and starts hitting him around the chest and shoulders.*)

CLIFF: You moron. Just because I'm dumb enough to fall for your cheap, pointless tricks.
    (J.P. *tries to control him, embracing him, attempting to dance with him, breaking into:*)

J.P.: When Irish eyes are smiling
    Sure it's like a morn in spring.

CLIFF: Fuck you!

*For full lyrics, see page 375.

J.P.: Come on!

CLIFF: Fuck you, you poor, washed-up, bloody inconsiderate maniac. Playing silly buggers with people's lives.

(*As their scuffling begins to subside,* ALISON *lets out a cry of rage, walks over to Teddy, grabs him, opens the mouth of the Aga and suspends him over it. The two men stop almost immediately and look at* HELENA. *She applauds lightly.* J.P. *moves rather uncertainly to the smoking Teddy and rescues him. As* ALISON *moves to go:*)

J.P.: Just a moment. Here. (*He produces a red and white football supporter's woolly cap and scarf.*) We mustn't let him depart without his colours.

(*He pulls the cap on his head and places the scarf around Teddy's neck.*)

Caparisoned thus: he will surely never walk alone. Don't you think?

(ALISON *goes out.*)

HELENA: You've no concern at all, have you?

J.P.: Concern? The busybody's gin – demonstrably not.

(HELENA *follows* ALISON *out.* CLIFF *mops Teddy down with a drying cloth and sits at the table.* J.P. *pours them both some wine, then goes to the window.*)

Well, they're all gone.

CLIFF: Fancy.

J.P.: You tomorrow?

CLIFF: That's right.

J.P.: Back to the real world.

CLIFF: It may be paved with cant and complaining. But no one tries to scare me to death.

(*A car door is slammed, outside.*)

J.P.: I had a card from Hugh the other day.

CLIFF: Yes?

J.P.: Doing a location recce for some television film, in some one-man, one-vote new democracy.

CLIFF: One man, one vote. The one man's the president and *he's* got the vote. I know. What did he say?

J.P.: Usual. Why don't I get out of this dead dreary land and come somewhere like this new, emerging country. I've been talking with the president. *With* the president.

CLIFF: I'm afraid you'll have to get used to that. Especially from Hugh.

(HELENA *appears*.)

HELENA: Used to what?

CLIFF: The fact that it's not 1956 any longer for a start. He didn't like that either. You wouldn't remember. After all this silly bugger's scrum, I'm going to watch something soothing and beautiful: highlights of the Wales–France match. (CLIFF *takes the woolly cap from Teddy and places it defiantly on his own head. Then goes.*)

HELENA: Alison told me to tell you she's sorry about Teddy.

J.P.: She was quite right. He's not at all interesting. I think he must go. Characteristically, he's already turned it to advantage. He's starting Abused Teddy Action Concern. Or is it Teddy-Line? Drink?

HELENA: I don't think so. They tell me you used to play the trumpet.

J.P.: For a while.

HELENA: Alison says you were very good.

J.P.: She can't remember. The Gatling gun of the guitar had mastered the world long before she was born.

HELENA: Don't you *ever* play it?

J.P.: Oh, on my own now and then. My old dog didn't like it too much. Before, it used to annoy the neighbours. Now I don't have any neighbours. My dog's gone but there's still the wild life. I shouldn't pollute the environment for *them*, should I? (*He opens a cupboard and takes out a case, places it on the table and takes out a trumpet, giving it a polish or two with his handkerchief.*) Anyway, I lost my puff. And it didn't seem an appropriate sound any longer. You really wouldn't enjoy it at all.

HELENA: No?

J.P.: No.

HELENA: Why not try me? There's no one here.

J.P.: I'm out of practice. Are you going too?

HELENA: Yes.

J.P.: I'll take you over.

HELENA: I've ordered a taxi.

J.P.: Very sensible . . . If I promise not to sing or tell jokes – would you delay your departure? Slightly? You'd be quite safe.

HELENA: I know.

J.P.: You're quite right. I'm very tired and you're very young. Irony. That English virtue that purifies our rowdy passion . . . (*Handles the trumpet.*) You wouldn't care for this – not ever . . .(J.P. *goes to window, his back to audience. Then he starts, tentatively, to play 'Lead, Kindly Light'.*)

HELENA: You've really fucked up your life, haven't you?

J.P.: Yes . . . With a little help. But it's not quite over yet. (*Puts down trumpet. Looks at the wine.*) Shall we finish this? Oh, it's almost dead. (*He pours out the remainder. Pause.*)

HELENA: You could open another.

J.P.: (*Raising his glass*) My old dog had the best idea. To caprice.

HELENA: To brave causes. Ecce il leone!

(*They drink.* J.P. *snaps on the tape recorder – 'Tornami a vagheggiar' from Handel's Alcina. A superb female voice seems to come from him as he mimes the aria, first front, then to her. He coaxes her to her feet, putting his arm around her. Amused a little, she moves with him, then slaps his face mockingly. In return, he kisses her lightly but warmly, as the orchestra takes over from his mime . . . Fade out.*)

The same. Some weeks later. Mid-day. CLIFF *and* J.P. *are seated in their respective armchairs.* HELENA *is standing behind the ironing board. She wears a T-shirt inscribed with the words* J.P. IS SCUM, OK. *Teddy is wearing a bandage.* J.P. *is wearing a gaudy tie which, from time to time, he fingers nervously.*

J.P.: (*Presently*) Why do I do this every Sunday?

CLIFF: No. Please not . . .

J.P.: Yes. It *was* a stupefyingly stupid question.

CLIFF: No more questions.

J.P.: No more *answers*.

CLIFF: You never had any.

J.P.: Never. I don't think I ever tried to stop anyone doing anything.

CLIFF: Erase the past. Right, Helena?

HELENA: Not so difficult. In my case.

J.P.: Don't miss what you've never had. Or thought you never had.

HELENA: You seem in a dull mood. Both of you.

CLIFF: I know. Come on, J.P. Sparkle a bit!

J.P.: *You* sparkle. Helena: sparkle.
(*Pause.*)
(*Noël Coward delivery*) I went round the world, you know.

CLIFF: How was that?

J.P.: The world? Developing.

CLIFF: And you? And have *you* developed?

J.P.: Not at all. Still, ultimately and finally a futile gesture.

CLIFF: Well, you can't repeat each cheap, easy success.

J.P.: No return bouts for El Cheapo. Why am I so modest, Whittaker?

CLIFF: You have every reason.

J.P.: Indeed, why did I not learn the art of immodesty?

352

CLIFF: You could have had two shows of your own on telly. Been an MP demanding inquiries.

J.P.: I do. I demand an inquiry. Good God, no I don't. Hand me the other one.

(CLIFF *does so*.)

CLIFF: Teddy's concerned –

J.P.: *I* thought there was going to be a moratorium on Teddy.

CLIFF: Was there? When?

J.P.: Helena?

HELENA: Weeks ago.

J.P.: All right then, let's get it over. What's the latest from the Ursine Rialto?

CLIFF: For one thing: he's concerned about the North–South divide.

J.P.: Tell him to forget it. He's in the Midlands.

CLIFF: Ah, but what about his *position*?

J.P.: Let him look to his infrastructure. It looks pretty ropey to me.

CLIFF: Yes, but do you think it makes a *statement*?

J.P.: Is it necessary?

CLIFF: Oh, it is. Particularly as he is caught in the poverty trap.

J.P.: Oh, a cardboard case, is he?

CLIFF: Well, not exactly. Yet. But he is dependent on your charity. Which is demeaning.

J.P.: Perhaps he should spend less on guzzling all those nasty buns?

CLIFF: Instead of making a cheap, wholesome soup out of stock and vegetables. What do you take him for? A peasant?

J.P.: He doesn't work, so I suppose he can't be.

CLIFF: He can't eat wholesome food. Capitalist society has seen to that. No, this is a matter of laying down first principles. What's required in our changing society is a Teddy's Charter.

J.P.: Indubitably.

CLIFF: But he needs your support.

J.P.: Counselling?

CLIFF: More. You see, our Ted has an astute mind *but* he's a poor communicator.

J.P.: So am I. Nobody understands a word I say.

HELENA: Telling me.

CLIFF: But you're privileged. How can he even contemplate bringing young bears into the world?

J.P.: Tell him – don't.

CLIFF: There's the pressing question of Fathers' Rights. What guarantee does he have?

J.P.: He wants to be rewarded for being a father? *And* being a Teddy?

CLIFF: Our society does nothing but place outmoded obstacles in his path.

J.P.: Couldn't he drop concrete blocks on a few intransigent cancer patients *en route* for the chemotherapy department?

CLIFF: I shall ignore that attempt at bad taste.

J.P.: I try my little best.

CLIFF: He wants to *participate*. That's why he's become such a totally convinced Euro-European.

J.P.: Gone native, has he?

CLIFF: He won't be put down by the likes of you any longer. No, that's why he's hopeful at this moment in time, at the end of the day, of learning the languages of the future: Urdu, Bengali, Gujerati . . . Welsh.

J.P.: Well, tell him to wash his mouth out afterwards.

CLIFF: He already has a firm grasp of New York Jewish humour and the international role of comedy in film –

J.P.: Oh yes, supporting wild life.

CLIFF: Damn it, J.P., he's only human –

J.P.: Damn *you*, that's just what he's not. It's what he's been told.

CLIFF: All he wants is to learn.

J.P.: His own way, you mean –

CLIFF: To create a better and more just society –

J.P.: Teddy on board. Keep your distance. Above all, like children, he must be dissuaded from any, but any, forms of self-expression.

CLIFF: You know, J.P., I really had come to believe that you had mellowed. Everybody says so.

J.P.: I am. Mellow, mellow, sere and yellow, a mushy, over-ripe and sleepy pear.

CLIFF: No. You're not. I was mistaken. You're bad. You're giving out very bad vibes. And it's very noticeable.

J.P.: Well, my free and everlasting vibe for Teddy and all his kind is simple. I wouldn't give him the sweat from my balls. Now –

CLIFF: What about some more Nicaraguan '89?

J.P.: You know where it is. My feet hurt.

CLIFF: Try washing your socks. This is quite good. Pity Alison's not here.

(HELENA *looks half-comically distraught.*)

HELENA: Which one?

J.P.: This tie is a frightful mistake. Sorry, Helena. I look like an executive.

HELENA: No. You don't actually.

J.P.: Ah 'actually' – try and put *that* in Gujerati. Here we are. 'This Sunday, Actress Janey Proudfoot opens her heart for the first time. "I've learned to minimize my stress," says Janey, forty-one, playing with her cottage-cheese salad and sipping Perrier.' Forty-one! Blimey, she was forty-one when we were contravening the Street Traders Act of 1956. '"Acting is indispensable to my personality. My work is filled with challenges and constantly having to communicate."'

CLIFF: She's been reading again.

J.P.: Have you ever seen any of this woman's films?

HELENA: Can't say I have.

J.P.: '"As an actress, sensuality and eroticism are something that I forge consciously." It is, she says, a structured approach.' Hear that, Teddy? '"Are you still vulnerable?" I asked. "Good God, yes. Everyone is. The difference is that I'm prepared to admit it. When I act, the danger and the fear are there until the day I die. I use my men as buffers against the world. I call it keeping Janey safe." She mentioned to her manager that it was time to go, rattling her discreet jewellery at me. "She really does go straight for it," he said. And she has no ego, which is a rare thing.'

CLIFF: Blimey!

J.P.: 'She turned to go and all eyes in the room swivelled towards us. She held out her hand in farewell. "I am into personal growth," she said.'

HELENA: Silly bitch.

CLIFF: What's on the telly?

J.P.: Wales versus France, no doubt. We don't want that.

CLIFF: Speak for yourself.

J.P.: What a gift from Zeus. Never to be bored by yourself. Only by others. Alison, the wife, was never happier than when she set out to become an actress. I bored her.

CLIFF: You did, captain. You did.

J.P.: Everybody bored her. Same with young Alison's mama. After she's extracted their own unique little piece of distinction or fame from someone and shot it up into her own system, it's on to the next. Every day brings a new baby seal to be lamented.

CLIFF: One thing, Porter, you were never a baby seal.

HELENA: Were you never bored with *them*?

J.P.: Oh, yes.

HELENA: You talk about them enough.

J.P.: (*Light, almost musical-comedy vein*) They are my pestilential years. How *can* I disregard them? Besides, I never had their godlike gift. A system of immunity to any later opportunity of self-boredom. What it must be to stand up and say, 'I am into personal growth.' If only

God were to make actresses and politicians of us all, borne aloft on the clouds of self-delight!

CLIFF: What's on?

J.P.: What have we here? Entertainment. What to watch out for. Well: the Hollywood star Perkin Schwarzkopf is to make an appearance in a new West End production of *King Lear*. 'Typical of his artistic approach to each part he plays, Perkin researched the role by living as an inmate in an old people's home for five months and underwent at least three weeks of enforced feeding and incontinence.' There's a box-office advance of £700,000 for the limited season. Ah, yes, on Good Friday the Great Midlands Leisure Complex is presenting a rock version of *Messiah*. A man of sorrow and acquainted with grief becomes a disoriented guy uncounselled in his stress. Top DJ Keith Katz says, 'Old George Frederic would have loved it! After all, he was the great pop musician of his day.' Several prominent churchmen enthusiastically agree, including –

CLIFF: The Rev. Ron.

J.P.: Wait for it. The –

CLIFF: Bishop of Bromley.

J.P.: Who says it makes the Christian message meaningful for young people in a pulsing idiom of today. 'After all, what is Christianity but the story of the one-parent family?'

CLIFF: He said what!

J.P.: I do not have the facility or energy for inventions. Why bother with art when every man's his own surrealist?

CLIFF: Perhaps we should go.

HELENA: I've booked tickets for you both.

CLIFF: There's a lady here complaining there's no such thing as a lesbian Tory.

J.P.: Blimey, she should come and live here. One ex-major, a sergeant and two ex-WAFs, the riding-school lady, a retired industrial psychologist and one joint MFH.

CLIFF: And that's just in the village. They all seem to like *me*.

HELENA: Why shouldn't they?

CLIFF: Why should they?

J.P.: If life's been hard on them, they don't blame it on J.P. Dominant Male Esquire.

CLIFF: You're about as dominant as Minnie Mouse.

J.P.: I was always a baby seal at heart. What are *you* smirking about?

CLIFF: I was just thinking of Janey in heaven.

J.P.: At least she's a non-smoker.

CLIFF: That should get her in.

J.P.: You say I'm negative, all gripe and no solutions. What *about* Young Folk's Homes? Pre-retirement homes for Junior Citizens? Senility is institutionalized. Why not adolescence?

HELENA: You don't like anyone, do you?

J.P.: Yes. But I may get round to it.

HELENA: *You* were never an adolescent?

J.P.: I wasn't a teenager.

CLIFF: They were before his time.

J.P.: Nor middle-aged. My school was stuffed with executives in short trousers already pining for their pensions. Missed both stages. It says here –

CLIFF: That's enough of that.

J.P.: 'Sir Anthony Wills, our foremost theatrical administrator and champion of the arts, admits freely to being a lifelong workaholic.' How disgusting. Admitting openly to work abuse.

CLIFF: What will *he* get up to in heaven?

J.P.: Chuck *my* money at a lot of no-talent con-persons. A superb politician – Politician! He looks like Guy Fawkes and they think he's smooth and subtle, is at his desk at 6 a.m. seven days a week, hates holidays . . . I can't bear it!

CLIFF: What's on the telly? Why can't you lead a full and useful life like that? Give it here.

J.P.: Well, let's have something cheerful, ducks. I can't say I really believe in this tie. It needs restructuring. Like a dead and alive hole like this place. Well, I've had quite enough upsets in my life, I can't stand any more. Yes. Well, you don't want any more, do you? *You've* had your share as well, haven't you?

CLIFF: I have.

(HELENA *leaves the ironing board and looks out of the window. A depressive mood is descending on all of them.*)

J.P.: Nemmind, duck. God pays debts without money.

CLIFF: That's right.

J.P.: *I've* never owed anybody anything.

CLIFF: You haven't, no.

J.P.: I was always an honest person.

CLIFF: You were.

J.P.: Always. Never owed anybody nothing. Still, they don't care, do they? They don't –

CLIFF: They certainly don't.

J.P.: It's a funny old world, innit?

CLIFF: That's right.

J.P.: Wouldn't do if we was all the same, would it?

CLIFF: My God. No.

J.P.: Still, it makes you think.

CLIFF: It does.

J.P.: Sometimes I sit on the toilet. They've still done nothing about that glass pane in my toilet.

CLIFF: No?

J.P.: I've written to the council.

CLIFF: They won't do nothing.

J.P.: 'Course they won't. Nobody cares about us.

CLIFF: This Government wants hanging if you ask me.

J.P.: Too good for 'em – eh? (*Chuckles.*) No, I sit on the toilet of a morning and I say to myself, 'Jim.'

CLIFF: Yes?

J.P.: You've got nothing to reproach yourself for. You can always hold your head up. Yes, you can. You know that time I was in hospital? Five operations I had.

CLIFF: Five.

J.P.: Five operations. And do you know – I always got to a vessel.

CLIFF: Always.

J.P.: Even Alison's mother remembers that. That time at Auntie Eva's when she was going on. I reminded her. You could write a play about me, you could.

CLIFF: You could.

J.P.: Can't help laughing though, can you?

CLIFF: No.

J.P.: Now Hugh, he always liked a nice play.

CLIFF: He did, didn't he?

J.P.: Oh yes . . . We all did. In *them* days.

CLIFF: Them days. Yes.

J.P.: Everybody did. Well, now you're talking, aren't you? Lots of music and dancing in them days. Real music. Don't get that now.

CLIFF: No. Not now.

J.P.: Just a lot of noise.

CLIFF: That's right.

(HELENA *returns wearily to the ironing board.*)

That was very depressing.

J.P.: It was.

CLIFF: I thought Helena had bucked you up a bit.

J.P.: She had.

(CLIFF *looks over to her for the first time and takes her in at the ironing board.*)

CLIFF: Good God!

J.P.: What?

CLIFF: What's she doing?

J.P.: Doing?

CLIFF: *Doing?*

(J.P. *looks round.*)

J.P.: What do you think? Ironing, of course.

CLIFF: That's your shirt. *Your* shirt.

J.P.: My dear Whittaker. My dear Whittaker, you chose the
perfect profession. You respond to nothing but
reportage and shared revelations. To you that object is a
bygone symbol of woman's drudgery. You can't detect
the whiff of burnt ironies given off by a mere ironing
board. Young Helena told me that when she was a
proud sixteen, she vowed that she would never be
prevailed upon or coaxed into the degradation of ironing
a man's shirt.

CLIFF: Don't tell me *you* moved her heart.

J.P.: May God in heaven forfend. We came to an agreement.

CLIFF: You mean you'd stop fooling around? All that gabble
and songs.

J.P.: That we'd pretend we were both human beings.

CLIFF: And you succeeded.

J.P.: *She* did. Triumphantly.

CLIFF: I'm sure. But what about you?

J.P.: Well, she's ironing my shirt, isn't she?

CLIFF: You've a hidden spring of generosity, all right.

HELENA: Call it a one-off caprice.

J.P.: The first and last. Never again, eh?

HELENA: That's right. There you are, one shirt. Male.
Somewhat flailing. For the use of.

J.P.: Thank you. Very much. I shall not wear this shirt. It
shall be kept in tissue in a drawer of memories. Smell it,
Whittaker, fresh and Edwardian crisp, as from an Italian
countrywoman's sunny basket.

CLIFF: What's *your* symbolic gesture then?

J.P.: I've run out of those. They won't wash. When you've
no expectations, the most faint and distant chimes peal
out like victory.

CLIFF: It won't last.

J.P.: The blood is up again. I'll take you both out to dinner.

HELENA: I'm catching the evening train.

J.P.: No matter. I'll sing you a song.

CLIFF: No. You promised.

(J.P. *taps a button on the tape recorder and assisted by the ironing board, hops on to a chair and sings to the tune of the Champagne Aria from* Don Giovanni:)

CLIFF: You've made him *worse*.

J.P.: Here stands Jimmy Porter . . .
Abused his son and only daughter.
Believed to be a fucked up person,
His old dog's died, his spirits worsen.
Porter's the name, I'm feeling quite gay,
In that little Gypsy tea-room across the way.
Mangy of look, but eyes of blue,
Pale of face and uncertain hue.
Looking for a dream that never comes true.
Drowns in sorrow once a week,
Chased by bullies up the creek.
Raped the lives of luckless wives,
Said sexist things they all despise.
His one and only paltry function,
Providing prigs with holy unction.

(CLIFF *turns off the tape.*)

CLIFF: That must have wasted a few hours.
(*Phone from outer kitchen rings.*)

J.P.: I'll get it. (*He goes.*)

CLIFF: God. He's reconnected to the world. You're off then?

HELENA: You didn't think I was staying, did you? And you?

CLIFF: In the morning.

HELENA: How *does* he manage?

CLIFF: Now then, Helena. It was never explained *why* he ran a sweet-stall, remember. I think old first father-in-law, the Colonel, settled a small sum. Intended as a secret. It sure toppled old Mummy Rhino into the grave. You know how sacred wills and entails are to those people. That must have been a one-off caprice too. One more stereotype fighting back.
(*Enter* J.P.)

Hello, whitey. Blimey, you *are* white. I was telling her about the Colonel.

(J.P. *goes to the fridge and takes out a bottle of champagne.*)

J.P.: He was a good old stick. Well, he was very nice to me, which is the yardstick we judge all people by, I suppose. After Alison left, I always got a Christmas card from him with just the initial R. Before the battalion band played him off to the smokeless regimental mess above. (*Opens the champagne and pours three glasses.*) Here's to him. He had all the patrician qualities: remoteness, detachment and magnanimity. Hugh was the same. Remoteness, especially. Here's to them both.

CLIFF: You look awful. Really past it.

J.P.: I am. And to the living. You, Helena. The Brave New – something very much.

CLIFF: What do you mean: Hugh was the same?

J.P.: You're not the only one whose father was a man. You're doing quite well. Hugh died in his sleep this morning. Gone to Captain Shanks and my dear old dog.

HELENA: I'm sorry.

CLIFF: What was it?

J.P.: What does it matter?

CLIFF: I knew it was a bad idea, you answering the phone.

J.P.: Something mysterious, I expect, knowing Hugh. Remote to the last. Ned, (*to* HELENA) his son, wasn't very coherent.

CLIFF: Was he upset?

J.P.: Very. I told him to come up here. He's my godson. Hugh was never keen on the idea, but we agreed finally. Hugh always denigrated him. The daughter was his favourite for some perverse reason. Complacent, tight-arsed little package but Hugh adored her. Ned's different.

HELENA: Less remote?

J.P.: He actually likes it *here*.

HELENA: Unlike your own children.

J.P.: He doesn't throw up at the sight of a little mess of muddled enthusiasm.

HELENA: He'll cry at the dog's burial?

J.P.: You can *all* go, please, all of you.

CLIFF: (*Rises*) I'll go back to Twickenham. (*Like TV reporter.*) How are you feeling now that your best friend is dead?

J.P.: I wish to be alone in my personal disasters.

CLIFF: (*To* HELENA) He'll be in need of some bereavement counselling. (*He goes.*)

J.P.: You'd better get your train. We don't want to tarnish our restrained little interlude. Cliff will take you to the station.

HELENA: You haven't learnt anything about me, have you?

J.P.: Hardly a thing.

HELENA: Did you expect to?

J.P.: No. I don't know much less than I do about my children, their mother. My ex-wife. I look for a glimpse of pleasure not enlightenment. Look at Teddy, he's quite a jolly little sphinx if you've a whimsical bent. But his secret's not worth the probing. I've looked for secrets where there were none. Everyone demands solutions, like happiness, as their right. You go to sleep at night and wake up with the same old *Giaconda* frown beside you. (*Sings to the tune 'Amapola':*)

Giaconda, my smiling Giaconda,
I like to watch and wonder,
I know I'll never get beyond its empty mystery.

I thought my first wife was concealing something. Something to declare *there*, I thought. Now she does, of course. To the whole world. Like Janey Proudfoot. I've no secrets. But I'm sometimes in the market for them. Like old T. Bear there. That's why he keeps changing his dumb little mind and it runs ever the same. Well, this won't buy the baby a new bonnet.

Replete of sin, devoid of guilt,
For holocaust I never built
A cheery, unrepentant sod,
Mine's an ad hoc relationship with God.

HELENA: (*Rising*) Well, I hope your new relationship with young Ned is a helpful one. For both of you. You've really become an awful unholy bloody clown, haven't you?

J.P.: Clowns don't laugh.
(*She kisses him on the forehead and goes to the door.*)
Oh, Helena . . .
(*She turns.*)
Thank you. Thank you for ironing my shirt.
(*She leaves as he shakily pours a glass of champagne. Music/song: possibly 'A Good Man Nowadays is Hard to Find', Bessie Smith. Slow fade, although some light remains on Teddy so that the pause before the next scene is minimal.*)

SCENE THREE

The same. Later that day. Only the oil lamp is burning. The French windows are open. Teddy wears a black armband. CLIFF *and* J.P. *in their respective armchairs,* J.P. *reading what looks like a prayer book.*

J.P.: (*As* Private Lives) I went round the world you know. After –

CLIFF: How was it?

J.P.: The world? Far too long.

CLIFF: Like plays.

J.P.: Either too long –

CLIFF: – or too short. Pity they don't have third acts any more.

J.P.: Quite, quite enough.

CLIFF: One does need a drink. (*Reverts to tone of last duologue:*) Ever see anything of Auntie Eva these days?

J.P.: No. Never writes. Think she'd send a postcard or something. Right opposite the post office. But never anything, not even on Alison's birthday. And she always thought the world of *her*.

CLIFF: Oh, yes, she was always the favourite.

J.P.: I was the *one* she wasn't keen on. Me.

CLIFF: Why was that I wonder?

J.P.: I never did her no harm. Still, there it is. People are funny.

CLIFF: They are.

J.P.: That poor Captain Shanks. All right one minute and then off up in the air somewhere.

CLIFF: Up in the air's right.

J.P.: Nemmind, eh, ducks?

CLIFF: Nemmind, eh, Ted?

J.P.: After all, what am I?

CLIFF: You're a cunt.

J.P.: I'm a contraflow.

CLIFF: Pour me some more wine.

J.P.: (*Rises to pour drink.*) I am a young couple, a young executive . . .

CLIFF: You're pissed.

J.P.: (*Rattles off*) . . . waiting twelve hours at the airport; I am a baggage handler on strike. I am a survey, an infrastructure; a mortgage wrapped about my inability to have an orgasm; I am a steamer, a government statistic, a gymslip mother; I am a Walkman with an inalienable right to hope and happiness and rights; above all I am a Right, to work, to guidelines, I am a grand object of public unconcern, an unscheduled delay, a workshop of new attitudes and ideas; the sounding brass of pop and charity, the rattle and the scarf, the boot, the Arts Council, banality and yoof; *Civis Britannicus* scum. Finally: I still am, after thirty-six years, a churlish, grating note, a spokesman for no one but myself; with deadening effect, cruelly abusive, unable to be coherent about my despair; uncomfortable and awkward. His only response a cynical guffaw. No real motivation, lashing out wildly in all directions, never identifying the shadows he is attacking. *We* are left to work out our own causes; futility is our only clue. Is this ugly, cheerless world supposed to be typical? By no means an artistic success despite some violent knockabout here and there. But, my friends, finally, finally and in the last examination, the total –

CLIFF: – gesture is –

J.P. *and* CLIFF: (*Together*) Altogether Inadequate.

J.P.: Perhaps, wait for it, *next* time –

CLIFF: *Next* time he will let us *know what* he is angry about . . . Pretty *déjàvu*. I'd say. You're still a cunt. You are – become very cold, Father Porter . . . the young Teddy said. And you're becoming increasingly cold.

J.P.: If I am cold, it is the cold that burns . . .
(*Pause.*)

CLIFF: Who's that?

J.P.: Who's what?
(*There is the sound of a car coming up the drive outside. It stops.*)
How do I know? Go and have a look.

CLIFF: Go yourself.

J.P.: I'm insufficiently motivated.

CLIFF: Oh, hell. (*He gets up to the window and peers out.*)

J.P.: Well – can't be anything good, can it? It's Vatman come for Teddy. (*To Teddy.*) Well, you would go into Europe. Now they've come for you. It's all that champagne he sloshes down his little socialist throat. Well, pay the man and you'll feel so much better.

CLIFF: It's the Rev. Ron.

J.P.: Well, he can fuck off back to St Bleeding Heart's and the liturgical leisure centre at once.

CLIFF: Someone's getting out.

J.P.: He can't think he's come to the Inner City. Actually, he has.

CLIFF: It's Alison. She's taking out a suitcase . . . She's back, James. Why don't you meet her at the door? Go on.

J.P.: We don't want to frighten her off. Do we?

CLIFF: You don't?

J.P.: I'm still dumb enough to believe in divinely flexible heroines. You go.

CLIFF: Be nice.

J.P.: I'm always nice. Tell the Rev. Ron we've got double glazing, and it doesn't work.

CLIFF: I shall be sickeningly polite.

J.P.: And tell her Ned's coming. To stay. That'll please her.

CLIFF: (*At door*) I wish you'd go yourself.

J.P.: Say I'm in here. Preparing the prodigal's baked meats.

(CLIFF *goes.* J.P. *goes to the fridge excitedly and produces a bottle of champagne, deciding between a Moët and a Dom Perignon. He chooses the latter. He glances out of the window hurriedly, picks up Teddy and places him on the table to face the door and places Alison's personal stereo earpieces on his head. There is the sound of voices and laughter from the hall. He opens the bottle and pours three glasses, then rifles through a pile of tapes on the sideboard, selects one and puts it in the machine. Perhaps 'The Sun Ain't Gonna Shine Anymore' by The Walker Brothers. Then, standing expectantly at the Aga – to which he makes the sign of the Cross – he begins to fill his pipe. Smoke pours forth from him as he waits. Presently,* CLIFF *enters. He looks across at* J.P., *then, turning off the tape player, he settles back into his armchair.*)

J.P.: Champagne?

CLIFF: Thanks. I could do with that.

(J.P. *hands him one of the three glasses, takes one for himself and moves slowly to the window and looks out.*

There is the sound of car doors slamming, voices, then the
car moving off. Silence. CLIFF *waits for a while before he*
speaks.)
She's left behind some of her tapes.

J.P.: Oh, yes?

CLIFF: Oh, and her personal stereo.

J.P.: Teddy's using it.

CLIFF: Yes. Well, I said you'd send it on.

J.P.: Of course.
(*He places the third glass of champagne in front of Teddy.*)
Cheers.

CLIFF: Cheers . . . What?

J.P.: I didn't say anything.
(*Pause.*)

CLIFF: What do you think – young Jim will do after his
community service?

J.P.: I don't know . . .

CLIFF: Do you think Alison will have an abortion?

J.P.: I've no idea. How was she looking?

CLIFF: Terrific. Shouldn't you find out?

J.P.: Why?

CLIFF: I should have thought pride was a bit LMC for you.

J.P.: I've no pride. Just a distaste for piety.

CLIFF: Well, there is –

J.P.: Young Ned will need my attention. He'll be upset
about the dog. Envy? I was too arrogant. Gluttony?
Certainly not. I refused to queue and despised second
helpings. Avarice?

CLIFF: No.

J.P.: Thanks, Whittaker. Wrath? Oh, not as much as people
thought. Lust? Now and then. Mostly then. Sloth? Oh,
yes, most certainly and grievously. Sloth. Do you
remember the brasserie and bars, the music-halls of
Sickert and La Goulu, lungs filling with carbon and
laughter and recklessness, defying clinical death and a
few unknowable extra years of antiseptic, germ-

banished, senior citizen's golden retirement and pensions schemes?

CLIFF: *You'll* be old one day. You see.

J.P.: I doubt it. (*Spoken in an almost soothing bedside manner.*) But, if I am ever propped up on state pillows, being catheterized and patronized by some hell's angel of check-out mercy, young Nurse Noylene, I shall rise like some last-gasp Lazarus of a bygone smoke-filled civilization; I shall rise from my bed of unheeding profligacy and if any frowning *Gauleiter* breathes their concern or care over my fetid and exhausted form, or any smarmy dietician dares lay her menu of lower-middle-class mush, asking old Mr Porter what putrid filth he'd like to pass through his National Health dentures for his dinner at noon – if –

CLIFF: (*To Teddy*) All memories of his hernia operation.

J.P.: (*Sweetly*) If anyone, any of these creeping refuse collectors, should refer to me as a senior citizen, they will get one last almighty smack in their sanitized mealy fucking mouth.

CLIFF: Swear box!

J.P.: When I was Junior, Junior Porter, I spake as a child, a child of hellfire and smoke, I swore to the gods of irreverence and dissent that even then spake within me: I will never be –

CLIFF: A member of the public. We know.

J.P.: A member of the congregation. Alone I am. Alone yet among many. But senior I am not. Senior to what? To whom? Seniority, the campaign medal of the dull and cowardly. Nor am I a *citizen* of the UK. Sounds like belonging to the Co-op. Underwashed, underendowed, unappealing, un-English. I live among the hills footmarked only here, here, in ancient English time.

CLIFF: Time you retired, Lord Sandy.

J.P.: Retirement, ah the red badge of mediocrity.

CLIFF: (*To Teddy*) He *used* to have a nice way with words.

But I'm afraid he's losing it. At least no one ever accused *you* of originality.

J.P.: No. But I don't assemble a lot of sloppy fads and serve them up as innovations. Do you know that before Auntie Wordsworth retired from his serious scribbling, people in their coaches used to pull down the blinds so that they didn't need to contemplate the landscape?

CLIFF: And what perception have *you* invented?

J.P.: None I can remember. Just perhaps the abiding expectation that more change means less improvement.

CLIFF: My feet hurt . . .

J.P.: You've said that already . . . (*He gets up, picks up the prayer book, takes his trumpet from the kitchen shelf and goes to the window.*)

CLIFF: Have I? Sorry, I'm sure.

J.P.: Keep thou my feet, I do not ask to see
    The distant scene; one step enough for me.
(*Puts the trumpet to his lips.*) I was not ever thus. (*He plays, uncertainly at first, 'Lead, Kindly Light'. At the second line, the trumpet is louder.* CLIFF *joins in.*)

CLIFF: (*Singing*) The night is dark and I am far from home.

J.P.: (*Stops*) I loved the garish day, and spite of fears
    Pride ruled my will; remember not past years.
(*The church bells peal out suddenly.*)

CLIFF: Those bloody bells!

J.P.: (*By the window sill*) Give us leave to depart the perils of this night, so that we may awake watchfully.

CLIFF: The Rev. Ron wouldn't go for that.

J.P.: And against the noise and clamour of those who would impose their certainties upon us.

CLIFF: Close the bloody windows.
    (J.P. *closes the windows.*)

J.P.: God *rot* their certainties.

CLIFF: That's more like it, Cornet.

J.P.: (*Very crisply, like battle commands*) Endow us with the courage of uncertainty. Accept an unruly but contrite heart. And in that frailty of disbelief we cannot overcome let us seek remedy from within ourselves and offer mercy that the world cannot give among the perils etcetera, etcetera.

CLIFF: Amen. Are you angry? That she didn't stay?

J.P.: (*Softly*) 'What's he angry *about*?' they used to ask. Anger is not *about* . . . It comes into the world in grief not grievance. It is mourning the unknown, the loss of what went before without you, it's the love another time but not this might have sprung on you, and greatest loss of all, the deprivation of what, even as a child, seemed to be irrevocably your own, your country, your birthplace, that, at least, is as tangible as death.
(*Long pause.*)

CLIFF: Teddy doesn't understand why it is that God allows so much suffering. In the world.

J.P.: He goes really straight to the heart of it, doesn't he?

CLIFF: Not when –

J.P.: When it's in his power to stop it?

CLIFF: Well, it's a fair question.

J.P.: 'I'd like so much to believe in God, but I'm afraid he just doesn't live up to my own moral necessities.'

CLIFF: What should I tell him?

J.P.: Tell him to go fuck himself. He didn't do his own son no favours. He can invent his *own* bloody collects.
(CLIFF *has the paper over his face.*)
(*To Teddy*) I should settle down if I were you. Pretend it isn't happening. You're a lucky fellow. Mediocrity is a great comforter, my furry little ursine friend. And very democratic. It's all yours. Oh, *lucky* bears!
(J.P. *thinks he hears Champagne Aria again.* J.P. *mimes to it, in his most ebullient fashion, using one of Teddy's arms to beat time. He ends with a grand operatic flourish, the most upward theatrical inflexion he can muster and stands*

defiantly. CLIFF *lies asleep beneath the newspaper.*
Blackout.)

(*In the unlikely event of audience dissent at the end of the
performance, the loud playing of martial music can be
effective. 'Molonello' played by the Grenadier Guards, the
quick march 'St Patrick's Day' or, to be more 'European',
the* 'Radetzky'.)

IT'S MY MOTHER'S BIRTHDAY TODAY

It's my mother's birthday today,
I'm on my way with a lovely bouquet,
For me it's the happiest day,
I won't be late at the old cottage gate.

I'll greet her with a kiss,
For that I know she yearns,
And then I'll say God bless you,
Many happy returns.

Those roses will soon fade away,
But she'll know what I mean to convey,
When I say,
It's *my* mother's birthday today.

My heart is singing a happy refrain,
Blue skies are smiling above,
I'm going home to my mother again,
Off to the one that I love.

There's a little devil dancin'
In your laughing Irish eyes,
And the little devil dances
Right into me heart.

There's a little bit of mischief,
In your laughing Irish eyes,
And it tells me you will give me
Such a grand surprise

Oh, I swear on me honour,
I'm a man who's a goner
And to prove what I can do,
You can put it in the papers
That the boys know, bejabers,
That I want to marry you.

But before we start romancing,
Darling, won't you put me wise
To the little devil dancin'
In your laughing Irish eyes?